Lucy A. Tedd · Andrew Large

Digital Libraries

Lucy A. Tedd
Andrew Large

Digital Libraries

Principles and Practice
in a Global Environment

K · G · Saur München 2005

Bibliographic information published by Die Deutsche Bibliothek
Die Deutsche Bibliothek lists this publication in the Deutsche Nationalbibliografie;
detailed bibliographic data is available in the internet at http://dnb.ddb.de.

⊗
Printed on acid-free paper
© 2005 K. G. Saur Verlag GmbH, München
Typesetting by Florence Production Ltd., Stoodleigh, Devon, Great Britain.
Printed and bound by Strauss GmbH, Mörlenbach, Germany.
ISBN 3-598-11627-6

Contents

List of Figures and Table

Table

Preface

The goal of *Digital Libraries: Principles and Practice in a Global Environment*, as its title suggests, is to introduce readers to the principles underlying digital libraries, as well as to illustrate these principles by reference to a wide range of digital library practices throughout the world. Much of what has been written about digital library developments, at least in English, refers to work carried out in English-speaking countries, and especially in the US and UK. Such developments are covered in this text, of course, but we have tried to cast our net somewhat wider by including examples from a broad range of additional countries. Furthermore, we have addressed explicitly the challenges of developing and implementing digital library systems in multilingual and multicultural environments; as it happens, we both live in bilingual communities and so are familiar with language issues in the provision of access to digital information. We have striven, then, to provide a concise and easily digestible introduction to a range of international, digital library-related developments.

Digital libraries can be treated from many points of view. We have tried to give an overview of their history and context, users and content, as well as dealing with a wide range of practical issues. It has not been our intention to write a detailed technical treatise on digital library design and implementation, but we have included some discussion of topics such as standardization, interoperability and interface design where these are central to an understanding of the principles and practices of digital libraries. Although this is not a book on information seeking, inevitably we have covered the ways in which users search and browse digital library collections. We recognize that the principles underlying digital libraries as well as their practical manifestations are relevant not only to institutions that call themselves libraries but also to a wide variety of other organizations, including archives, museums and art galleries. It must be conceded, however, that it is difficult to provide equal balance across all these institutions in the confines of one short book, and undoubtedly libraries do dominate.

This domination in part is a consequence of the primary target audience for *Digital Libraries: Principles and Practice in a Global Environment* – graduate and undergraduate students in Library Science, Information Science or Computer Science (and related) programmes around the world, as well as information professionals working in libraries and information units who wish to update their knowledge in this rapidly developing field.

The opening chapter, Digital Libraries in Context, provides an overview of digital libraries, thereby setting the scene for the chapters to follow. It introduces readers to the typical characteristics and formal definitions of digital libraries, reviews their brief history and situates them in the broader historical and global context of libraries and information media. Chapter Two focuses upon digital library users and the services that are offered them. It covers topics such as the different kinds of institutions that provide digital library services, the personalization of these services for various specific user groups, the role of digital reference services, information literacy, and the barriers that still can impede access by users to the digital library services. The third chapter offers an overview of the various kinds of information sources typically found in digital libraries and provides details of some of the suppliers of these sources. In addition the chapter discusses briefly issues related to the development of the 'open access' movement as well as digitization, that is, creating digitized versions of existing print, photographic, audio or video materials.

Chapter Four provides an overview of the many standards and protocols with which digital libraries must cope in the context of interoperability. In Chapter Five the discussion takes a more practical flavour, with a review of software that might be used in the development of digital libraries, including the use of open source software. Chapter Six then turns to interface design, and here includes consideration of issues that arise in multilingual and multicultural environments. The critical searching and browsing functions of digital libraries are given their own chapter, which also has sections on searching both multilingual and multimedia collections.

Further practical issues are covered in Chapter Eight, with an emphasis on the tasks of planning, installing, operating and evaluating digital libraries. It also discusses intellectual property rights and preservation in relation to digital libraries. Finally it reviews staffing aspects and enumerates principles for digital library development.

The last chapter comprises eight case studies drawn from Canada, England, India, Italy, Singapore, Sri Lanka, the US and Wales. These case studies are used to illustrate in actual settings many of the points made in earlier chapters. We should like to thank the following people who were kind enough to discuss their institutions with us and verify the accuracy of our resulting case studies: Piero Cavaleri and Laura Ballestra (Università Carlo Cattaneo), Gordon Burr (McGill University), Allison Druin (University of Maryland), Ruvini Kodikara and Ruwan Gamage (University of Moratuwa), Shalini Urs (University of Mysore), Ai Cheng Tay (National Library Board, Singapore),

John Watts Williams and Lyn Lewis Dafis (National Library of Wales), and Anne Ramsden, Patricia Heffernan and Gill Needham (Open University).

We are especially indebted to Jamshid Beheshti (McGill University) and Fred Guy (formerly of the National Library of Scotland and now an independent consultant) for their willingness, despite heavy schedules, to read through and comment upon an early draft of *Digital Libraries*. Their critique undoubtedly has made this a better book, though for any remaining shortcomings, it goes without saying, we must bear all responsibility.

Digital Libraries: Principles and Practice in a Global Environment contains many screenshots from digital libraries around the world; in all cases these were active as of December 2003. Permission accorded to us by their owners has been acknowledged individually throughout the following chapters, but here we should like to express our gratitude to all the copyright holders whose work has been reproduced in the book. Inevitably, the digital libraries described, and especially the screens reproduced, will develop over time, but the principles relating to digital library development and implementation will prove much more durable.

The origins of this book are to be found in a course jointly offered by us in 2001 at the International Graduate Summer School, hosted by the Department of Information Studies, at the University of Wales Aberystwyth. This was by no means, however, our first collaborative endeavour. We have jointly authored, with other colleagues two books on information seeking, as well as presenting workshops on digital library related issues for the Soros Foundation (Open Society Institute) in the Czech Republic, Estonia, Kazakstan, Romania and Slovenia, and advising on the development of a Unesco ICT training package for library and information professionals in Asia and the Pacific rim. Individually, we have acted as consultants for a number of prominent international agencies as well as presenting conference papers and training courses in many parts of the world. Although we hate to admit that our ages make this possible, we also have between us almost 60 years of teaching experience in library and information studies where we ourselves have learnt much from teaching students from very many countries.

Our work in preparing this book has been greatly facilitated by our respective periods of sabbatical leave from our teaching commitments, and we express gratitude to our universities (the University of Wales Aberystwyth and McGill University, Montreal) for this. In addition our families have been a great support. With all but one of our respective children being no longer 'home-based', our spouses have had to tolerate the brunt of our day-to-day working on this book. To Mike and Valerie, we can only say a big 'thanks'.

Lucy Tedd and Andrew Large
January 2004

Chapter 1

Digital Libraries in Context

1.1 Treasures from the World's Great Libraries

What better way to begin a book about digital libraries than with an example. And as our concern is with digital libraries in a global environment, we should choose one that illustrates both through its structure and content the opportunities as well as the challenges offered for international resource sharing by digital libraries.

Treasures from the World's Great Libraries is a digital library created by the National Library of Australia to celebrate its centenary in December 2001, and is accessible to users via the Web (http://www.nla.gov.au/worldtreasures). The 161 items from 38 collections located in 24 countries are arranged under seven themes (see Figure 1.1) and the collection "presents an extraordinary sample of the cultural treasures to be found in libraries throughout the world, ranging from ancient texts and forms of writing to electronic books".

Treasures from the World's Great Libraries can be used to illustrate many features typically encountered in a digital library. Digitized versions of priceless artefacts that are located in many different physical collections distributed around the world can be visited virtually by linking to a host computer sited in Canberra, Australia. The visitors themselves might be anywhere from Albania to Zanzibar, and it does not matter what make of computer they use, what operating system is installed on that computer, which service provider is linking it to the Internet, nor which network route is followed to Canberra. Thanks to internationally agreed standards, a connection can be established between the user's local Internet access point and the digitized collection at the National Library that permits the user to 'enter' and explore the digital library collection.

This collection itself has a focus – world treasures – and the constituent items have been carefully selected by professional staff at the National Library of Australia. In this case the potential user community is very broad, but even so certain characteristics can be assumed with a reasonable degree of confidence: users are likely to be interested in art, music, literature, religion, exploration or science; they most probably will not be experts in these domains (the collection has been assembled for amateurs rather than professionals); and they might well be teachers or students (as there is a special section for teachers to assemble digital artefacts for the specific needs of their students). This is a multimedia digital library, containing text, colour images, and sound sequences (like Bessie Smith's 1929 recording of *Wasted Life Blues*). It is arranged so as to facilitate retrieval of individual images as well as to permit browsing through parts or all of the collection. The creators of this digital library have taken account of potential copyright issues by including a Copyright Statement; it emphasizes that although the material may be downloaded, stored in a cache or displayed, it must not be altered, and cannot be used for commercial purposes. The collection can be accessed from a main menu (shown in Figure 1.1) or from a list of all the items to be found under the library's seven themes. Some items can be scrolled from left to right in order to provide a panoramic view, or viewed in close up; captions can be opened or closed; and a tour through the collection is no more than a mouse click away. Links are also provided to the more than 30 library sites around the world in which the physical items comprising the collection themselves are kept. Finally, the digital library has an interactive component where 'visitors' can submit their own comments on the digital library via an online form, and read comments that have been submitted by others. In short, then, a spectacular and informative collection that otherwise could be viewed only by travelling to many cities in many countries.

Figure 1.1 Treasures from the World's Great Libraries, National Library of Australia (reproduced courtesy of the National Library of Australia)

From a global perspective, however, this digital library also presents certain problems. The first relates to language. The text is available only in one language – English. The beauty of Treasures from the World's Great Libraries' many images can be appreciated by anyone, but what exactly these images represent would remain a matter for conjecture to a viewer unable to read the English-language captions. Furthermore, the images would have to be located using trial and error by those who cannot read the English-language menus and hyperlinks embedded in the interface (accompanying icons are pretty but unlikely to enlighten users without aid from the text captions). A long and fascinating introduction to the collection is available, but again only in English.

This particular digital library comprises artefacts representing various world cultures in different time periods – an ancient Chinese statue, an early Arab translation of *Euclid*, an Ethiopian manuscript book, a German translation of the *Old Testament* made by Luther, Jane Austen's manuscript of *Persuasion*, a letter from Groucho Marx, and so on. Yet even in such a multicultural collection, selection criteria have been applied that from some points of view might suggest cultural biases. Furthermore, the interface to the digital library, in its choices of colour and layout, hints at the West European tradition through its visual similarities to a medieval European manuscript. Such cultural differences, going beyond the limits of language, can affect users' reactions to digital libraries: icons, colours, terminology and metaphor, for example, can all exhibit cultural biases that are no less invidious for often being unwittingly introduced by digital library designers.

A different set of problems concerns technology. Two versions of the digital library are available: a standard version and an animated version (where the images can be manipulated more fully). However, even in the standard version, visitors confined to a low bandwidth connection will find Treasures from the World's Great Libraries exasperatingly slow at best, and simply unusable at worst. The wealth of images available places significant demands upon bandwidth, as is emphasized in Treasures' opening screen. The curator's notes are available only in Portable Document Format (PDF) that may take a long time to download and even longer to print; sound sequences also will be very slow to download and disappointingly disjointed when heard. As a consequence, visitors to the digital library who cannot employ a reasonably powerful processor and a high-speed connection will become second-class users, or even non-users. Treasures from the World's Great Libraries, therefore, is available via the Web, but its potential can only be fully realized by those with sufficiently powerful computing and telecommunications tools. In other words, a digital divide opens between those with such tools and those without, a divide that may be based upon disparities within a society or disparities between different societies.

We shall encounter many more examples of digital libraries in the chapters to follow, but Treasures from the World's Great Libraries will suffice here to provide a glimpse of the promise as well as the challenge posed by digital libraries in a global context.

1.2 The Rise of Digital Libraries

Many examples of digital libraries can be found around the world, conferences regularly are held on them, numerous books, articles and even entire journals are dedicated to their discussion, and they can attract reports in the popular press, on radio and on television. Their rapid growth has been encouraged by the publication of digital materials, and by large and small digitization projects that have converted items originally available in other forms into digital versions. Such rapid diffusion of both the concept and reality of digital libraries is all the more remarkable given their brief history.

A good place to begin a historical discussion of digital libraries is with four individuals whose vision and actions helped shape their emergence. In July 1945 an article entitled "As we may think" appeared in the *Atlantic Monthly*. Its author, Vannevar Bush, was at various times Professor of Electrical Engineering at the Massachusetts Institute of Technology (MIT), Director of the US Office of Scientific Research and Development, and President of the Carnegie Institution in Washington, DC. Bush was concerned about information overload as even then encountered by scientists: "our methods of transmitting and reviewing the results of research are generations old and by now are totally inadequate for their purpose." He suggested several technological solutions that in the future might overcome this problem, and in particular described an imaginary machine that he called a Memex that would store an individual's books, records and communications, and could be consulted at high speed and with great flexibility. He imagined it as comprising a desk on top of which are slanting translucent screens on which material could be projected for convenient reading (he had in mind not a computer but a kind of microfilm reader whose images would be coded so that a light scanner could retrieve the data as they passed at high speed through a film transport mechanism). He envisaged the Memex as "a sort of mechanized private file and library" from which "any given book ... can thus be called up and consulted with far greater facility than if it were taken from a shelf" (Bush, 1945).

One of the many people influenced by Bush's ideas was Douglas Engelbart, who read "As we may think" in the late 1940s and became an early believer in the concept of a machine that would aid human cognition. Together with colleagues he developed in the 1960s at the Stanford Research Institute in California the first implementation of what was to be called 'hypertext'. Engelbart was particularly concerned with collaboration among geographically distributed teams, and to this end also developed the mouse pointing device, a windows software environment, online help systems and promoted the concept of consistency in user interfaces. His online information system, demonstrated live in 1968 (http://sloan.stanford.edu/mousesite/1968Demo. html), provided a visual environment for information sharing and shared-screen collaboration by two people at different sites communicating over a network with an audio and video interface. Engelbart's work directly influenced research at the Xerox Corporation's Palo Alto Research Center (Xerox PARC) in California that conducted pioneering interdisciplinary research in the physical, computational and social sciences (http://www.parc.xerox.com).

Ted Nelson in turn was influenced both by Bush and Engelbart. He coined the term 'hypertext' in the mid-1960s and emphasized the interconnectedness of knowledge that hypertext can convey. His Xanadu project was envisaged as a universal, democratic hypertext library and publishing tool that would put all information within the reach of all people. Although it failed to materialize, Xanadu played a major role in the evolution of hypertext systems.

Tim Berners-Lee, while a consultant software engineer in 1980 at CERN, the European Particle Physics Laboratory in Geneva, Switzerland, wrote a program for storing information using random associations. In 1989 he took hypertext a step further by proposing a global hypertext project designed to allow people to work together by combining their knowledge in a web of hypertext documents; he called it the World Wide Web.

The ground-breaking ideas of these four men in the realms of automated information systems, interface design, hyperlinks and the Web, together with technological developments in computer processing and data transmission, laid the ground for the early experiments in organizing and manipulating large quantities of digital information in institutional settings that were the immediate forerunners of digital libraries. Without these ideas, indeed, it would be hard to envisage current digital libraries that are overwhelmingly accessible via the Web, rely heavily upon hypertext to link documents both within and across digital libraries, and employ user friendly, windows-based interfaces.

The earliest digital library experiments all involved the digitization of journal articles. The Mercury Electronic Library project at Carnegie Mellon University in Pittsburgh, Pennsylvania, was an early attempt (1989–1992) to establish a campus-based digital library of journal articles on computer science (http://www.cs.cornell.edu/wya/papers/Mercury6.doc). It was followed by the Chemistry Online Retrieval Experiment (CORE) involving Bellcore (Bell Communications Research, now a part of Telcordia Technologies), Cornell University, OCLC (a major international provider of digital information services), the American Chemical Society, and the Chemical Abstracts Service. CORE digitized some 400,000 pages from chemistry journals published by the American Chemical Society. Between 1991 and 1995 the publisher Elsevier Science, through The University Licensing Project (TULIP), provided nine leading universities in the US with digitized content from 43 of its journals. TULIP's objective was to test systems for networked delivery and use of journals at the user's desktop, and the focus was on technical issues, user behaviour, and organizational and economic questions (the TULIP Final Report can be found at http://www.elsevier.nl/homepage/about/resproj/trmenu.htm). Mercury, CORE and TULIP helped demonstrate the feasibility of realizing digital libraries and the benefits that could emerge from them.

During the 1990s both research and professional interest in digital libraries continued to grow rapidly. One of the earliest meetings to focus attention on this topic was the "Future Directions in Text Analysis, Retrieval and Understanding" workshop held in the US in 1991, though at this time the phrase 'electronic libraries' was employed (Fox, 1993). It was followed by more workshops that led to the launch in 1994 of the first four-year Digital Library Initiative (subsequently called DLI-1) by three US federal agencies – the National Science Foundation (NSF), the National Aeronautical and Space Agency (NASA), and the Defense Advanced Research Projects Agency (DARPA). DLI-1's mandate was to develop methods to collect, store and organize information in digital forms and make it available for searching, retrieval and processing in user-friendly ways via communication networks. It supported research in several critical areas for digital libraries that will be more fully explained later in this book, including digitization, metadata, browsing and searching software, and networking. Six research projects were funded under DLI-1:

- the University of California at Berkeley developed a large digital collection about California's environment;
- the University of California at Santa Barbara dealt with maps and geospatial information in its Alexandria project;
- Carnegie Mellon University's Informedia project researched digital video retrieval;
- the University of Illinois Interspace project focused on repositories of scientific and engineering journals;
- the University of Michigan was concerned with intelligent agents for information location;
- Stanford University's Infobus project developed interoperation mechanisms among heterogeneous digital libraries.

More information on these projects can be found on the DLI-2 website (http://www.dli2.nsf.gov/dlione).

The second phase of the Digital Library Initiative (DLI-2) followed in 1998 (http://www.dli2.nsf.gov/announce.html) and was sponsored by several US agencies, including new partners that had wider interests than those involved in Phase I such as the National Library of Medicine (NLM); the National Endowment for the Humanities; the Library of Congress (LC); and the NSF's Division of Undergraduate Education. Its objectives were to:

- selectively build on and extend research and testbed activities in promising digital library areas;
- accelerate development, management and accessibility of digital content and collections;
- create new capabilities and opportunities for digital libraries to serve existing and new user communities, including all levels of education;
- encourage the study of interactions between humans and digital libraries in various social and organizational contexts.

A list of 36 projects funded between 1999 and 2004 can be found on the DLI-2 website (http://www.dli2.nsf.gov/projects.html). To give just one example, the University of California Davis project, "A Multimedia Digital Library of Folk Literature", worked with an archive of Judeo-Spanish ballads, lyric poetry, folktales, proverbs and riddles. It focused on the creation of a multimedia digitized corpus that could be made more widely available and used more effectively for textual analysis.

Digital libraries were also being established in many other developing as well as developed countries as the necessary technological support became available around the world. Examples include:

- The African Digital Library, freely accessible to anyone living in Africa, providing information on African education and development in the form of electronic books (ebooks), electronic journals (ejournals) and other materials (http://africaeducation.org/adl).
- In Brazil, the Biblioteca Virtual em saúde (the Virtual health Library) includes a network of health information resources from the region (http://www.bireme.br); the home page can be viewed in English and Spanish as well as Portuguese (the default language).
- The Canadian Initiative on Digital Libraries is an alliance of Canadian libraries and other organizations that are collaborating to ensure better use of digital information and better services to users (http://www.nlc-bnc.ca/cidl/cidle.html); an example of a resource provided under this Initiative is Collège de Joliette: 150 ans d'éducation (1846–1997), a collection of archival documents – photographs, letters, and so on, with commentaries – that tells the story of life in this Seminary (http://collections.ic.gc.ca/joliette).
- In Ireland the Corpus of Electronic Texts (CELT) comprises an online resource for the academic study of Irish history, literature and politics (http://www.ucc.ie/celt).
- The New Zealand Digital Library (NZDL) project at the University of Waikato (http://www.nzdl.org) was conceived to develop technology, examine novel interfaces, enhance information presentation and assess potential subject areas for public-domain collections, as well as to survey and critique other digital library projects.
- In Thailand the digital library of the Child Institute Foundation (http://www.childthai.org) supports its institution's objective to help strengthen family bonding and develop a better quality of life for children and their families.
- In the UK the Electronic Libraries (eLib) Programme, initiated in 1994, fostered digital library development in areas such as digitization, digital preservation, and electronic document delivery. A list of the more than 70 projects funded until 2000 can be found on the Web (http://www.ukoln.ac.uk/services/elib/projects) and the ejournal, *Ariadne* (http://www.ariadne.ac.uk), includes many articles that discuss various aspects of the eLib Programme.

Early discussions of what became known as 'digital libraries' were dominated by computer scientists. DLI-1, for example, focused upon information architecture and information retrieval, and had little to say about libraries as understood by librarians. That is to say, scant attention was devoted to matters such as collections and their custodianship, user services, conservation of material, and ethical concerns relating to access and use. Soon, however, librarians along with other information professionals were engaging in the debate. By DLI-2 far more concern for social, behavioural and economic aspects was being demonstrated alongside continuing technical issues. The eLib Programme in the UK from the outset focused upon the development of services for users rather than on fundamental research with a technological slant (Rusbridge, 1998). Libraries rather than departments of computer science were the primary institutions involved here. Digital libraries, though still in their early developmental stage, are now very much a part of the library environment around the world whether viewed from a research or an operational perspective.

1.3 The Traditional Library

It is no easy task to define what constitutes a 'traditional' library. We might agree, however, that it does occupy one or more physical buildings; when we talk of going to the library, perhaps first of all we think of heading for a building of brick, steel, concrete or glass. It is a building whose primary task in most (but not all) cases is to store printed documents – books, journals, newspapers, and so on – but also non-print documents such as photographs, films, videos, and music CDs. A library, however, is more than just a documentary storehouse. The documents will have been carefully selected according to a collection policy that in turn is based upon the identified needs of the library's users. Moreover, this collection will be organized in such a way that the users easily can find what they are looking for, whether they search by creator, title or subject. The organization involves physical arrangement of the documents on shelves or other storage devices, and in various rooms, but also it requires a catalogue comprising records for all these documents that can be arranged in other ways so as to permit multiple approaches to finding information about the collection. A typical library will offer not only its selected and organized collection, but also a range of services. These might include an inter-library loans service that extends the physical collection by bringing to users documents from other libraries, a reference service to answer a wide variety of informational questions from users, and services for special user categories such as children's reading circles or home delivery of documents to the housebound. Finally the physical space occupied by the library also offers a warm (or cool, depending on the external climate) and light environment to sit and read, work on school assignments, hold meetings, and so on.

Libraries do not only provide a range of services to their contemporary generation of patrons. Some, and especially national and university libraries, also play a major role in preserving the documentary heritage of previous generations so that it will be available for future ones. Without libraries, it is difficult to believe that all the historical and cultural assets assembled in Treasures from the World's Great Libraries, discussed at the opening of this Chapter, would have survived the ravages of time.

It is important to note that even in a traditional library it is possible for users to request and borrow material that is held in other libraries, or to e-mail or telephone reference questions to the library from their home or office. In other words, services do extend beyond the library's physical walls. The concept of library cooperation also did not originate with digital collections, although they have greatly facilitated resource sharing. Cooperative acquisition policies were adopted by German university libraries after the First World War (1914–1918), later to be followed by other forms of cooperation such as inter-library loan services and union catalogues. Likewise, librarians have demonstrated a willingness to embrace information and communication technologies (ICTs) when they enable the more efficient collection, storage, retrieval and dissemination of documents. This precedes the emergence of digital libraries. From the 1960s onwards computers played a growing role in cataloguing, acquisitions and circulation, and online information services of various kinds were offered to users.

Libraries are not the only institutions involved in safeguarding our cultural heritage. Archives, museums and art galleries collect and preserve documents and other artefacts for current and future use. As we shall see throughout this book, these institutions also can make available digital collections of various kinds. One example is Our Future, Our Past: The Alberta Heritage Digitization Project (http://www.ourfutureourpast.ca). It provides access to digitized versions of historical documents – photographs, maps, newspapers, government documents and local histories – relevant to the history of this Canadian province. The partners include university libraries, museums and archives.

1.4 Libraries and Information Media in Historical Context

The advent of digital libraries has provoked debate about the future of libraries, some of it heated. This debate is very much entangled with prognostications concerning the survival or demise of printed documents in a digital environment. Some predict revolutionary shifts that will result in profound transformations of society, including the imminent replacement of printed documents by electronic media, and radical transformations of such institutions as archives, museums and libraries. Others adopt an evolutionary stance, believing that such institutions will have to adapt their practices to the new media, but that print will continue to co-exist with them (see Borgman, 2000). The following statement, interestingly made by two computer scientists rather than librarians, expresses well this point of view:

> We do not believe that digital libraries are supplanting existing bricks-and-mortar libraries – not in the near-and medium term future . . . And we certainly don't think you should be burning your books in favour of flat-panel displays! Digital libraries are new tools for achieving human goals by changing the way that information is used in the world. We are talking about new ways of dealing with knowledge, not about replacing existing institutions (Witten and Bainbridge, 2003).

In fact, the emergence of digitized information is but the latest in a long list of technological developments to impact information media and libraries that stretches back into antiquity. In the third millennium BC the Sumerians were using soft clay (then hardened into tablets or walls) and a wedge-shaped stylus or pointed stick to record their information in cuneiform characters. The heavy clay tablets favoured the collection of permanent records in central sites, and the Sumerians established temple libraries, and probably also municipal and government libraries, though they might be likened more to archives that stored commercial records than to modern libraries. Stone or clay tablets were slow to work, bulky to store and difficult to transport, and therefore the Egyptian invention of papyrus around 2500 BC represents a major communication media development. Papyrus, made from a plant, was extremely light in contrast with stone, and sheets could be glued criss-cross to form scrolls. Other civilizations also adapted plant products as a communication medium – in China and Japan paper was made from the bark of mulberry trees, in Southern Asia it was palm leaves, and in Central America the Mayans used the inner bark of certain trees.

The Romans, like the Egyptians and Greeks before them, mainly recorded documents on papyrus rolls. The early Christians, however, favoured a different medium – parchment. For centuries parchment coexisted alongside papyrus. It was made from sheep, calf or goat skin that was both highly durable and widely available. Furthermore, it could be rolled as scrolls or sewn into books, it could be written on both sides, and scraped and re-cycled (although it was harder work to write on than papyrus).

Paper had been made in China since the second century AD, but the skill of paper making reached Europe only in the twelfth century. Like many new communication technologies, paper making was regarded with suspicion by conservatives; nevertheless, its importance quickly grew as it was cheaper than parchment and took ink better – although it was more fragile. But the same labour intensive and error prone copying was necessary with paper as with parchment.

Printing with moveable type in fact had been practised in China from the eleventh century, but the idea does not seem to have spread to Europe from China. It had to be invented afresh, in the mid-fifteenth century, when the technology of the goldsmith's punch was combined with that of the wine-press to produce the printing press. Printing spread rapidly across Europe, despite initial resistance to printed books from collectors who saw them as cheap and inferior imitations (printers tried to counter this by making their products look like hand-copied manuscripts – using, for example, the same kinds of letter design and other decorative techniques found in manuscripts). Scribes did not suddenly disappear and hand copying continued for many years, even though more expensive. Nor were printed books immediately more portable than copied manuscripts; early versions were large folios bound in boards that were heavy and difficult to carry. Only around 1800 did the iron printing press, easier to operate and producing better copies, replace wooden presses, followed in 1886 by the first mechanical composing machine – the linotype. Alongside these advances in printing, paper production also was mechanized, and the appearance of wood pulp as a cheap alternative to rag pulp led to a dramatic fall in price.

The rapid development of new information technologies (to apply a modern term to an older phenomenon) was not confined to printing. As a precursor of multimedia, in 1827 the first photograph was developed after an exposure of eight hours! Rapid improvements in photography followed, and although the equipment remained bulky and heavy for many years, photographs were common in newspapers by the end of the nineteenth century.

In the visual realm, from the 1920s onwards microfilm and microfiche permitted the reproduction of print documents on film, thereby providing a much more compact storage medium than paper that was also easier to preserve. Another development in the late 1950s – photocopying – also revolutionized storage and transmission of printed documents, further enhanced with the arrival of the fax machine.

Digital computers first appeared in the late 1940s and 1950s, but their application to storing and retrieving large stores of textual information came somewhat later, in the 1960s and 1970s. At this time a number of online search services emerged, such as Lockheed Dialog, and Medline from the NLM, offering databases containing abstracts and later the full texts of journal articles, conference papers, research reports, patents and other information sources. Such databases could be searched remotely by users located in other countries or continents via data communication networks that were becoming more reliable and less expensive.

These new networks depended upon a technology called packet switching, developed in the late 1960s initially for military communications by DARPA. The resulting ARPANET network had its first public demonstration in 1972. Like computing technology, networking underwent dramatic technical developments leading to much higher bandwidths that enable more data, including moving images and sound as well as text, to be transmitted at high enough speeds for real-time use. The emergence from ARPANET of the Internet – a vast collection of inter-connected networks that all use a shared protocol to communicate between themselves called TCP/IP (Transmission Control Protocol/Internet Protocol) – provided an opportunity for information transfer on a scale hitherto unimagined.

Earlier in this Chapter we saw how the pioneering work of Bush, Engelbart, Nelson and Berners-Lee had led by the 1990s to hypertext systems, windows-based operating systems, improved interface design and the Web. Three new developments were incorporated into the Web: HTML (HyperText Markup Language) used to write the web documents, HTTP (HyperText Transfer Protocol) to transmit the pages, and a web browser program, such as Netscape Navigator or Internet Explorer, to receive and interpret data and display results. A critical aspect of the browser's user interface is its consistency across all types of computer platforms so that users can access information from any type of computer. With the appearance of the Web, the technological stage was now set for the rapid diffusion of digital libraries. The use of satellite transmission has eliminated the need for land-based cabling in remote or harsh terrains, thereby opening geographically remote regions to data transfer and enabling us to talk of a truly global information environment.

During the 1980s a new digital data publishing and storage medium appeared – the optical disc in the form of CD-ROMs and later DVDs. They were used to assemble multimedia collections of still images, moving images and sound as well as text for on-site access. The stand-alone nature of optical discs (although they also can be networked) made them particularly useful in developing countries lacking cheap and reliable telecommunication networks.

Important technical advances were also made in fields such as optical character recognition and digital scanning, enabling printed text to be converted into digital format much more quickly and cheaply than was possible when relying upon manual keying. Scanning also made it feasible easily to digitize images, and digital recording had similar implications for analogue sound recordings. Moreover, digital capture became the normal method initially to handle text, or music and voice recordings, regardless of the medium or media on which they subsequently would appear.

What can we learn from this history that will help us better to understand the implications of the changes currently in progress, and especially to appreciate continuity and change in libraries? To begin, the full possibilities of an invention rarely are obvious immediately. Indeed, in some cases it takes a long time before its role becomes apparent. The many ramifications of the printing press, for example, would not have been apparent to an observer in the early sixteenth century. And the story goes that the engineer who developed the IBM Mark I computer predicted in 1947 that only six would satisfy the needs of the entire US.

In contrast, the power of an invention to transform radically organizational and human behaviour also can be greatly exaggerated. A good example is provided by microforms. Their appearance led not a few observers from the 1920s onwards to predict the transformation of libraries, notwithstanding the unpopularity of microforms with many readers. They were lauded as the most significant development in text communication since the printing press. Microfilms, microfiche and the machines required to use them, can still be found in libraries, but their revolutionary impact failed to materialize.

Technological change can induce widespread adjustments in work practices, reducing or eliminating the need for some skills while introducing a demand for others. In the case of libraries, computerized generation of cataloguing records (instead of hand-written or typed records) coupled with an efficient way to exchange such records and the adoption of standards for their creation, for example, has reduced the number of professional staff in a typical library's cataloguing department. At the same time, new library departments have emerged to develop, maintain and manage the automated library systems that are now crucial to most libraries' operations. Users also must acquire new skills in order to exploit, for example, the automated catalogues and other information systems that are a typical feature of the academic, public or special library.

Digitized information can be accessed by users over great distances; the user need no longer make contact with the stored item; an image of it will be delivered to his or her screen, wherever it happens to be. The book printed on paper was much more portable than parchment manuscript, let alone the clay tablet, but libraries normally have served a user community defined perhaps by occupation or interest, but also in geographical terms. The library served its locality, however narrowly or broadly defined, because typically users would have to visit the library in person to avail themselves of its services. Improvements in people transportation did relatively little to modify this reality. Furthermore, the library reflected in its collections and services the shared cultural heritage of its local community. Digital libraries now have the opportunity to serve much broader geographical communities – worldwide communities, in fact. Observers such as Marchionini (1998) see this as representing a fundamental shift for libraries and for human culture more generally.

Information containers dramatically affected the durability of information. The papyrus roll was light and relatively simple to transport from place to place. But it was also fragile, and much more easily damaged by use than parchment. Paper also was less durable than parchment, but when hand-made from rags could still be preserved over centuries. The introduction of cheap but acidic paper manufactured from wood pulp made books, journals and newspapers much more affordable, but over time has created major problems for libraries that must try to preserve them. Digital information is raising new doubts concerning preservation; for example, will technological developments render earlier equipment obsolete, in turn making it impossible to access information for which that obsolete equipment is required?

Harris (1995) distils the essence of libraries over the centuries into a brief formula: a library is "a collection of graphic materials arranged for relatively easy use, cared for by an individual or individuals familiar with that arrangement, and accessible to at least a limited number of persons." In this sense there has been continuity over several thousand years. The precise form in which the library has appeared, however, has changed dramatically over time. The medieval monastic library, in which small numbers of manuscript books were chained to tables for safe keeping, has little in common with modern lending libraries only too happy to circulate their stock to the widest range of clients. The early centuries of library development knew nothing of national, university, special or public libraries as we know them today. The distinction between a library and an archive has not always been apparent; the libraries of Sumeria and ancient Egypt, for example, might just as well be described as archives. Digital libraries once again are beginning to blur such organizational specializations.

The graphic materials used to store information always have strongly influenced how libraries function. Different media have raised individual problems for libraries in terms of acquisition, storage, organization, circulation and preservation. In turn, these considerations have influenced the design of the library building, the ways in which items are stored, the kinds of equipment required to access the information contained in these items, the cataloguing and circulation policies to be adopted, the conservation techniques that must be applied to them, and so on. This will be no less true for libraries that now must cope with digitized information stored on computer servers. It in turn will influence the ways in which libraries are structured and function. For these reasons, indeed, Levy and Marshal (1995) think that the term 'digital' library is unnecessary. Today's library, they argue, is dealing with a heterogeneity of materials, this time including digital ones, and essentially is no different from its predecessor with its clay tablets and papyrus rolls, or parchments and printed books.

1.5 Digital Libraries as a Global Resource

Although research and development relating to digital libraries, as discussed above, initially was focused in certain developed parts of the world, in fact digital libraries already are a global phenomenon. First, digital libraries in an institutional sense are being established in developed and developing countries, big and small countries, and countries in the north, south, east and west. Second, many digital libraries, regardless of content location, can be entered virtually, searched or browsed, and information retrieved by users from all over the world. Third, the content itself that has been selected and assembled as a unified digital collection may physically be stored on computers in different parts of the world. And fourth, cheap and effective digitization processes are offering diverse cultures the opportunity to organize, preserve and make available to users their own local text, image and sound artefacts in ways that were previously unthinkable (Worcman, 2002). Given the right resources, digital libraries through their multimedia collections can collect, record, disseminate and conserve locally generated information in the vernacular languages for the benefit of both the immediate community and wider audiences.

In developing countries, especially, digital libraries offer an opportunity to leapfrog the print collection era in which their libraries often suffered woefully because of lack of financial resources to acquire books and journals to support education, research, industry, commerce, government or leisure. Speaking of Africa, for example, Ojedokun (2000) believes that "digital libraries can play a major role in promoting knowledge or enhancing education" and that "the introduction of digital libraries will be of great benefit to library and information services delivery." People the world over have a need for timely and relevant information, even if the specific needs and kinds of information differ from community to community.

This is not to minimize the problems that can be encountered in such endeavours. In late 1999 Muswazi (2000) undertook a random sample of 47 libraries in southern Africa. Only 20 had official home pages, and even fewer – nine – had made their online catalogues available via the Web. As he concludes, digitization still was a rarity. First and foremost is the need for financial resources either to establish and maintain digital libraries locally or to access remotely those at a distance. Given such resources, technological problems can be tackled: satellite communication or distribution of collections on CD-ROM or DVD can offset inaccessible terrain, though infrastructure shortcomings such as a reliable electricity supply, unstable telecommunications networks, and insufficient bandwidth can still pose enormous problems in many parts of the world. Information must be made available in languages that local people can read, and illiteracy will still remain an obstacle to text-based information services. Muswazi (2000) reminds us that in southern Africa the 14 countries use 17 official languages and 139 ethnic or national languages, and that the average literacy rate across the region is 67%. In addition to language issues, interfaces must be designed with the needs of individual user communities in mind, and this means taking into account cultural differences. Finally, personnel with the requisite management and technical expertise are needed (Ojedokun, 2000). These various problems will form the focus of later chapters, as we explore the role of digital libraries in a global environment.

Such problems have led some observers to ask whether ICTs in fact are widening rather than narrowing the gap between the rich and the poor nations. Researchers at Harvard University and MIT created in the late 1990s DigitalDivide.org (http://www.digitaldivide.org) to help close the digital divide between those able to benefit from digital technologies and those who cannot. The phrase 'digital divide' refers to the division between those societies with access to digital infrastructure and services, and those without and it can also refer to the divide within a particular country between those people with access and those without. More details on aspects related to the digital divide can be acquired also from the Digital Divide Network website (http://www.digitaldividenetwork.org). Paul (2002) discusses, from a southeast Asian perspective, this divide in terms of digital connectivity, the level of e-commerce locally available, the skills capacity of the society, the level of investment in ICTs, the cultural openness to new digitally based lifestyles, the extent to which various sections of society are involved in overcoming digital divides, the level of cooperation between different sectors of society to exploit new opportunities, and the extent to which digital content from a country, about a country and in the language(s) of that country is available.

One observer pessimistically concludes that "it is in the nature of any new technology to exacerbate the existing divide between the rich and the poor." He considers that the rapid changes in the way information is published, stored retrieved and disseminated have worsened the relative deprivation of researchers in the developing world. In order to reverse this, information content should be freely available on the Web, and technology should be in place in poorer as well as richer countries to take advantage of this content: "then access to information for research will truly become democratic and the divide between the rich and the poor would be considerably reduced" (Arunachalam, 2003). One of the major issues facing digital libraries globally is whether they can rise to the challenge posed by such have-nots in order to ensure that access to information really is broadened rather than narrowed by their existence. Witten et al. (2002) suggest that digital libraries represent a key technology for developing countries as they can enable them to capture and exploit local information sources of direct relevance to them in fields such as health, hygiene, agriculture and nutrition:

> Disseminating information originating in the developed world is a very useful activity for developing countries. However, a more

effective strategy for sustained long-term human development is to disseminate the capability of creating information collections, rather than the collections themselves. This will allow developing countries to participate actively in our information society, rather than observing it from outside.

1.6 Digital Library Definitions

So far in this Chapter we have avoided the thorny issue of defining what exactly is a digital library. There is good reason for such prevarication. The problem does not lie in any dearth of definitions; Schwartz (2000) reports that students in a digital library course found 64 different definitions. Rather, the difficulty is a lack of consistency between them. Bawden and Rowlands (1999) concluded from their examination of the literature that there is little agreement on the basic assumptions underlying the concept of the digital library. Despite any such misgivings, in this book we must arrive at working definition of its central concept!

Borgman (2000) believes that one reason for the confusion of terminology is that research and practice in digital libraries are being conducted concurrently at each stage of the continuum from basic research to implementation. She adds that the variety of concerns within the digital library research community also reflects the interdisciplinary nature of the topic. Librarians see libraries as organizations that select, collect, organize, conserve, preserve, and provide access to information on behalf of a community of users. From their point of view, libraries are employing yet another delivery system for another information form. In this sense digital library connotes 'future library' and carries a sense of continuity with the past (a point of view discussed earlier in this Chapter). But definitions from the research community, especially from computer scientists, tend to take a narrower view of 'library' that emphasizes databases and retrieval at the expense of the broader library service and conservation roles (Borgman does point out, though, that these two communities are not mutually exclusive – some library practitioners participate in research teams, and some researchers are interested in practical issues).

What, then, are the characteristics of a digital library? The rapid pace of developments ensures that here we are aiming at a moving target. Rather than formulate yet another definition, we shall draw upon that presented by Borgman and her colleagues initially in 1996 in their Final report to the National Science Foundation, widely cited by many authors, and quoted in Borgman (2000):

> Digital libraries are a set of electronic resources and associated technical capabilities for creating, searching, and using information. In this sense they are an extension and enhancement of information storage and retrieval systems that manipulate digital data in any medium (text, images, sounds . . .) and exist in distributed networks. The content of digital libraries includes data, metadata that describe

various aspects of the data ... and metadata that consist of links or relationships to other data or metadata, whether internal or external to the digital library.

Digital libraries are constructed – collected and organized – by [and for] a community of users, and their functional capabilities support the information needs and uses of that community ... In this sense they are an extension, enhancement, and integration of a variety of information institutions as physical places where resources are selected, collected, organized, preserved, and accessed in support of a user community. These information institutions include, among others, libraries, museums, archives, and schools, but digital libraries also extend and serve other community settings, including classrooms, offices, laboratories, homes and public spaces.

Despite the detailed nature of this long definition, it is worth further discussion to clarify this controversial issue.

A digital library must contain information in a digital state (electronic resources, in the above definition). This may sound like a truism, but it still must be stated explicitly. Furthermore, such information may be represented as text, still images, moving images or audio sequences, or some combination of these different media. That is to say, digital libraries in practice very often include multimedia content. This leaves aside one contentious issue: can a digital library contain non-digital as well as digital content? For example, can a university library that maintains large print collections alongside ejournals and ebooks be considered a digital library? For Bawden and Rowlands (1999) a "significant proportion of the resources available to users" must exist in digital form. In contrast, Chowdhury and Chowdhury (1999) remind us that a characteristic of many digital libraries is that a large percentage of materials still are to be found in non-digital form. Marchionini (1998) says that to be modified by the term digital, a library must have some electronic content and services. The phrase 'hybrid library' rather than digital library has been used by some authors, especially in Europe, to emphasize that the collection may include non-digital alongside digitized documents. Oppenheim and Smithson (1999), for example, see a hybrid library as a means to integrate the traditional library with the digital library. Some of the digital libraries used as examples in this and subsequent chapters do provide access only to digital content, but in practice, many digital libraries also include non-digital (and especially print) documents alongside their digital holdings and no doubt will continue to do so for many years to come.

The next point in the definition is that digital libraries exist in distributed networks. That is to say, users can gain access to them via telecommunication networks (typically the Internet or organizational intranets) from myriad locations. Marchionini (1998) says that in practice a digital library makes its digital content and services accessible remotely through wide area or local area networks. Borgman (2000) herself concedes a lack of consensus on this point when stating that it is especially in the US that the necessity for a digital library to exist in distributed environments is asserted. Chowdhury and Chowdhury (1999) state that the users of a digital library *usually* (our italics) are somewhere other than the information they need. Witten and Bainbridge (2003), however, cite as an example of a digital library the Human Development Library containing just over a thousand digitized books and periodicals stored on a single CD-ROM and used in a Ugandan village without Internet access. Another example is The Essential Electronic Agricultural Library (TEEAL), a collection of more than 140 agricultural, environmental and related science periodicals developed at the Mann Library at Cornell University and the Rockefeller Foundation in the US in cooperation with many bibliographic database producers and journal publishers, and contained on 381 CD-ROMs. The aim of TEEAL is to help institutions in developing countries expand their journal collections despite the prohibitive cost of journal subscriptions, and it is used in 34 low and middle income countries (Dauphiné, Ochs and Koos, 2003).

The content of a digital library comprises both data and metadata describing that data (such as their authors, titles, year of publication, and a summation of their subject coverage). Libraries traditionally have called such metadata 'bibliographic information'. Metadata is discussed in Chapter Four, and is critical to the organization and retrieval of data. The definition also refers to metadata links to other data or metadata that might be contained within the digital collection or relate to digital content held elsewhere (revealing the importance of the Web and its hyperlinked environment for digital libraries). Chowdhury and Chowdhury (1999) agree that a significant part of the information in a collection typically will be metadata about the actual items, while Bishop and Star (1996) place the emphasis the other way around: the content cannot be entirely bibliographic but must include at least some full-text information.

A very important characteristic of a digital library is that its collection has been selected and organized for an identifiable user community. The collection will have been assembled and will be developed in future according to a policy, much as a traditional library typically has a collection development policy for its non-digital collection. Such a collection policy, whether formal or informal, will have been established with a specific user community or communities in mind. For this reason alone, the Web as a whole cannot be considered a digital library: although it provides access to multimedia information in digital form, this information has not been selected according to an established policy, but is simply made available by whomever so wishes to create a site (the Web also contains, of course, millions of pages to which no metadata have been assigned). The service component is also an important feature of the digital library as of the traditional library. The needs of the community are to be met not merely through the digital collection itself but also by means of reference and other services offered to virtual users.

The definition then goes on to point out that digital libraries can be extensions or enhancements of, or integrated into, a variety of institutional types including libraries but also other information-related organizations such as museums and archives. Furthermore, they can be used from a wide variety of locations other than these institutions: places of work, play or travel (wireless Internet connections make it possible to enter a digital library, at a price, from places like airport terminals or railway stations). In a traditional library, the collection is defined by its physical presence and ownership, whereas in a digital library it is defined by access, both technical and economic.

Two points not explicitly covered in the above definition need to be considered. First, despite the distributed nature of the content, many digital library definitions emphasize the importance of collection stability for digital libraries much as for traditional libraries: a distinguishing characteristic of any library is that its information resources are preserved for future as well as present use. For example, Deegan and Tanner (2002) emphasize that a digital library must treat its contents "as long-term stable resources" and "ensure their quality and survivability." The Digital Library Federation (http://www.diglib.org/dlfhomepage.htm), a consortium of libraries and related agencies "pioneering in the use of electronic-information technologies to extend their collections and services" has as one of its objectives the maintenance of "long-term access to the digital intellectual scholarly record." Certainly this is a major issue for digital libraries and is discussed in Chapter Eight. Second, the definition says nothing about collection size: must the collection attain a certain minimum size, and if so, what is this size? For Arms (2000), size is not an issue: digital library collections can range from tiny to enormous. Witten and Bainbridge (2003) implicitly suggest the same by including a CD-ROM-based library alongside, for example, the NZDL with which they are closely involved. Other authors (for example, Waters, 1998) state or at least imply that digital libraries will have substantial collections (and certainly more than could be held on one or two CD-ROMs).

It is hard to disagree with Deegan and Tanner (2002) when they write: "there are many different kinds of digital libraries creating, delivering and preserving digital objects that derive from many different formats of underlying data, and it is very difficult to formulate a definition that encapsulates all of these."

Before leaving definitional issues, mention must be made of the phrases 'virtual library', 'library without walls', 'electronic library', 'cyberlibrary', 'cybrary' and 'ebrary', all used by some authors to describe the digital library concept.

Two other related terms are 'gateway' and 'portal'. Following Peterson (2002), a gateway provides a list of resources, pre-selected to meet users' likely requirements, that are accessed by users via hyperlinks from the gateway to the resource that is located elsewhere; a portal accepts requests from users and *itself* interrogates information services believed to hold appropriate resources; the requests are then sent to those services and the retrieved information returned to the portal that processes it and presents it to the user. In essence, the user never leaves the portal. In many cases though the terms gateway and portal are used interchangeably. An example of a gateway from the University of Illinois is shown in Figure 1.2 (http://door.library.uiuc.edu). It provides links to a variety of digital information sources both on and off campus. In Figure 1.3 the subject portal for basic and agricultural sciences at the University of Wageningen (http://gateway.library.uiuc.edu/index.html) is shown.

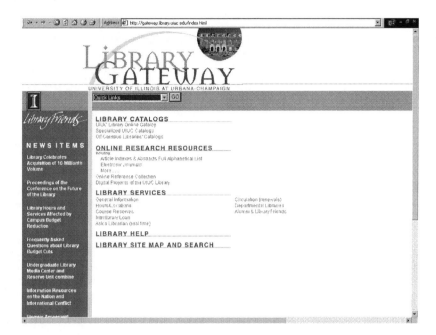

Figure 1.2 Library gateway, University of Illinois at Urbana-Champaign, US (reproduced courtesy of the University of Illinois)

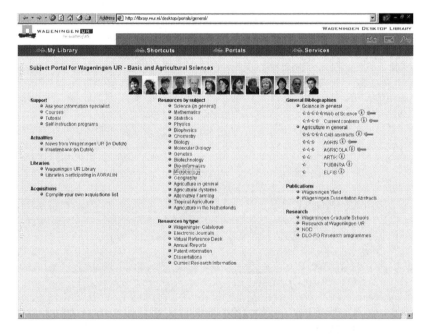

Figure 1.3 Subject portal, University of Wageningen, Netherlands (reproduced courtesy of the University of Wageningen)

Miller (2003), in an attempt to develop a typology for portals, refers to various definitions for them and suggests that the defining characteristics of a portal are that it can be customized and personalized so as to provide relevant content and functionality from a number of different information sources. The main message is that portals, as digital libraries, are in a process of development.

1.7 Why Digital Libraries?

What do digital libraries offer users that cannot be found in a traditional bricks and mortar library? First and foremost, they often are able to provide access through distributed networks to a range of information that would prove impossible for the greatest of the world's traditional libraries. It is no longer necessary for a library to find the economic resources to own its entire collection, nor to find the physical space to house it. High on the list of attractions for many users also is the opportunity to consult digital libraries from multiple locations such as the home, school, university, office, cybercafe or hotel room, rather than only from the library, archive or museum premises. Furthermore, they can be consulted at any time of the day or night everyday of the year (except for any computer downtime caused by maintenance or malfunctions). Items are never inaccessible because they have been loaned, sent to the bindery, wrongly shelved or stolen.

Digital libraries also can provide enhanced search and browse features, and enable documents to be downloaded, or cut and pasted directly into other documents. They can provide services to support activities such as distance education (e-learning) and e-commerce, and facilitate collaborative work among people who are geographically scattered. As Marchionini (1998) expresses it, "digital technology offers the potential to radically change who may use a library, when they do so, and what types of services are offered." These advantages offered to users by digital libraries will be explored in more detail in subsequent chapters.

Information professionals appreciate these same service enhancements: bigger collections, wider accessibility, reduced storage costs compared with the storage of traditional documents on library shelves, and more powerful retrieval capabilities. Digital documents also help with preservation as they can be consulted without the need to handle rare and fragile originals. As Allard (2002) says, "digital libraries can be viewed as extensions and augmentations of traditional libraries by extending the resources that can be offered and augmenting how people can seek and express information."

It should be emphasized, however, that the growth in digital records and digital libraries has not eliminated, as some predicted, the rule of paper. Not only do millions of print volumes from the pre-digital era remain unconverted, but the number of print publications continues to rise year by year, as does the quantity of paper consumed by computer printers! Both the publishers of academic journals and their readers have taken readily to digital versions, for example, but in many cases a traditional print version continues to co-exist alongside its digital equivalent.

Digital libraries, or at least their digital collections, unfortunately also have brought their own problems in areas such as:

- Equity of access – the digital divide
- Interoperability between systems and software
- User authentication for access to collections
- Information organization
- Interface design
- Intellectual property rights
- Preservation of digital data over time
- Staff re-skilling and training

Both the positive and the negative aspects of digital libraries will be explored in subsequent chapters and therefore will not be dwelt upon further here.

Information-related institutions like libraries, archives and museums traditionally have stressed the building in which their activities are conducted rather than the skilled professionals who work within them. Digital libraries may be de-emphasizing the former, but there is no reason to do likewise with the latter. Witten and Bainbridge (2003), although, or perhaps because, they are computer scientists, emphasize the importance for digital libraries of the traditional skills of the librarian. They believe that the librarian's functions are often overlooked by digital library proponents (at least in the research community to which they belong) but it is in the selection and organization of information by librarians that digital libraries are distinguished from the Web.

Fred Lerner in *The Story of Libraries* (1998) shares this view: whatever changes take place in libraries, librarians themselves will remain essential. He reminds us that libraries never have been static institutions; rather, they have wrestled many times with changing environments, including technological revolutions that have had a profound impact upon them:

> So long as human beings continue to use the knowledge they have inherited from their ancestors and learned from their contemporaries, so long as human ingenuity and creativity increases the store of information, there will be a need for persons and institutions to collect, to catalog, to preserve, and to guide. Books, and libraries, have changed over the thousands of years since the invention of writing ... But the essential task of the librarian has remained the same: to collect and preserve the record of human accomplishment and imagination, and to put this record in the hands of those who would use it.

References

Allard, S. (2002) Digital libraries: a frontier for LIS education. *Journal of Education for Library and Information Science*, **43** (4), 233–248

Arms, W. Y. (2000) *Digital Libraries.* Cambridge, MASS: MIT Press

Arunachalam, S. (2003) Information for research in developing countries: information technology – friend or foe? *Bulletin of the American Society for Information Science and Technology*, **29** (5), 16–21

Bawden, D. and Rowlands, I. (1999) Digital libraries: assumptions and concepts. *Libri*, **49** (4), 181–191

Bishop, A.P. and Star, S.L. (1996) Social informatics for digital library use and infrastructure. In M.E. Williams, ed. *Annual Review of Information Science and Technology*, **31**. Medford, NJ: Information Today, 301–401

Borgman, C. L. (2000) *From Gutenberg to the Global Information Infrastructure: Access to Information in the Networked World.* Cambridge, MASS: MIT Press

Bush, V. (1945) As we may think. *Atlantic Monthly*, **176** (1), 101–108. Available at: http://www.theatlantic.com/unbound/flashbks/computer/bushf.htm

Chowdhury, G.G. and Chowdhury, S. (1999) Digital library research: major issues and trends. *Journal of Documentation*, **55** (4), 409–448

Dauphiné N., Ochs, M. A. and Koos, N. K. (2003) Bringing scientific literature to the developing world: the essential electronic agricultural library – TEEAL. *Online Information Review*, **27** (1), 51–54

Deegan, M. and Tanner, S. (2002) *Digital Futures: Strategies for the Information Age.* London: Facet Publishing

Fox, E. A., ed. (1993) *Sourcebook on Digital Libraries: Prepared and Sponsored by the National Science Foundation.* Available at: http://fox.cs.vt.edu/DLSB.html

Harris, M. H. (1995) *History of Libraries in the Western World.* 4th ed. Metuchen, NJ: Scarecrow Press

Lerner, F. (1998) *The Story of Libraries: From the Invention of Writing to the Computer Age.* New York: Continuum

Levy, D. M. and Marshal, C. C. (1995) Going digital: a look at assumptions underlying digital libraries. *Communications of the ACM*, **38** (4), 77–84

Marchionini, G. (1998) Research and development in digital libraries. *Encyclopedia of Library and Information Science*, Volume 63. New York: Dekker, 259–279

Miller, P. (2003) Towards a typology for portals. *Ariadne*, **37**. Available at: http://www.ariadne.ac.uk/issue37/miller/

Muswazi, P. (2000) Digital library and information services in southern Africa. *Information Development*, **16** (2), 75–81

Ojedokun, A. A. (2000) Prospects of digital libraries in Africa. *African Journal of Library, Archival and Information Science*, **10** (1), 13–21

Oppenheim, C. and Smithson, D. (1999) What is the hybrid library? *Journal of Information Science*, **25** (2), 97–112

Paul, J. (2002) Narrowing the digital divide: Initiatives undertaken by the Association of South-East Asian Nations (ASEAN). *Program*, **36** (1), 13–22

Peterson, L. (2002) Digital versus print issues. In G.E. Gorman, ed. *The Digital Factor in Library and Information Services.* London: Facet Publishing, 26–44

Rusbridge, C. (1998) Towards the hybrid library. *D-Lib Magazine*, **7** (7/8). Available at: http://www.dlib.org/dlib/july98/rusbridge/07rusbridge.html

Schwartz, C. (2000) Digital libraries: an overview. *Journal of Academic Librarianship*, **26** (6), 385–393

Waters, D.J. (1998) What are digital libraries? *CLIR Issues*, **4**. Available at: http://www.clir.org/pubs/issues/issues04.html

Witten, I. H. and Bainbridge, D. (2003) *How to Build a Digital Library*. San Francisco: Morgan Kaufmann

Witten I. H., Loots, M., Trujillo M. F, and Bainbridge, D. (2002) The promise of digital libraries in developing countries. *Electronic Library*, **20** (1) 7–13

Worcman, K. (2002) Digital division is cultural exclusion. But is digital inclusion cultural inclusion? *D-Lib Magazine*, **8** (3). Available at: http://www.dlib.org/dlib/march02/worcman/03worcman.html

Chapter 2

Digital Libraries: Users and Services

2.1 User Access to Digital Libraries

In Chapter One we presented a definition of digital libraries that included
". . . a set of electronic resources and associated technical capabilities for creating, searching and using information" and that ". . . are constructed – collected and organized – by [and for] a community of users and their functional capabilities support the information needs and uses of that community." As in the development and maintenance of traditional collections of materials in libraries, museums, archives and so on, users are very important when developing and implementing digital libraries. In this chapter we shall concentrate on why people use digital libraries, their use in various types of institution, what services are offered, why some users face particular challenges and how these may be overcome. Questions relating to the What? of digital library sources and the How? they may be implemented are covered in later chapters.

The early digital library research projects introduced in Chapter One were based in university environments in the so-called developed world, and primarily in the US. Since the late 1990s, however, there has been a rapid growth in the number of digital libraries around the world. There are various reasons for this:

- People are being encouraged to learn throughout their lives and not just while formally studying within traditional educational establishments. This is often referred to as lifelong learning (or learning from the cradle to the grave), and digital libraries may be developed by public libraries, or other institutions, to provide relevant learning resources.
- Developments in teaching and learning within education establishments at all levels are becoming more student-centred, with project-based or

problem-based teaching methods. In such environments digital libraries are integral to providing access to appropriate digital information sources.

- Professional users have higher expectations of services provided by libraries. They have become used to searching the Web for entertainment, travel and other information, and so are now expecting to be provided with quality digital information sources also for their professional work.
- Researchers in universities around the world have become used to online communication and are keen to enable the flow of scholarly thought via published papers in digital form that might be held in repositories in digital libraries.
- The need to preserve cultural and historical heritage collections of fragile and precious artefacts has encouraged many museums, archives and galleries around the world to develop digitized collections for users from all over the world to access and study.
- The technology for developing digital libraries is available throughout the world: organizations in developing countries can use appropriate technology and provide comparable digital library services for their users as for those in developed countries. Also users who might have similar interests but are geographically dispersed can be provided with a collection of relevant digital information sources via a digital library.
- Governments of many countries aim to provide access to relevant information for their citizens and the development of digital libraries is seen as one way of achieving this. Further developments, such as e-voting and so on, are a move towards e-government.
- And finally, the fact that digital libraries can assist in the transformation of data into information and thence to knowledge is seen as being of value in the knowledge-based economies of many countries.

There is a wide spectrum of users for digital library services in academic, national and public libraries, and these users are described in subsequent sections. In other situations the users of a particular digital library are linked through a shared interest in a subject rather than being 'members' of some organization that offers a more traditional library or information service. The Tibetan and Himalayan Digital Library, for instance, is being developed at the University of Virginia in the US as an international archive of knowledge (including multimedia learning resources and multilingual studies) about Tibet and the Himalayas, and brings together scholars, librarians and others from all over the world (http://www.thdl.org). Figure 2.1 shows the opening page of the website of this digital library. The site is available in Tibetan, Nepali, Chinese and Japanese as well as in English (Germano, 2002).

In some cases the users of a digital library are defined by their age. Adkins (2002) provides an overview of developments with respect to digital libraries and younger users. Stories from the Web (http://www.storiesfromtheweb. org) is a Reader Development Programme which has been developed by Birmingham Libraries with a number of partner public library authorities in the UK. Figure 2.2 shows the homepage for the collection of digital information sources for 8–11 year olds. More information on the development of a digital library for children is given in a case study in Chapter Nine.

Figure 2.1 Tibetan and Himalayan Digital Library, University of Virginia, US (reproduced courtesy of the Tibetan and Himalayan Digital Library)

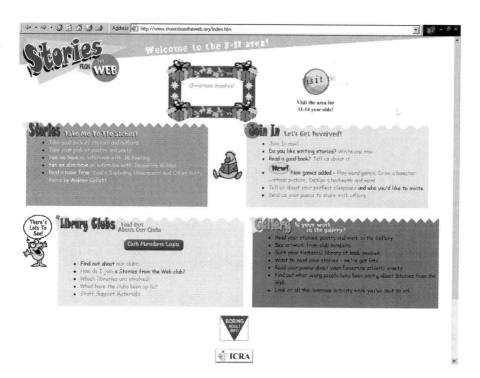

Figure 2.2 Stories from the Web – a digital library for younger users, UK (reproduced courtesy of Re:Source and contributors)

There are also many users of digital libraries at the other range of the age spectrum. For example, the National Institutes of Health (NIH) in the US, in conjunction with the US National Library of Medicine, the US Department of Health and Human Services and the National Institute on Aging, has developed NIHSeniorHealth (http://nihseniorhealth.gov), a digital library of health information sources of relevance to older people (60 plus). The interface for this digital library has been designed in a senior-friendly way: with large print, short, easy to read segments of information; with the ability to enlarge the text and to alter the contrast (from normal (black or green text on a white background) to high (yellow or white text on a black background)); and with a spoken word version also available as can be seen in Figure 2.3.

Some of the general advantages that digital libraries offer as well as the challenges faced were discussed in Chapter One. For any individual user the reasons for using a digital library can include:

- the information is available on the desktop or laptop computer. This saves physically visiting the library or information centre and is particularly useful for remote or distance-learning students of universities as well as for users with mobility problems who may be housebound.
- the 'library' is open 24/7 (or all day and every day).
- the information retrieved is in digital form and so can be incorporated into appropriate documents, such as student assignments, research reports, company information and so on. The issue of intellectual property

Figure 2.3 NIH SeniorHealth – a digital library for older users, US (reproduced courtesy of the US National Library of Medicine)

rights, however, must be understood and adhered to so that plagiarism and copyright infringement do not happen.

- a possible greater awareness, through a well-designed user interface, of the information sources that have been collected and made available in an appropriate manner. Such sources might be text-based (including ebooks and ejournals) and also multimedia as described further in Chapter Three.
- much increased chance of being able to access the required information (that is, no problem with another user also using the resource at the same time).
- improved facilities for resource discovery and location of information.
- specific services of potential relevance may be offered.
- access to up to date information (as long as the collection of digital information sources is managed appropriately and individual sources are kept current).
- possibility of gaining access to information sources that are not accessible to an individual over the Web but which are available through a digital library from a specific institution, such as a public or academic library.

2.2 Digital Libraries in Various Institutional Environments

The digital libraries that exist around the world are many and varied. In this section we shall concentrate on digital libraries developed for users linked to five types of organizations: museums, national libraries, public libraries, research establishments, and teaching and learning institutions. Details of the information sources which might be used within these digital libraries are provided in Chapter Three.

2.2.1 Museums

Many culture-based organizations, such as museums, are developing digital collections of their holdings which can be accessed freely by individuals (as well as by schools or higher education institutions) around the world. The State Hermitage Museum in St. Petersburg, Russia, for instance, since 1997 has been involved in a variety of projects with the computer manufacturer IBM to provide access to the huge collections of the museum using a variety of digital technologies (http://www.hermitagemuseum.org). These digital collections, accessible in both Russian and English, include a gallery of 3D images, virtual excursions, and virtual exhibitions as well as the ability to search using IBM's Query by Image Content technology.

Many museums and galleries have found that visitors to their physical buildings and collections have increased following searching and browsing of their digital collections. The homepage of the Virtual Library museums pages (VLmp), a distributed directory of museums around the world with digital collections and which is supported by the International Council of Museums, is shown in Figure 2.4 (http://vlmp.museophile.com). Bowen

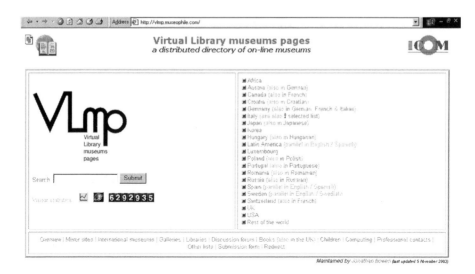

Figure 2.4 Virtual Library museums pages, UK (reproduced courtesy of Jonathan Bowen)

(2002), using tracking software, surveyed the use made of VLmp and covered aspects such as the location of users, software browsers used, times of access and search keywords. He found, amongst other results, that although by 2002 many users were converging on a small number of platforms and browsers to access museums' digital information sources, a significant minority used non-standard facilities. He suggested this might increase with the development of devices such as mobile telephones, interactive television and specialized browsers for disabled people.

2.2.2 National libraries

National libraries often house important collections of archives, printed materials, and photographs related to a particular country, and also function as a central point for information about the culture and heritage of that country. Their users may come from within the country or from elsewhere, and in the past often had to travel to the physical national library building. With the development of digital libraries users can now view and study the collections from all over the world and these collections therefore can be used by a much wider range of people. Treasures from the World's Great Libraries, developed by the National Library of Australia and described in Chapter One, is an example of a digital library developed within a national library. The use of digital technologies to provide users with access to the 'treasures' of the British Library, has been underway since the Turning the Pages project of the mid-1990s. This project incorporated a novel interface design for accessing images from a number of sources including the *Lindisfarne Gospels*, the *Diamond Sutra*, the *Sforza Hours*, the *Leonardo Notebook* and the *Sultan Baybars' Qur'an*. Although initially only available through a special viewing station within the British Library, users around the world may now view these sources on the Web (http://www.bl.uk/collections/treasures/treasures.html). The use of digital technology to help in the preservation function of national libraries is also very important – and is discussed further in Chapter Eight. Digital libraries within national libraries provide their users with a wide range of services, and Figure 2.5 shows some of the digital information sources made available from the Det Kongelige Bibliotek – the National Library of Denmark.

Library and Archives Canada (formerly the National Library of Canada) in partnership with the Canadian Institute for Historical Microreproductions and the National Archives of Canada, has produced a digital library called Early Canadiana Online/Notre Mémoire En Ligne (http://www.canadiana.org). This digital library comprises over 3,000 English-language and French-language books and pamphlets published before 1900, and is particularly strong in literature, women's history, native studies, travel and exploration, and the history of French Canada. Cherry and Duff (2002), members of the user-based evaluation of digital libraries research group at the University of Toronto, surveyed users of this digital library in 2000. Of the 159 respondents, approximately half were using the resource for personal interest/genealogy, 21% for scholarly research, 12% for professional purposes and 6% for teaching. The investigators concluded that "digital library research should take into account the types of tasks carried out, as well as

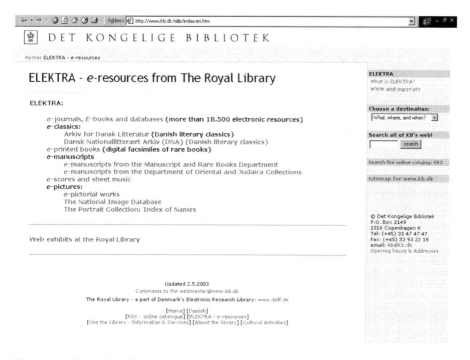

Figure 2.5 Digital information sources from Det Kongelige Bibliotek, Denmark (reproduced courtesy of Det Kongelige Bibliotek)

the culture of different user groups". They believe that digital libraries of historical materials such as this have the potential to attract new user groups who may use the collection to support unexpected tasks. Other national libraries are also finding that digital library developments are broadening their range of users.

2.2.3 Public libraries and institutions

In many countries the role of public libraries in the new 'knowledge economy' or in the globalization of services is being defined. In Singapore, for instance, staff at the National Library Board (NLB), which covers public libraries as well as the National Library of Singapore, view a digital library as playing:

> a key role in providing a knowledge network that equips individuals and corporations with the necessary resources to tap into the information highway and transform raw information into economic value. (http://www.elibraryhub.com/libraryServices/libraryServices.asp).

Further information about the development of digital library services in the public libraries of Singapore is given in a case study in Chapter Nine. Staff from the NLB are involved with colleagues from public libraries in Australia, Canada, Denmark, Finland, France, Germany, the Netherlands, New Zealand, Sweden, the UK and the US in the International Network of Public Libraries project (http://www.public-libraries.net/en/). The project, which runs from 1996 to 2004, aims to pool international 'know-how' and develop appropriate solutions for their users. Poustie (1999), who is involved in this project, notes how public library managers in Australia and the UK are seeing a new role for public libraries as a "centre for lifelong learning and self-directed learning, utilizing the new technologies and making them available to the public". In the UK this development has been fostered by funds of 240 million euros from the Government to public libraries in an initiative known as the People's Network (http://www.peoplesnetwork.gov.uk). Public libraries in the UK, as elsewhere, have often been considered 'street corner universities' without necessarily having the requisite resources. However, with funds from the People's Network, by the end of 2003 all 4,000 or so British public libraries had the necessary equipment (including some 30,000 PCs) to enable free access via the Web, library staff had received appropriate training to assist users, and work on developing relevant content for users was underway. The People's Network has been judged a great success and public libraries are receiving further funding to provide new online services such as access to e-government services, e-learning resources, community information and virtual reference sources for their users. Through the People's Network members of public libraries in the UK can gain access to various licensed digital information sources; for instance many public libraries in Wales provide their members with free access to Oxford Reference Online – a digital collection of over 120 language and subject reference works. In Canada, members of the Virtual Reference Library at Toronto Public Library (http://vrl.tpl.toronto.on.ca) can also access free and licensed

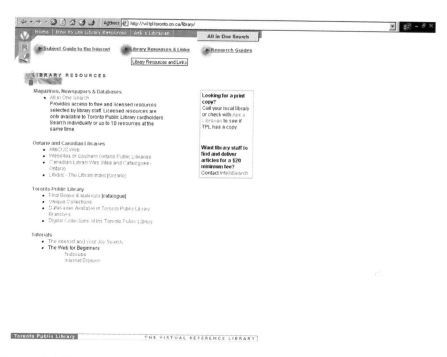

Figure 2.6 Virtual Reference Library, Toronto Public Library, Canada (reproduced courtesy of Toronto Public Library)

sources – including bilingual (English/French) encyclopaedias, the full texts of magazines and newspapers, *The Canadian Theatre Record*, *The Toronto Official Plan* and local history digital collections as well as links to catalogues in the geographic (Toronto, Ontario and Canada) area as described by Scardellato (2001) and shown in Figure 2.6.

2.2.4 Research establishments

In the research sector users require access to research carried out by colleagues worldwide made available in articles published in refereed scholarly journals, in books, or in unpublished sources such as doctoral dissertations or research reports. There has been growing consternation within universities and research establishments in recent years about the increasing costs of scholarly journals and the lack of funds within libraries to acquire access to the appropriate materials. The solution seen by many is the development of 'Open Access' sources, and these are described in Chapter Three. Figure 2.7 shows some of the information sources that are made available to users at CERN, the European Particle Physics Laboratory in Geneva, Switzerland. The CERN Document Server provides users with access to a large number of bibliographic records, almost half of which provide access to the full text of materials such as preprints, journal articles, reports and theses. In addition there are records for photographs, presentations, videos, press cuttings and archives.

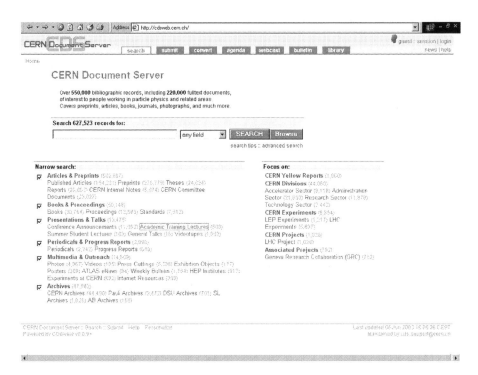

Figure 2.7 CERN Document Server, Switzerland (reproduced courtesy of CERN)

2.2.5 Teaching and learning establishments

With the teaching of students at all levels becoming more user-centred there needs to be an appropriate learning environment infrastructure to support them. In many establishments the concept of user-centred learning is being achieved with the adoption of various managed learning environments (MLEs) and virtual learning environments (VLEs). MLEs comprise the whole range of information systems and processes of the institution (including a VLE if its exists) that contribute directly, or indirectly, to learning and learning management including the student record system, learning resources and so on whilst VLEs encompass the components in which students and lecturers participate in online interactions of various kinds. Software, such as WebCT and Blackboard, have been developed to integrate online methods of delivering course material and links to appropriate digital information sources that can then be accessed 24 hours a day, seven days a week (24/7) by students, as well as providing computer-based communication software (chat rooms, e-mail, bulletin boards, and so on). In the UK the Joint Information Systems Committee (JISC) is supporting a range of projects in this area and has prepared an MLE Information Pack (http://www.jisc.ac.uk/mle). Library and information staff in institutions involved in using this technology have an important role to play, and the DELIVER (Digital Electronic Library Integration within Virtual EnviRonments) project, jointly undertaken by the London School of Economics and Political Science (LSE) and De Montfort University, is one example of a project which has explored this further by linking the VLE with the library management system (http://www.angel.ac.uk/DELIVER/). Within DELIVER, practical software tools have been developed for the creation and integration of course-based reading lists within the WebCT VLE. Many courses at LSE now have e-based course packs containing e-readings which have to be copyright cleared and made available in digital form. DELIVER was just one of 10 projects funded by JISC to investigate linking digital libraries with VLEs. JISC (http://www.jisc.ac.uk) is an independent advisory body supporting further and higher education in the UK. JISC provides strategic guidance, advice and opportunities to use ICT in teaching, learning, research and administration and also funds a number of projects related to digital library developments.

User-centred learning has always been a feature of distance education and open learning courses. Institutions such as the Open University (OU) in the UK (http://www.open.ac.uk), Sukhothai Thammitharat Open University in Thailand (http://www.stou.ac.th) and Yashwantrao Chavan Maharashtra Open University (http://www.ycmou.com) in India have pioneered these approaches in their respective countries for several years. Rowntree (1990) refers to open learning as an all-embracing philosophy which places control and choice in the hands of learners so that they can learn at the time, pace and place which satisfies their individual circumstances and requirements. For many years the libraries located in open universities were mainly for use by their academic staff in teaching and research rather than for the many thousands of students who were enrolled in the courses. ICT developments are changing this situation, and these libraries are becoming much more designed to meet the needs of all their students as well as researchers and staff and are available on a 24/7 basis. The case study on the OU in the UK in Chapter Nine provides further details of the range of services offered by its digital library. Figure 2.8 shows the information sources available to students, via the Electronic Library, at the Open University of Hong Kong.

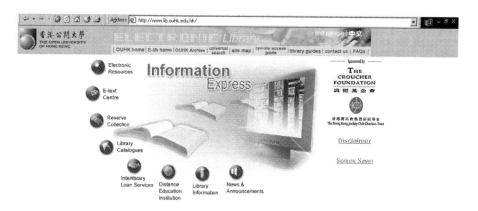

Figure 2.8 Electronic Library, Open University of Hong Kong, China (reproduced courtesy of the Open University of Hong Kong)

The English interface is shown in the figure and a Chinese-language version and a text-only version (for visually impaired users) are also available by clicking on the appropriate option at the top right hand corner of the screen.

A three-year study (1999–2002) on the uptake of digital information sources by users in higher education establishments in the UK is reported by Urquhart and others (2003). A main trend identified was that academic staff support for use of digital information sources may increasingly be formalized through the use of VLEs. Staff in library and information centres need to develop new skills in working with academic staff who themselves may be unaware how key their role is in encouraging use of digital libraries by students.

A user survey of 1050 college students in the US found that during their most recent digital library visit the digital information sources used were:

- full texts of ejournals (67%);
- library catalogue (57%);
- databases and journal indexes (51%);
- ebooks (21%).

In response to a question on what the campus library could do to help with study assignments users suggested:

- make it easier to use and access library resources;
- have more materials available (both in print and electronic);
- offer interactive maps, study tips and guides;
- provide links to other library and research sites (OCLC, 2002).

2.3 Personalized Digital Libraries

For some users, a major advantage in using a digital library is the ability to 'personalize' the information that appears on their desktop or laptop computer. Personalization (or customization as it is sometimes called) was a major trend identified in 1999 by ten expert members of the Library and Information Technology Association (LITA) of the American Library Association:

> library users who are web users, a growing group, expect customization, interactivity, and customer support. Approaches that are library-focused instead of user-focused will be increasingly irrelevant. The University of Washington's MyGateway and North Carolina State University's MyLibrary@NCState are examples of customized portals (http://www.lita.org/committe/toptech/mw99.htm#customization).

Staff at the University of Washington Library describe why users should use MyGateway in the following way:

- enables the organization of frequently-used web resources in a way similar to bookmarking but, unlike bookmarks, they are independent of the workstation used;
- provides links to new resources of potential interest to a specific user which have been added to the library's 'collection' since the user last logged in;
- allows users to add items from the results of a search directly to MyGateway;
- avoids the need to add further personal information after logging in to MyGateway. (https://www.lib.washington.edu/resource/help/MyGateway.html)

MyLibrary@NCState also allows users to create their own personal web interface. This software has been used by many other institutions both within the US (for instance at Virginia Commonwealth University, Los Alamos National Laboratory, Cornell University Library) and without (for instance at the Central Medical Library of the University of Ljubljana in Slovenia, Toronto Public Library in Canada and Lund University in Sweden). In developing the personalized medical library portal at the University of Ljubljana in Slovenia, staff reviewed various software options and chose MyLibrary @NCState as described by Rozic-Hristovski, Humar and Hristovski (2003). This software was written for English-language speakers, but communicating with the digital library in the user's native language is an important feature of any personalized system. The Slovenian team therefore decided to develop the functionality of the software so that other languages could be covered along with a facility for multilingual support. Staff at the Università Carlo Cattaneo (LIUC) in Italy (see the case study in Chapter Nine) also felt that users needed to communicate their personal preferences in their native language and so developed an Italian interface for this software as shown in Figure 2.9 (http://mylibrary.liuc.it).

2.4 Digital Reference Services

One possible disadvantage of digital libraries is that users need not visit the physical building and so are not able to call upon the staff within the library for face to face help in finding information. In order to overcome this, some institutions provide digital reference services. The two basic models for digital reference are:

- Asynchronous. In such services the user will e-mail a request to the library, or fill in a specific web form outlining the specific request and, in due course an answer will be provided by e-mail.
- Synchronous (real-time, text-based or chat). In these services there is a two-way communication between user and librarian using 'chat' software or video technology.

Sometimes libraries collaborate with others, either in the same country, or perhaps in different parts of the world, to assist in the 24/7 approach to

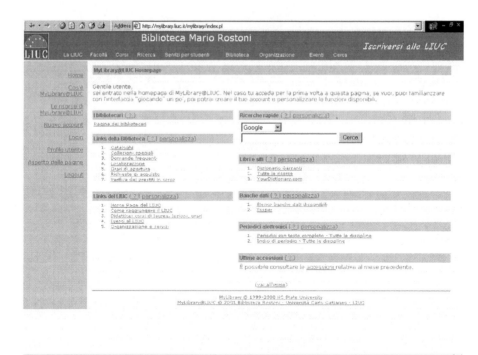

Figure 2.9 MyLibrary, Biblioteca Mario Rostoni, LIUC, Italy (reproduced courtesy of Biblioteca Mario Rostoni)

offering digital reference services for their users. Examples of collaborative digital reference services include:

- VRC – Virtual Reference Canada/ Référence Virtuelle Canada (Gaudet and Savard, 2002). This service involves a large number of libraries, archives, museums and research institutions across Canada providing a free and bilingual collaborative digital reference service (http://www. nlc-bnc.ca/vrc-rvc). Ask A Librarian in the UK involves about 70 public libraries (http://www.ask-a-librarian.org.uk). It developed from early work (in the mid-1990s) in public library collaboration relating to digital library services (Berube, 2004).
- QuestionPoint- Cooperative Virtual Reference, being developed by the Library of Congress and OCLC in the US with input from participating members of the Global Reference Network – a group of libraries and institutions worldwide that are committed to digital reference (http://www. questionpoint.org). In the Netherlands a Dutch version of QuestionPoint – known as Al@din (Algemeen Landelijk Dekkend Digitaal Informatie Netwerk) – is being developed and made accessible via the Dutch Public Libraries website (http://www.bibliotheek.nl).

It is often important for users in bilingual or multilingual communities to be able to ask questions of digital reference services in their 'mother' tongue and receive responses in that language and Al@din hopes to achieve this for Dutch users (Visser, 2003). Staff at the University of Illinois at Urbana are compiling a worldwide list of such collaborative digital reference services (http://www.lis.uiuc.edu/~b-sloan/collab.htm).

2.5 Information Literacy

It is necessary for users to have the requisite skills to obtain relevant information quickly and effectively from digital library sources and become what is often referred to as 'information literate'. What exactly are these skills? A number of definitions have been formulated; for example, in the UK a working group of SCONUL – the Society of College, National and University Libraries – developed what have become known as the Seven Pillars of information literacy:

- The ability to recognize a need for information.
- The ability to distinguish ways in which the information 'gap' may be addressed, that is, knowledge of appropriate kinds of resources; selection of resources with 'best fit' for the task at hand; and the ability to understand the issues affecting accessibility of sources.
- The ability to construct strategies for locating information (for instance, to articulate the information need to match against resources; to develop a systematic method appropriate for the need; and to understand the principles of construction and generation of databases).
- The ability to locate and access information (that is to develop appropriate searching techniques (such as the use of Boolean operators); to use appropriate ICTs; to use appropriate indexing and abstracting services, citation indexes and databases; and to use current awareness methods to keep up-to-date).
- The ability to compare and evaluate information obtained from different sources and to have an awareness of bias and authority issues as well as an awareness of the peer review process of scholarly publishing, and to be able to extract information matching the particular need.
- The ability to organize, apply and communicate information to others in ways appropriate to the situation, and to cite bibliographic references in project reports and theses; to construct a personal bibliographic system; to apply information to the problem at hand; to communicate effectively using an appropriate medium, and to understand issues of copyright and plagiarism.
- The ability to synthesize and build upon existing information, contributing to the creation of new knowledge (SCONUL, 1999).

The above definition is just one of many, and numerous organizations (such as the Australian and New Zealand Institute for Information Literacy, and the Association of College and Research Libraries Institute for Information

Literacy in the US) as well as individual libraries in many countries are working to make their users information literate. Research in information literacy at Sheffield University in the UK has resulted in a website with links to many information literacy developments around the world (http://dis.shef.ac.uk/literacy/). In addition an international conference on eliteracy, which covers both information literacy and IT literacy, is held annually (http://www.elit-conf.org).

In an academic environment (school, college or university) information literacy training for students might be provided through a compulsory component, or module, which, ideally, should be closely related to the subject content of their studies. For instance, the OU in the UK has a distance learning, credit-bearing module on information literacy called MOSAIC (Making Sense of Information in the Connected Age) which covers key aspects of information literacy (recognition of information need, searching, evaluating, using information, and so on) and is assessed by a portfolio which documents a search process (http://www.open.ac.uk/mosaic/). This module takes about 12 weeks to complete and is open to non-professional library staff as well as students. Students completing the course satisfactorily can gain credits that can be used towards their degree. Voluntary training classes can also be provided, though attendance tends to be lower (and frequently those most in need of training are least likely to volunteer!). It is often only by making courses compulsory that students will actually pay any attention to them. Another approach is to provide self-help guides or tutorials. In addition to MOSAIC, the OU has also developed a tutorial SAFARI – Skills in Accessing, Finding and Reviewing Information (http://sorbus.open.ac.uk/safari/signpostframe.htm) that is freely available for anyone to use. Via SAFARI, users can work their way through the stages of understanding information sources, planning a search, carrying out a search and evaluating a search. The whole tutorial takes about 14 hours to complete.

2.6 Barriers to User Access

2.6.1 Visual or other physical impairment affecting access

Users with a range of disabilities are provided, through legislation in force in many countries around the world, with rights to ensure access to digital information services on the Web. The policies in a number of countries (including Australia, Canada, Denmark, Finland, France, Germany, Ireland, Italy, Japan, New Zealand, Portugal, the UK and the US) with respect to such web accessibility are maintained by the WAI – Web Accessibility Initiative (http://www.w3.org/WAI/Policy). For instance, in Australia the Disability Discrimination Act of 1992 has a section (No. 24) that makes it unlawful for websites to be inaccessible to the disabled, and so the State Library of New South Wales provides a variety of adaptive (or assistive) technology to assist users in accessing electronic information resources. Examples include:

- Screen reading software so that a 'voice' speaks the content on the screen – needed for blind people.
- Image magnification software – needed for those with low vision so as to enable them to read information on the screen.
- An alternative mouse – needed for those who have problems with hand control (http://www.sl.nsw.gov.au/access/technology.cfm).

Users can have a range of visual impairments which affect their use of digital libraries. An annual conference is held on Technology and Persons with Disabilities at California State University, and a paper from the 2003 conference briefly describes a management system for a digital library being developed at the Silesian University of Technology (Bzorza, 2003). Figure 2.10 shows a record for a digitized version of a Polish translation of a book by the English author Alastair McLean held in the digital library, developed using the Silesian software, for the Laski School for the Blind.

Apart from those registered as blind or partially sighted, some users may be colour blind. Colour blindness affects one in 20 people and the Vischeck website (http://www.vischeck.com) provides good examples of what it is like to be colour blind with an inability to differentiate between red and green, although there may also be other troublesome combinations. More generally, anyone with less than perfect vision, and older users especially are likely to fall into this category, may encounter problems with small font sizes, or poor colour combination.

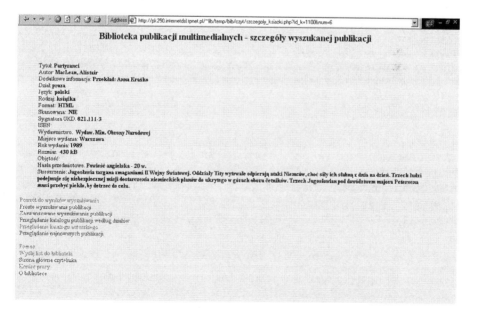

Figure 2.10 Catalogue record, Biblioteka publikacji multimedialnych, Laski School for the Blind, Poland (reproduced courtesy of the Polish Blind Union, Polski Związek Niewidomych)

Information staff need to ensure that their digital libraries are as accessible to the visually impaired users as to other users. A wide variety of assistive technology exists, such as text enlargers, synthetic voice output and so on, that can help those with visual impairments. Two examples of relevant centres for information are:

- BIKA Competence Centre (Barrier-free ICT for all) in Germany (http://access.fit.fraunhofer.de/bika/home.xhtml?lang=en) which is part of the Fraunhofer Institute of Applied Information Technology, and amongst other activities is involved in European Union –funded projects as part of the Information Society Technologies programme.
- TechDIS (www.techdis.ac.uk) in the UK, a service funded by JISC.

Practical guidance on providing accessible library websites for visually impaired people is provided, and updated, by a number of web sources such as the WAI and the Royal National Institute for the Blind in the UK (http://www.rnib.org.uk) as well as by printed sources such as Mates (2000). Interface design issues for users with visual problems are discussed further in Chapter Six. Some institutions have implemented their own guidelines on accessibility issues. For instance, at MIT developers of websites or web-based software are expected to follow specific guidelines to ensure that the products meet the minimum level of accessibility to persons with disabilities (see http://web.mit.edu/atic/www/sw/developweb.html).

As noted earlier, the majority of digital libraries are accessed via the Web and the following quote by Tim Berners-Lee, the inventor of the Web, is as applicable to digital libraries as it is to the Web: "The power of the Web is in its universality. Access by everyone regardless of disability is an essential aspect". This quote appears on the home page of the WAI based at MIT (http://www.w3.org/WAI/). The WAI is an International Program Office within the World Wide Web Consortium (W3C) that works, in coordination with organizations around the world, to pursue accessibility through five primary areas:

- technology;
- guidelines;
- tools;
- education and outreach;
- research and development.

2.6.2 No appropriate technology

The concept of the digital divide and the unequal pace of developments in societies with respect to accessing digital libraries between the developed and developing world as well as within individual countries was introduced in Chapter One. Annual reports, such as those published by the Global Digital Divide Initiative, provide information about the digital divide among and between nations. The Global Digital Divide Initiative was set up in 2000 by the World Economic Forum to build partnerships between public and private sector communities to bridge the divide between those who can make effective use of ICT to improve their lives and those who cannot. Here are some details from the 2001–2002 report:

- industrialized countries with some 15% of the world's population are home to 88% of all Internet users;
- by 2003 Asia will have over 200 million Internet users, surpassing the US and Europe;
- Norway has Western Europe's highest penetration rate at 49%, with Italy at the other end of the spectrum at 15%. (http://www.weforum.org/pdf/ Initiatives/Digital_Divide_Report_2001_2002.pdf)

Overcoming the digital divide is a challenge that is being faced in many countries, and further insights into such issues were discussed (between participants from China, Malaysia, New Zealand and the University of the South Pacific and Sri Lanka) at a conference organized by the Sri Lankan Library Association in early 2003 (http://www.nsf.ac.lk/slla/papers.htm). It was felt that library staff in many countries had a role to play in bridging the digital divide by creating appropriate digital libraries and by ensuring that their users were information literate.

To address the problem of users without easy access to the Internet a café called Cyberia was set up in London in 1994 where users, for a fee, could sip a cup of coffee and access the Internet. This was the world's first cybercafe, and there are now thousands of such establishments in over 140 countries (http://www.cybercafes.com). The People's Network in the UK, described earlier, is another attempt to provide access to the Internet for all within a community. Appropriate computing equipment and access to the Internet through a reliable service provider are prerequisites for using digital libraries. In some countries, for instance Malaysia, 'smart' homes are being designed with wireless broadband telecommunications links which offer very high speed access to the Internet (http://www.cyberjaya-msc.com).

2.6.3 ICT illiteracy

If users are unable to read, or to type, or to use a mouse then they will face a major challenge in using a digital library. Many organizations, especially public libraries, involved in developing digital libraries are also involved in running training courses on basic IT or ICT literacy for their users. IT or ICT literacy is different from the Information Literacy described earlier. In Singapore there has been a major National IT Literacy programme (http://www.nitlp.com.sg) where the government aim is to reskill and retrain Singaporeans for a knowledge-based economy. The training programme is available in the four national languages of Singapore: English, Malay, Mandarin and Tamil. Public libraries are just one of a number of venues where participants can access the e-learning courses for this IT literacy programme. In many countries the European Computer Driving Licence

(ECDL), and the linked International Computer Driving Licence (http://www.ecdl.com), are recognized as a qualification for those who wish to become IT or ICT literate. The ECDL comprises a number of modules covering functions including word processing, use of spreadsheets, and accessing the Internet. Providing school children with the opportunity to gain appropriate ICT skills is common in many countries. In Thailand, for instance, the human resource development programme of 2000 provided all teachers, college lecturers and professors, and school and college students with the opportunity to gain familiarity with ICT as an enabling tool for accessing information, and knowledge acquisition through self-paced learning.

2.6.4 Language barrier

Users may feel that a particular digital library is a challenge to use because it does not contain appropriate information sources in a language that can be easily read and understood. To overcome this many institutions involved in developing digital libraries are also very active in creating appropriate content for their users in relevant languages. However, this may not always be easy. In Vietnam, for instance, Hung (2001) describes how there is no standard Vietnamese character font, there is a lack of software for digitizing materials in Vietnamese using Optical Character Recognition (OCR) scanners, and a lack of digital content in the languages of the 54 ethnic groups. Nevertheless, Hung describes the work of the National Center for Scientific and Technological Information Documentation (NACESTID), an important digital content creator and digital information source provider in Vietnam. The home page of NACESTID is in Vietnamese but with English and French language options, as illustrated in Figure 2.11 (http://www.vista.gov.vn/main.htm). Even from the Vietnamese version of the website there are some links to English-language sources (such as the ACM Digital Library and databases from Cambridge Scientific Abstracts), as shown in the menu on the right-hand side of the screen.

NACESTID is just one of seven libraries involved in the InterCity Digital Library project in the Asia Pacific region. Others include: Shanghai Library, the National Library of Singapore, the National Library of Malaysia, the National Library of Vietnam, the General Sciences Library of Ho Chi Minh City, and the Biblioteca Central de Macau.

There are many instances of groups of people within a country or community for whom the main language of the country is not their language. In many parts of the UK the public library may be serving a community of people who are not able to communicate in English and so appropriate digital as well as print information services need to be made available. For instance, in the London Borough of Westminster there is a large Chinese community, and Figure 2.12 shows part of the website where links to relevant Chinese digital information sources are provided. As will be described further in Chapter Four the display of characters in different fonts is not always possible and in this case the correct font to display the Chinese characters is not available. It is however, available on the PCs within the Westminster Libraries.

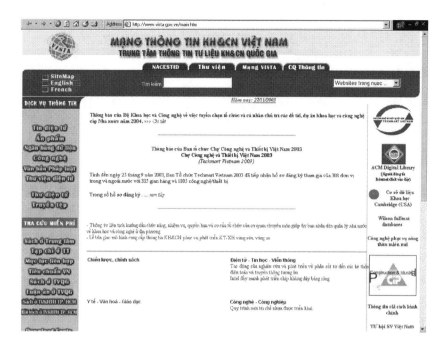

Figure 2.11 National Center for Scientific and Technological Information Documentation, Vietnam

Figure 2.12 Chinese Library, Westminster City Council, UK (reproduced courtesy of Westminster City Council)

Digital libraries, then, are being developed in a variety of institutions, in many countries and for a range of users. When implementing digital library systems it is important to think of the needs of the users and to provide appropriate features and facilities for those who may face particular barriers. Increasingly users are expecting to be able to access information in digital form. A major survey was carried out for the Digital Library Foundation and the Council on Library and Information Resources in 2001/2 which involved 3,234 faculty members, graduate students and undergraduate students in 392 doctoral research universities in the US. The general conclusion was that:

> Responses to the survey confirm, in the aggregate, that electronic information use is substantial and growing in the nation's major universities and liberal arts colleges, without much of the "drag" that some might have expected from methodologically entrenched professors and book-loving humanists. Respondents to the survey are highly comfortable with digital resources, are making use of them for research, teaching, and coursework, and have equipped themselves well to do so (Marcum and George, 2003).

References

Adkins, D. (2002) The digital library and younger users. In G.E. Gorman(ed.) *The Digital Factor in Library and Information Services. International Yearbook of Library and Information Management 2002/2003*. London: Facet Publishing, 133–155

Berube, L (2004) Collaborative digital reference: an Ask A Librarian (UK) overview. *Program*, **38** (1), 29–41

Bowen, J. P. (2002) Weaving the museum web: the Virtual Library museums pages. *Program*, **36** (4), 236–252

Bzorza, P. (2003) Virtual multimedia library accessible to blind people. *Centre on Disabilities Technology and Persons with Disabilities Conference 2003*. Northridge: California State University. Available at: http://www.csun.edu/cod/conf/2003/proceedings/75.htm

Cherry, J. M. and Duff W.M. (2002) Studying digital library users over time: a follow-up survey of Early Canadiana online. *Information Research*, **7** (2). Available at: http://informationr.net/ir/7-2/paper123.html

Gaudet, F. and Savard, N. (2002) Virtual Reference Canada: a Canadian service in a multicultural environment. Paper presented at 68th IFLA Council and General Conference, August 18–24. Available at: http://www.ifla.org/IV/ifla68/papers/004-128e.pdf

Germano, D. (2002) The Tibetan and Himalayan Digital Library. *D-Lib Magazine*, **8** (5). Available at: http://www.dlib.org/dlib/may02/05inbrief.html#GERMANO

Hung, T. B. (2001) Bridging the digital divide in Vietnam. *Astinfo Newsletter*, **16** (3), 10–13

Marcum, D.B. and George, G. (2003) Who uses what? *D-Lib Magazine*, **9** (10). Available at: http://www.dlib.org/dlib/october03/george/10george.html

Mates, B. T. (2000) *Adaptive Technology for the Internet: Making Electronic Resources Available to All*. Chicago and London: American Library Association

OCLC (2002) *How Academic Librarians can Influence Students' Web-based Information Choices*. OCLC White paper on the Information habits of college students. Available at: http://www5.org.oclc/downloads/community/informationhabits.pdf

Poustie, K. (1999) *A Knowledge Centre for the Community: a New Role for the Public Library*. Gütersloh: Bertelsmann Foundation Publishers. Available at: http://www. public-libraries.net/en/x_media/pdf/poustie_engl.pdf

Rozic-Hristovski, A., Humar, I. and Hristovski, D. (2003) Developing a multilingual, personalized medical library portal: use of MyLibrary in Slovenia. *Program*, **37** (3), 146–157

Rowntree, D. (1990) *Exploring Open and Distance Learning* London: Kogan Page

Scardellato, K. (2001) Experiences in developing and maintaining the Virtual Reference Library at Toronto Public Library. *Program*, **35** (2), 67–180

SCONUL (1999) *Information Skills in Higher Education*. London: SCONUL. Available at: http://www.sconul.ac.uk/pubs_stats/pubs/99104Rev1.doc

Urquhart, C., Thomas, R., Armstrong, C., Fenton, R., Lonsdale, R., Spink, S. and Yeoman, A. (2003) Trends in the uptake and use of electronic information services in higher education: results from JUSTEIS 1999–2002. *Program*, **37** (3), 168–180

Visser, F. (2003) Bringing the Dutch public online: the story of al@din, the public libraries' online reference desk. In Lewis J. (ed.) *Online Information 2003: Proceedings*. Oxford: Learned Information Europe, 187–191

Chapter 3

Digital Information Sources

3.1 Introduction

In this Chapter we shall describe some of the information sources that might be made available as part of a digital library and answer questions such as What are the types of sources? and Where do they come from?

The digital information sources in libraries, museums or archives are various and depend on factors such as the needs of the users and the aims of the institution. Some sources involve the acquisition, or licensing of already digitized content whereas other sources involve digital content being developed locally – perhaps covering local materials or material in local languages. Some digital information sources will be freely accessible for anyone to use whereas others, perhaps because of cost issues or licensing implications, will only be available to authorized specific users. Some sources will contain the 'full' information (such as the full text of a book, report, journal, or an archive) whereas others will contain metadata or information about material in a collection (such as a library catalogue or an archive index). Some sources will be digital versions of material already existing in printed form whereas other sources will have first appeared in digital form, often referred to as being 'born' digital (such as a website or a word-processed document). Issues of intellectual property rights affect the use of all digital information sources and these will be covered in Chapter Eight.

Figure 2.8 showed the opening page from the digital library of the Open University of Hong Kong which has links to a number of digital information resources including:

- Electronic resources (including electronic journals, electronic dictionaries and encyclopaedias, electronic directories and handbooks, indexes and abstracts).

- Electronic texts (including electronic books in English and Chinese).
- Reserve collection (including electronic versions of past examination papers, dissertations and other reference materials).
- Library catalogues.

Such a range of types of material is typical in the digital libraries of academic institutions throughout the world. There is a mixture of 'public' materials such as ejournals and ebooks as well as materials emanating from within the institution such as past examination papers, course packs, students' theses and dissertations. Many digital libraries within academic institutions also provide a subject approach to their digital information sources. Figure 3.1, for instance, shows the digital information sources for architecture (with an appropriate 'house design' border) available via LEARN (Library Electronic Academic Resources Network) at the University of Auckland in New Zealand (http://www2.auckland.ac.nz/lbr/).

In public libraries the range of digital information sources made available is usually very broad to cater for the possible needs of users. For instance, newspapers and magazines form part of the Virtual Reference Library at Toronto Public Library, as described in Chapter Two. Some public libraries bring together relevant sources in a particular language. For instance, at the public library of the Pompidou Centre in Paris (Bibliothèque Publique d'Information) links are provided within its digital library to selected current news articles in French from a variety of digital sources around the world (http://www.bpi.fr).

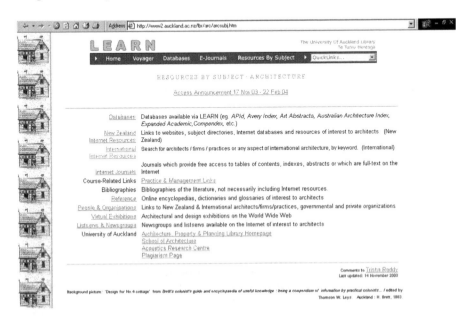

Figure 3.1 Menu of architectural digital sources, Library Electronic Academic Resources Network, University of Auckland, New Zealand (reproduced courtesy of the University of Auckland)

In this Chapter we shall describe some of the types of digital information sources that might be selected for inclusion in a digital library and then consider ways in which such sources might be made available for the digital library. There are, of course, very many more types of sources found within digital libraries such as patents, international standards, statistics and geographic information systems that we have not discussed here. We have concentrated on the major kinds of sources that are found in digital libraries around the world.

These sources could be classified in a variety of ways and we have chosen the following:

- 'Full-text' material to cover ejournals, open access and open archive collections, ebooks and e-newspapers.
- Metadata sources to cover catalogues, indexes and abstracts, or sources that provide 'information about information'.
- Multimedia material.
- Websites.

Some of the sources described are freely available on the Web and so access via a digital library is not absolutely necessary. However, for other sources access may only be possible for an individual user through a specific digital library. Not all digital libraries will include access to all these types of information sources but many, as evidenced in the various screenshots of digital libraries included in this book, provide access at least to several of them.

3.2 Full-text Materials

3.2.1 Scholarly ejournals

Scholarly journals first appeared in the mid-seventeenth century and quickly became a basic tool for the communication of scientific information. Until the mid-twentieth century these were mainly produced by not-for-profit learned societies and copies were made available to members as part of their annual subscription. Now, however, many scientific, technical and medical (STM) journals in particular are published by commercial organizations. Details of the average costs of printed journal subscriptions are monitored each year by Swets Blackwell based on journals published in a number of countries or regions (http://www.swetsblackwell.com/custsn-about.htm). For many years there has been an annual increase in subscription costs, sometimes quite substantial. Libraries, as major buyers of scholarly journals, have been greatly affected by the continuous cost increases, especially when library budgets in many cases have decreased in real terms, and so many have had to cancel subscriptions.

A number of publishers (for example, the American Chemical Society, Elsevier Science and the Institute of Physics) started to experiment with the production of digital versions of their printed scholarly journals during the early 1990s. As well as the advantages (including 24/7 availability) linked to being delivered via digital libraries identified in Chapter Two, ejournals can add value to printed scholarly journals in a number of ways, for instance, by:

- adding colour;
- being available rather than lost or at the bindery;
- including high-quality graphics;
- incorporating sophisticated searching facilities;
- presenting information using multimedia technologies (such as sound or video);
- directly linking to other related material (such as relevant websites or other published materials);
- enabling 'feedback' between authors of articles and their readers.

The majority of ejournals, still have linked printed counterparts although the content may vary between the printed and the digital version. For instance, the digital version of the international weekly journal of science, *Nature*, contains more material than its printed counterpart (http://www.nature. com/nature/free-issue.html). One major challenge facing library and information professionals in making ejournals available is that an individual library often does not own the ejournal but has a licence for its use. If that library decides to stop subscribing to the journal then access to the back issues may be denied. This obviously is different from the situation with printed journals where the library would have the printed copies of back issues on its shelves in perpetuity. Nevertheless, very many libraries are moving, or have moved, to providing access to ejournals and, in some cases, are only providing e-access even if a printed version also exists.

The majority of scholarly ejournals cover material written in English. However, there are instances of ejournals appearing in other languages and, of course, these would be of most interest to native speakers of those languages. Figure 3.2 shows part of a journal article in Bahasa Indonesia that is available from the Ganesha Digital Library from the Institut Teknologi Bandung in Indonesia (http://digilib.itb.ac.id/index.php).

3.2.2 Open access, eprint collections and open archives

In recent years many librarians and academic authors have become concerned at what is seen as the 'commercialization' of scholarly journal publishing and the requirement for authors to sign over the copyright of a paper to the publishers prior to publication. Libraries need to pay increasingly large sums (as indicated in the previous section) to subscribe to the printed copies of the journals or to acquire licences for access to electronic versions of them or else cancel subscriptions which results in researchers failing to have access to necessary source materials. The result has been a growth of the 'open access' movement. Open Access is a system of providing users access to the full text of quality, peer reviewed research articles which uses a funding model that does not charge users or their institutions for

Figure 3.2 Ejournal article, Ganesha Digital Library, Indonesia (reproduced courtesy of Institut Teknologi Bandung)

access. In some instances authors may be charged a 'processing cost' for their article to be published. In general this open access can be achieved in one of two ways:

- *Open Access Publishing.* Scholarly journals such as those covering the digital library area (*Ariadne, D-Lib Magazine* and *First Monday*) would be included in this category.
- *Open Access Self-archiving.* In this situation authors, or the institutions within which they work, create an archive, or repository, of published materials in addition to such materials being published in the existing journals. Some, but not all, journal publishers accept this activity.

A major development in the open access movement was the setting up, in 2002, of the Budapest Open Access Initiative (BOAI) by the Open Society Institute (OSI). Since 1993 the OSI in Budapest has developed and implemented a number of programmes in the areas of educational, legal and social reform in former Soviet republics and countries of central and eastern Europe. OSI's Information Programme has committed one million US dollars (about 800,000 euros) per year for three years to support a number of projects relating to open access including:

- the development of business models and plans for self-archiving and open access publishing;
- the use of library networks to mobilize support for open access;
- support for authors in low and middle income countries to publish in open access journals;
- the development of software tools and templates for open access publishing, self-archiving, indexing and navigation;
- the promotion of the open access philosophy.

A further impetus came in late 2003 when a group of European researchers were signatories to the Berlin Declaration (http://www.zim.mpg.de/openaccess-berlin/berlindeclaration.html) which noted that "the Internet offers the chance to constitute a global and interactive representation of human knowledge, including cultural heritage and the guarantee of world-wide access" and that this challenge needs to be addressed through content and software tools "that must be openly accessible and compatible".

So what does all this mean for information sources in digital libraries? In research and higher academic environments many institutions are beginning to make the published output of their researchers available as part of their digital library and are creating links to other such collections. For instance, Figure 3.3 shows a gateway to eprint collections available worldwide via

Figure 3.3 Gateway to ePrint repositories, Cybrary, University of Queensland, Australia (reproduced courtesy of the University of Queensland Library)

the Cybrary at the University of Queensland in Australia (http://www.library.uq.edu.au). As stated in the screenshot, the term eprint is used to cover the electronic version of the preprint of articles as well as the electronic postprints or versions that have been published in peer-reviewed scholarly journals.

The first major collection of eprints, known as arXiv (and included in Figure 3.3), was set up at the Los Alamos National Research Laboratory in New Mexico, US in 1991 and comprised preprints of articles published in the area of high-energy physics. The phrase 'open archive' was used to describe this collection. In order for users to be aware of, and access, eprints residing in similar distributed collections in various digital libraries, the Open Archives Initiative (OAI) was formed in 1999 to develop various standards for interoperability and to promote the use of these types of collections worldwide (http://www.openarchives.org). As well as an OAI standard for describing the eprint (the metadata), there is the Open Archives Initiative Protocol for Metadata Harvesting (OAI- PMH) which collects the metadata and enables it to be searched. OAIster (http://oaister.umdl.umich.edu/o/oaister/), one of the cross-archive search tools included in Figure 3.3, is a project of the University of Michigan Digital Library production services. OAIster provides facilities, using OAI-PMH, to search eprint collections in almost 250 institutions worldwide. Harnad (2003) has been an active proponent of open access and the setting up of institutional archives, and all his papers on this topic, not surprisingly, are available on his website (http://www.ecs.soton.ac.uk/~harnad/intpub.html).

Open access solutions, as identified in this section, need to be sustainable but they do present an attractive information source for those implementing digital libraries in developing countries as well as in developed countries (Chan and Kirsop, 2002). Also, open access publishing in developing countries will help to make research carried out in those countries become accessible to those in developed countries. For instance, Marcondes and Sayão (2003) describe the work of the SciELO (Scientific Electronic Library Online) a digital library comprising the full text of selected scientific journals from Brazil, Latin America and the Caribbean that are published in Portuguese, Spanish and English and with metadata that is compliant with OAI. In the Netherlands a project (funded with a grant of two million euros) is being undertaken to make the published output from Dutch universities digitally accessible. The project is known as DARE (Digital Academic Repositories) and involves Dutch national organizations such as the Royal Library, the Royal Netherlands Academy of Arts and Science, and the Netherlands Organization for Scientific Research as well as Dutch universities (http://www.surf.nl/en/home/index.php).

3.2.3 Ebooks

The development of electronic versions of printed books (or ebooks) can be seen as part of the whole e-publishing phenomenon that began in the 1970s. The main challenge has been the delivery mechanism as few users wish to 'read' books via a screen. Another challenge relates to copyright issues.

Nevertheless ebooks are considered important information sources in many digital libraries. Some ebooks are freely available. For instance, Project Gutenberg in the US (http://gutenberg.net) provides access to digitized versions of over 6,000 books which are categorized as being light literature (such as *Peter Pan* or *Alice's Adventures in Wonderland*), heavy literature (religious texts or the works of Shakespeare) or reference sources (almanacs,encyclopaedias and dictionaries). There are mirror sites of Project Gutenberg in a number of countries including Denmark, Germany, Mexico and South Africa. The works covered by Project Gutenberg all lie outside US copyright and are thus freely available. An Australian version of Project Gutenberg, Project Gutenberg of Australia (http://gutenberg.net.au) provides access to about 10,000 books which are in the public domain in Australia or are of specific Australian interest.

Ebooks are now predominantly available from companies which license their use via the Web, and further details of these are given later in this Chapter. At the turn of the millennium there was a lot of optimistic 'hype' concerning ebooks, with various companies producing special hardware or 'readers' to allow users to view them on these handheld devices. However, many of these companies have ceased to exist as users were unhappy with the reading technology. More standard ways of reading ebooks, either on Personal Digital Assistants (PDAs) or on PC screens, have become the norm and are being accepted by users. A further alternative is to print the ebook on request – a facility referred to as Print on Demand. Many public libraries have investigated making ebooks available as part of a digital library. Saunders (2002) describes the experiences at Yarra Plenty Regional Library in Melbourne, Australia and notes that " ebooks enable libraries to provide 24/7 access to information with enhanced content features". After experiencing hand-held reading devices for ebooks she now advocates only using ebooks that are downloadable for use on PCs and states that ebooks are "best suited to reference and non-fiction titles, such as study guides to literature, titles which are not read from cover to cover". Public libraries in the UK are also adding ebooks to their collections of digital information resources. Figure 3.4 shows information about ebooks that are available at the London Borough of Richmond-upon-Thames (http://www.richmond. gov.uk/libraries).

Many academic libraries also provide their users with access to ebooks via their digital library. These may be basic textbooks that have been published in ebook format as well as in 'normal' format or they might be specially developed reference works such as encyclopaedias, dictionaries, almanacs and so on. Although many ebooks were originally published in English, ebooks in other languages are now appearing. The National Library Board in Singapore, for instance, provides access for its users to some 200,000 ebooks in Chinese.

The advantages of using ebooks are similar to those outlined earlier for ejournals, and they have a place in the provision of digital information sources in many types of digital library. Some of the specific advantages of ebooks are:

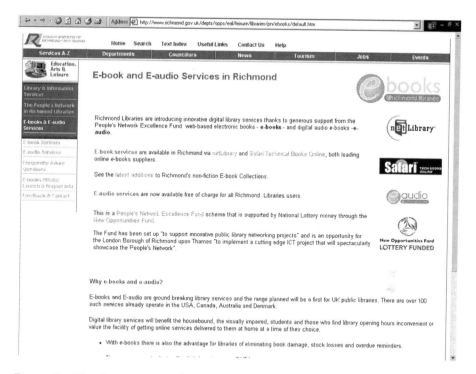

Figure 3.4 Ebook services, Richmond Libraries, UK (reproduced courtesy of the London Borough of Richmond upon Thames)

- They can include animation, images, sound and graphics and this can be very useful, say, in medical texts to explain the workings of various organs, or in technical manuals to explain the functioning of a specific part of a machine.
- For the visually impaired user the 'audio' features can provide access to the book's content so that it might be 'read' by special text-audio equipment.
- They may be cheaper than their printed equivalents.
- They can be delivered instantly.
- They are searchable.
- They do not deteriorate over time.

However, ebooks are not necessarily appropriate for all reading material and not all users like the thought of ebooks. The world 'appetite' for reading printed books is not diminished by the availability of ebooks, indeed in many countries the number of published printed books continues to rise annually. Nevertheless, within a digital library ebooks can be a relevant information source for some users.

The Open eBook Forum is an international trade and standards organization for the ebook industry (http://www.openebook.org). The Forum fosters the development of applications and products that will benefit creators of content, makers of reading systems, as well as consumers.

3.2.4 Electronic newspapers

Local, national and international newspapers are important information sources for current affairs and some newspapers have existed since the eighteenth century. Providing access to back copies of newspapers is sometimes achieved through microfilm versions. Some newspapers began to appear digitally on CD-ROM in the late 1980s and were early examples of full-text digital information sources. With the advent of the Web it was natural for newspaper publishers to make their products also available on it. After the major political changes in Eastern Europe and the former Soviet republics of the early 1990s, web-based versions of many newspapers in the newly independent countries became a key source for keeping the respective diaspora aware of developments. As with ebooks, e-newspapers are not necessarily liked by all and there appears to be no diminution in the sales of printed newspapers because of the existence of digitized versions which are now available from countries all around the world. An indication of this is provided in the Yahoo directory (http://dir.yahoo.com) that provides links to newspapers in over 120 countries ranging alphabetically from Andorra to Zimbabwe. As with ejournals, web editions of newspapers do not always contain the same information as their printed counterparts and often provide more features such as links to related news items and so on.

Some digital libraries include news clippings services for users to be kept up-to-date with current affairs. Such services may be found in special libraries, and the development of such a service for staff in the National Informatics Centres in India is described by Matoria et al. (2003) who outline the advantages of such a system as:

- instant access to news clippings over the Web through a common user interface;
- global access to news clippings in real time by remote users;
- access to full-text news supplemented with graphics, charts, tables, and so on;
- up-to-the-minute updated access to news;
- dynamic updating of the back-end database from many locations;
- provision of a high level of search options for news archive retrieval;
- instant feedback from users;
- unlimited downloading and printing;
- environmentally friendly.

Although creating such a news clipping service requires a fair amount of human resources, the authors note that this is much reduced from the amount of resources needed to provide the previous print-based news clipping service. The University of Moratuwa Library in Sri Lanka, as described in the case study in Chapter Nine, includes the output from a commercial news clipping service in its digital information sources.

3.2.5 Theses and dissertations

Within any university the results of research undertaken by doctoral and masters students and presented in theses and dissertations are important information sources not only for other researchers within the university but also elsewhere. As with ejournals, eprints, ebooks and e-newspapers there has been a move towards the development of electronic versions of theses and dissertations (ETD). This concept was first aired at a meeting in 1987 run by UMI (formerly known as University Microfilms) an organization with a long history of involvement (since the 1920s) in making the full text of university dissertations available on microfilm (http://www.umi.com). In order to support the development of ETD, a Networked Digital Library of Theses and Dissertations (NDLTD) is being developed at Virginia Tech in the US (http://www.ndltd.org). Its objectives are to:

- improve graduate education by allowing students to produce electronic documents, use digital libraries, and understand issues in publishing;
- increase the availability of student research for scholars and preserve it electronically;
- lower the cost of submitting and handling theses and dissertations;
- empower students to convey a richer message through the use of multi-media and hypermedia technologies;
- empower universities to unlock their information resources;
- advance digital library technology.

NDLTD has spearheaded the development of ETD in many countries, organized annual international conferences, and maintains a searchable union catalogue of the dissertations held by its 190 or so member institutions. Examples of other organizations which are involved with ETDs include:

- Australia Digital Theses Project (http://adt.caul.edu.au);
- Digitale Dissertationen at Humboldt University of Berlin (http://dochost. rz.hu-berlin.de/epdiss/index_en.html);
- Helsinki University of Technology Electronic Academic Dissertations (http://lib.hut.fi/Diss/);
- McGill University, Montreal Electronic Thesis Initiative (http://digital. library.mcgill.ca/ethesis/);
- Uppsala University, Sweden (http://publications.uu.se/theses/).

Providing access to the full text of theses and dissertations presents challenges of copyright, and many academic institutions are only beginning to address such issues and incorporate ETD into their digital libraries. More information on some of these issues is provided in the case study on Vidyanidhi in Chapter Nine.

3.2.6 Archives

In the archives area many local and national archives are beginning to move from providing computer-based catalogues and finding aids to their collections, to linking to digitized versions of the archives. In the UK, the National Archives (http://www.nationalarchives.gov.uk/) brings together the collections of the Public Record Office and the Historical Manuscripts Commission to form one of the largest archival collections in the world, spanning 1000 years of British history, from the Domesday Book to contemporary government papers released each year to the public. The National Archives has plans to provide access to digital copies of the documents in a number of areas including:

- the 1901 census of England and Wales which can be used for genealogical research;
- 800,000 probate wills from 1650 to 1858;
- the Cabinet papers from Harold Macmillan's Government (1957–1963);
- medieval seals and how they were used;
- immigration experiences from the 1940s to the present day.

At an international level Unesco launched its Memory of the World programme in 1992 to encourage the preservation and dissemination of heritage and archive holdings reflecting the diversity of languages, peoples and cultures around the world (http://www.unesco.org/webworld/mdm/en/index_mdm.html). Figure 3.5 shows some of these including:

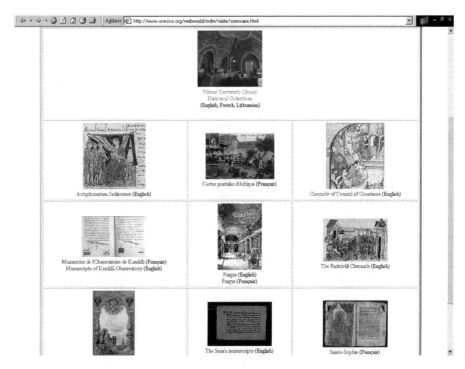

Figure 3.5 Thumbnail images, Unesco's Memory of the World programme (reproduced courtesy of Unesco)

- Manuscripts at Vilnius University demonstrating European contributions to scientific advancement between the 15th and 18th centuries.
- 3,000 old postcards from the 16 countries of the Economic Community of West African States.
- 1300 Kandilli manuscripts on astronomy in three languages (Turkish, Persian and Arabic) held in the library of the Kandilli Observatory and Earthquake Research Institute of Bogaziçi University in Istanbul.

By 2003 some 68 projects from 40 countries were included in the Memory of the World Register. Within the framework of this programme Unesco (along with IFLA – the International Federation of Library Associations and Institutions) is also involved in compiling DigiCol – a database of documentary heritage collections digitized throughout the world (http://www.unesco.org/webworld/digicol). Examples include:

- Archives Aequatoria (historical documents in French and Dutch relating to the equatorial region of the Congo).
- Napoleonica (working papers, in French, of the French Council of State 1800–1815).
- Memoriae Mundi Series Bohemica (Jesuit manuscripts in Czech and English relevant to the history of Central Europe).
- Early Kazak newspapers (1913–1918) in the Arabic alphabet.
- Brazilian Government Documents issued (in Portuguese) primarily in the nineteenth century.

An overview of guides and directories to national and international projects related to archives is provided by Mattison (2002). He notes that many such projects which cover original material in languages other than English are a reaction to the dominance of US culture and information on the Web.

3.3 Metadata Sources

The availability of full-text digital information sources is comparatively recent with sources appearing on CD-ROM in the mid-late 1980s and the Web during the 1990s. Before then searching for information about material collected by libraries, museums or archives was normally done by searching metadata sources, that is information about the information contained in the physical collections. Such information sources are still useful in digital libraries as, in many cases, the 'whole' collection is not available in a digitized format.

3.3.1 The catalogue

Writing in 1876 Charles Ammi Cutter defined a library's catalogue as an efficient instrument intended to achieve the following objectives:

- to enable a person to find a book of which either the author, the title or the subject is known;

- to show what the library has by a given author, or on a given subject or in a given kind of literature;
- to assist in the choice of a book as to its edition or as to its character.

These objectives were incorporated into a set of cataloguing principles agreed by an international conference of cataloguers in Paris in 1961. At that time the physical format of the catalogue was a set of catalogue cards. However catalogues became a popular application for computers in libraries during the 1960s and 1970s and by the late 1970s the OPAC – or Online Public Access Catalogue – appeared. The OPAC to any collection, be it of books and journals in a library, artefacts in a museum, or pictures in a gallery, comprises a database of descriptions of the items held in the collection. OPACs have developed over the years to form a key module in the web-based library management systems used by many libraries or in similar collection management systems in museums or galleries. A common standard for the description of a book in an OPAC is the MARC (Machine-Readable Catalogue) format which is described in more depth in Chapter Four. However, in some instances fuller information is provided to improve subject searching of an OPAC by including extra information such as the Table of Contents. The functionality of OPACs around the world is similar, and even if the language of the interface is not known it is often possible to carry out a search. Figure 3.6 shows the result of searching the OPAC at the University

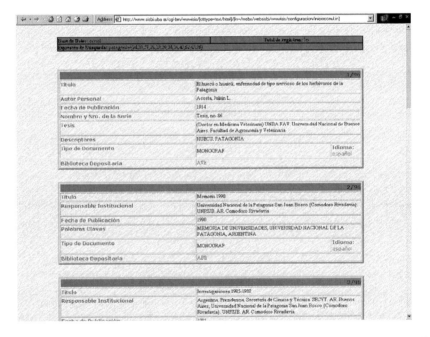

Figure 3.6 OPAC record, Sistema de Bibliotecas y de Información de la Universidad de Buenos Aires, Argentina

of Buenos Aires in Argentina, and accessible through its digital library (http://www.sisbi.uba.ar/) for items about Patagonia.

Catalogues are important digital information sources and are often included in the collection of sources made available through digital libraries. As well as incorporating links to local catalogues, digital libraries might include links to other catalogues in the geographic or subject area or to collections of catalogues such as:

- Gabriel (Gateway and Bridge to Europe's National Libraries) – provides links to the websites and catalogues of the 41 national libraries which are represented at the Conference of European National Libraries (http://portico.bl.uk/gabriel/index.html).
- LIBDEX the online index – provides links to the web addresses of 18,000 OPACs in many countries of the world (http://www.libdex.com).
- COPAC, the OPAC of CURL (Consortium of University Research Libraries) in Britain – provides access to the physically merged union catalogues of the libraries of 24 CURL members including the Universities of Birmingham, Cambridge, Edinburgh, Glasgow, London and Oxford as well as the catalogues of the British Library and the National Library of Scotland (http://copac.ac.uk).
- Virtual union catalogues, sometimes called clumps – may be developed for libraries in a particular region or covering a particular subject area. In this case no actual physical merging of catalogue records has taken place and the catalogues of each library are searched separately using appropriate software making use of the Z39.50 protocol (as described in Chapter Four).

3.3.2 Abstracting and indexing databases

In the late nineteenth century, in an attempt to overcome the perceived information overload of the day, abstracting and indexing (A&I) publications (such as *Index Medicus* from NLM) started to appear. These printed publications provided shortened forms, or abstracts, of articles published in scholarly journals as well as author and subject indexes to the articles. Computers began to be used for typesetting these A&I publications in the mid-1960s. It quickly became apparent that having digitized the abstracts and indexes, computers could then search this digitized information. Many such publications (for example *Art Abstracts, Chemical Abstracts, Engineering Index*, and *Psychological Abstracts*) became available as computer databases during the 1970s and 1980s. Figure 3.7 shows an example of a record from the Medline (Medical Literature Analysis and Retrieval System Online) database which is an online A&I database developed at the NLM in the US. The records are structured into fields (such as title, author, journal name, language of publication, abstract, and descriptors (taken from a special list of Medical Subject Headings)). Medline contains over 12 million records covering journal articles published, since 1966, in the life sciences in 4,600 journals covering 30 languages.

Figure 3.7 Extract of a record from the abstracting and indexing database Medline (reproduced courtesy of the National Library of Medicine)

Abstracting and indexing databases can be very useful in making users aware of what has been published. However, if access to the full text of potentially relevant material is not easy then users may become frustrated.

3.3.3 Indexes to archives

Metadata in the form of indexes are frequently used to search archive collections either individually or in a given region. Access to Archives (or A2A), for instance, enables users to search and browse information about archives, dating from the 900s to the present day, in collections housed in about 330 repositories including local record offices, libraries, universities, museums and national and specialist institutions across England (http://www.a2a. org.uk/). Figure 3.8 shows the result of a search of A2A using the phrase *football club*.

The phrase football club appeared in 344 different indexes and an example of an archive record from one of these, the Elizabeth Munns collection of photograph albums within Bedfordshire and Luton Archives and Record Office, is shown in Figure 3.9.

Figure 3.8 Search results, A2A (Access to Archives), The National Archives, UK (reproduced courtesy of The National Archives, UK)

3.4 Multimedia Material

Multimedia materials covering stand-alone still images (such as photographs, prints and paintings), moving images (such as films and videos), sound recordings, and animation are important sources of information in many subject areas and so are included in digital library collections. Many museums, art galleries and libraries are digitizing their collections of images, or creating digital images of their cultural heritage collections, so as to make them available for a wide audience. Digitized moving images, as well as still images, may be incorporated into the VLEs that are appearing within educational institutions. An overview of some of the projects in British higher education involving the networking of moving images is provided by Atkinson (2001). The techniques for storing and retrieving visual images are very different from those for text-based information sources and more on this will be found in Chapter Seven.

Digital information sources covering speech and music are of great interest in a variety of educational and academic situations as well as public libraries. Figure 3.4 shows that Richmond Public Library in the UK provides access to e-audio materials as well as to ebooks. The e-audio books are seen as equivalent to the talking books service which is of great importance to

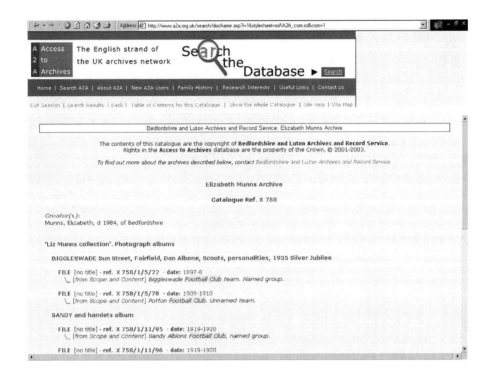

Figure 3.9 Archival record, Bedfordshire and Luton Archives and Record Service, UK (reproduced courtesy of Bedfordshire and Luton Archives and Record Service)

visually impaired users. In implementing digital libraries, information professionals may well need to provide access to appropriate databases of sound recordings. There are many examples of national organizations, such as museums, libraries and archives which have, for many years, been collecting their nations' sound 'output' – such as that broadcast on national radio or television. The British Library Sound Archive comprises a million discs, 185,000 tapes, and many other sound recordings from all over the world including music, oral history and wildlife sounds. The recording technologies range from cylinders made in the late 19th century to the latest digital techniques. However, the amount of audio information that is accessible via digital libraries is still comparatively limited. Figure 3.10 shows some of the digital audio recordings that can be heard from the digital library of ScreenSound Australia, the National Screen and Sound Archive (http://www.screensound.gov.au).

In some academic institutions digital recordings are made of lectures which may then be linked to other course materials within the digital library. As with text collections, developing appropriate metadata to describe the content of multimedia materials collections is an important aspect of providing these information sources in digital libraries.

Figure 3.10 Digital audio recordings, ScreenSound Australia (reproduced courtesy of ScreenSound Australia, the National Screen and Sound Archive (Canberra, Australia))

3.5 Websites and Quality Issues

For many people the only digital information sources they think about using are websites and they do not use digital libraries even though relevant information sources may be available. The Pew Research Center regularly surveys Internet use in the US and found that:

> With over 60% of Americans now having Internet access and 40% of Americans having been online for more than three years, the Internet has become a mainstream information tool. Its popularity and dependability have raised all Americans' expectations about the information and services available online. When they are thinking about health care information, services from government agencies, news, and commerce, about two-thirds of all Americans say that they expect to be able to find such information on the Web. Internet users are more likely than non-users to have high expectations of what will be available online, and yet even 40% of people who are not Internet users say they expect the Web to have information and services in these essential online arenas (Pew Research Center, 2002).

Although web search engines index a very large number of pages (by its fifth birthday in 2003 Google indexed 3,300 million web pages) nevertheless, this is only part of the Web – that which is freely accessible. A whole 'other' area, sometimes referred to as the deep web, the hidden web or the invisible web, for various reasons (including subscription charges, format of source, dynamic web pages) is often not indexed. Some of the digital information sources already described in this Chapter (such as catalogues, and abstracting and indexing databases) may not be indexed by the search engines.

The Web traditionally, has been dominated by information in English and from the US. So, it is important that digital information sources of relevance to other communities served by libraries, and in languages that can be easily understood by people in those communities, are developed. Mutula (2002) notes that, in 2000, less than 0.05% of the Web's content was produced by the 54 African countries, although all have some form of Internet connectivity. In many countries government information is being made available online as part of e-Government initiatives, and Muir and Oppenheim (2002) provide a review of initiatives in a number of countries including Australia, Canada, members of the European Union, Hong Kong, New Zealand, South Africa, and the US.

Since anyone can publish anything on the Web the quality of information available varies greatly. A clearly written guide to finding quality information on the Internet is provided by Cooke (2001). Aspects to consider include:

- authority and reputation of the author(s);
- is there an obvious bias? (say to a particular political point of view);
- currency of the information (if no details are provided as to when the site was last updated, chances are that it might not be very recent);
- accuracy of the information (if this can be judged);
- presentation and arrangement of the information.

Many digital libraries include links to relevant websites that have been selected by those implementing the digital library. These websites may have been 'hand-picked' by library and information professionals as sources of recognized quality information. Funding for the development of various gateways in specific subjects (including biomedicine, engineering and social sciences) formed part of the eLib Programme in the UK in the 1990s. These gateways have now evolved into the Resource Discovery Network (RDN), a collaboration of over 70 educational and research organizations, including the Natural History Museum and the British Library. RDN gathers together websites that have been carefully selected, indexed and described by specialists in the partner institutions (http://www.rdn.ac.uk). The RDN is one of the national organizations participating in Renardus (http://www.renardus.org) which aims to provide a trusted source of selected, high quality Internet resources for those teaching, learning and researching in higher education in Europe. Other participating organizations include:

- DAInet – the German agricultural information network (http://www.dainet.de);

- DutchESS – the Dutch Electronic Subject Service (http://www.kb.nl/dutchess);
- Finnish Virtual Library – the Finnish Internet gateway to selected Internet sources (http://www.jyu.fi/library/virtuaalikirjasto/engvirli.htm);
- NOVAGATE – the Nordic gateway to information in forestry, veterinary and agricultural sciences (http://novagate.nova-university.org/).

Renardus was initially developed as part of a European Union-funded project during 2000–2002 and is now hosted at Niedersächsische Staats – und Universitätsbibliothek, Göttingen, Germany. It can be searched in Dutch, English, Finnish, French and German.

The Virtual Library or VL (http://www.vlib.org) is the oldest gateway of selected quality websites in specific subjects, having been started by Tim Berners-Lee, the creator of the Web. It is run by a loose confederation of volunteers, who compile pages of key links for particular areas in which they are expert. Mirror websites of the VL are based in Argentina, Switzerland and the UK.

3.6 Suppliers of Some Digital Information Sources

Anyone involved in the collection management of digital information sources needs to be aware of the range of organizations that provide such sources or access to such sources. In this section an introduction to some of these is given.

3.6.1 Scholarly ejournals

Subscription agencies (such as Blackwells, Ebsco and Swets) developed services, during the twentieth century, to assist libraries in the 'management' of subscriptions (in a variety of currencies) to print-based journals from a range of different publishers in various parts of the world. In more recent years, there has been a growth of organizations providing 'aggregated' access to the full text of a range of electronic scholarly journals. The term aggregator was used originally during the 1980s and referred to organizations (such as Ebsco Publishing, Gale and ProQuest) that used the increased storage capabilities of CD-ROM to deliver full-text information (licensed from the original publishers) as well as abstracting and indexing databases. With the arrival of the Web in the 1990s many journals are now available from the original publishers as well as from one, or often more, aggregators which provide a common interface for searching and retrieving the articles as well as a number of other 'value-added' services. Brief descriptions of some of these services are given here to provide a 'feel' for this fast-developing area.

a) ACM Digital Library (http://www.acm.org/dl)
The Association for Computing Machinery (ACM) was formed in 1947 and is the world's oldest and largest educational and scientific computing society with members in over 100 countries. Its Digital Library provides a

full-text collection of every article ever published in the various ACM journals, newsletters and conference proceedings – some 103,000 items by late 2003.

b) Ebsco (http://www.ebsco.com)
This Alabama-based organization provides a range of 'packages' of digital information sources for different types of libraries in specific countries– full-text scholarly journals for academic libraries, reference and literacy digital information resources for school libraries, and so on. Ebsco is used in many countries and its interface is available in French, Spanish and German. In addition Ebsco uses special translation software, Transparent Language's Transcend, to translate, on request, articles originally written in English into these languages. In the late 1990s the OSI negotiated a 39-country contract with Ebsco to provide databases to countries in central and eastern Europe, former Soviet republics and in Africa.

c) Emerald (http://www.emeraldinsight.com)
This British company publishes some 150 or so English-language journals, mainly covering management and library and information science. Its full-text database, Electronic Management Research Library Database (hence the name Emerald), comprising some 40,000 articles, was set up in 1996 and its contents are also available via a number of other electronic delivery services such as Ebsco, ingenta and Swets Blackwell.

d) ingenta (http://www.ingenta.com)
This British company was launched in 1998 and now provides full-text access to some 5,500 publications and table of contents services to a further 20,000 publications from over 230 academic and professional publishers. It is used widely throughout the world, providing access to users in more than 10,000 academic, research and corporate libraries.

e) JSTOR (http://www.jstor.org)
Many of the electronic versions of scholarly journals are only available for material published since the 1990s. JSTOR (Journal Storage) emerged from a project to provide access to older materials, thereby easing the increasing problems faced by libraries seeking to maintain stack space for their long backfiles of printed scholarly journals. JSTOR was established as a not-for-profit organization in the US in 1995 and digitizes the content of journals while simultaneously improving access to the journal content. It was also hoped that the project might offer a solution to preservation problems associated with storing paper volumes. The JSTOR database is unique as the complete archives of a number of core scholarly journals in arts, humanities and social sciences, as well as in STM, have been digitized, starting with the very first issue, some of which date from the 1800s. By 2003 JSTOR was being used by 1,500 institutions in 71 countries to provide access to two million articles from 322 journals. General information handouts describing JSTOR are available in a range of languages including Chinese, French, German, Japanese and Russian.

f) ScienceDirect from Elsevier (http://www.sciencedirect.com)
This Dutch company, with a long history of STM publishing, launched its ScienceDirect service in 1999. ScienceDirect provides access to articles in some 1,800 STM journals published by Elsevier as well as to journals from 120 other publishers. ScienceDirect is used by many organizations throughout the world, including countries in Asia such as China, India, and South Korea.

g) Swets Blackwell (http://www.swetsblackwell.com)
Swets Blackwell was formed in the 1990s as a merger between the Swets Subscription Service (a division of the Dutch firm, Royal Swets and Zeitlinger) and Blackwells Information Services (a division of Blackwell Ltd of Oxford, UK) with both organizations having long histories and strong track records in providing services to libraries and information centres worldwide. Swets Blackwell now provides a range of serials-based services, including the SwetsWise subscription service, to 60,000 academic, medical, corporate and government libraries worldwide based on the products from 65,000 publishers and covering 250,000 journal titles.

Any one institution might use more than one of these suppliers to provide access to ejournals. Oxford University Libraries in the UK (http://www.lib. ox.ac.uk/) uses the TDNET software from Teldan (http://www.teldan.com) to manage access to its ejournal collection. Figure 3.11 shows part of the alphabetic display of the ejournal holdings, coverage and so on, and although access to specific journal titles might be via separate organizations such as Ebsco, ingenta, JSTOR or SwetsWise, the titles are all presented in a unified format so as to make searching the collection easier.

In Germany, the University of Regensburg was one of the first libraries in the country to face the challenges, and opportunities, of providing its users with access to ejournals in 1996. Staff developed a database-driven service, Elektronische Zeitschriftenbibliothek (EZB), which is now a cooperative system used in 238 German libraries as well as in seven other countries (http://www.bibliothek.uni-regensburg.de/digibib/ebib.htm). EZB uses an innovative metaphor of traffic lights (red, amber, green) to indicate the accessibility to the user of the full text of a particular journal's articles.

3.6.2 Open access, eprint collections and open archives

The Directory of Open Access Journals (DOAJ) provides a good source of information on quality controlled scientific and scholarly journals that are published in open access mode in a range of subjects and languages. By late 2003 it included records for about 700 journals (http://www.doaj.org). DOAJ was set up in 2002, is funded by OSI in Budapest and is also supported by SPARC – the Scholarly Publishing and Academic Resources Coalition. SPARC was set up by the US-based Association of Research Libraries (ARL) and has members and supporters from many countries in Asia, and Europe as well as in Australia and New Zealand. Its objective is to introduce new solutions to scientific scholarly publishing through ICT (http://www.arl. org/sparc).

Address http://tdnet.bodley.ox.ac.uk/Journals/Journal_List_Frames.asp?Letter=B&PN=1

A B C D E F G H I J K L M N O P Q R S T U V W X Y Z   All

Journal Title	Online Coverage	Full Text Access	Print Holdings	Table of Contents	
				Local	Publisher
PA News		☑	☑		
PA TIMES [EBSCO (Business Source Premier)]	01/1997 - /	☑			
Pacific Affairs [JSTOR UK]	/1928 - /1998	☑	☑	◉	◉
[Periodicals Contents Index (PCI Full Text) UK]	/1927 - /1990	☑	☑	◉	◉
Pacific Basin Finance Journal		☑	☑	◉	
Pacific Economic Review [EBSCO (Business Source Premier)]	02/1998 - /	☑	☑	◉	◉
[Ingenta]	/1997 - /	☑	☑	◉	◉
Pacific Journal of Mathematics		☑	☑	☑	
Pacific Philosophical Quarterly [Ingenta]	/1997 - /	☑	☑	◉	◉
Pacific Review , The [SwetsWise]	/1988 - /	☑	☑	◉	◉
Pacing and Clinical Electrophysiology [Synergy]	/2003 - /	☑		◉	◉
PACKAGEPRINTING [ProQuest (ABI - INFORM Global)]	01/1998 - /	☑		◉	
Packaging Digest [EBSCO (Business Source Premier)]	07/1999 - /	☑		◉	◉
[ProQuest : ABI - INFORM Global)]	01/2002 - /	☑		◉	◉
PACKAGING MAGAZINE [EBSCO : Business Source Premier)]	06/2002 - /	☑		◉	
PACKAGING TECHNOLOGY AND ENGINEERING [EBSCO (Business Source Premier)]	01/1997 - 10/1999	☑			
Packaging Technology and Science	01/1997 - /	☑	☑	◉	◉
Paediatric Anaesthesia [Synergy]	01/1999 - /	☑	☑	◉	◉
Paediatric and Perinatal Epidemiology					

Figure 3.11 Extract of the alphabetic list of electronic journals, Oxford University, UK (reproduced courtesy of the University of Oxford Libraries)

A number of organizations provide free (or very reasonably priced) digital collections of scholarly publications in specific subject areas and such sources are often included in digital libraries. Lambert (2003) reports on developments within the biomedical community and provides brief descriptions of the following services:

- BioMed Central (http://www.biomedcentral.com) is an open access publisher which charges authors an 'article-processing' fee. BioMed Central provides free access to peer-reviewed articles covering biomedical research.
- Highwire Press (http://www.highwire.org) from Stanford University provides access to over 330 journals, mostly biomedical, on behalf of more than 60 learned societies. Some are accessed by subscription, some as pay-per-view, some are free to institutions in developing economies and some, such as the *British Medical Journal*, are just free.
- PubMed Central (http://www.pubmedcentral.org) is the NLM's digital archive of free life sciences journal literature.
- SPARC and BioOne (www.bioone.org). BioOne comprises a database of full-text peer reviewed bioscience journals from small scientific societies.

Prosser(2003) provides an overview of various open access initiatives and developments in eprint collections.

Another example of a freely accessible collection of more popular journal articles is FindArticles (http://www.findarticles.com). This collection is provided by a commercial publisher, the Gale Group (part of the Thomson Corporation) and LookSmart, which provides the search infrastructure. FindArticles comprises 3.5 million articles from 700 publications on a range of topics, including business, health, society, entertainment and sports.

3.6.3 Ebooks

The sources used for ebooks in Richmond Libraries as shown in Figure 3.4 are netlibrary and Safari. NetLibrary (http://www.netlibrary.com) was set up in Boulder, Colorado in 1998 and aimed to be the world's premier provider of ebooks to academic, public, corporate and special libraries. Since 2001 netLibrary has been part of OCLC, the worldwide library cooperative based in Dublin, Ohio. NetLibrary offers a free collection of over 3,000 out-of-copyright titles, and Richmond also subscribes to about 300 non-fiction titles covering economics, ICT, management and psychology. Safari Technical Books Online (http://safari.oreilly.com/) provides access to ebooks on ICT and management published by O' Reilly & Associates and which are particularly suitable for home PC users. Netlibrary and Safari are used as suppliers of ebooks by very many libraries around the world. As with ejournals, some institutions have come together to form consortia for sharing access to ebooks. For instance, the Korean Education and Research Information Service (KERIS) has formed a consortium of over 70 universities to share access to more than 8,000 ebook titles from netLibrary.

Many other publishers are entering the ebook field and providing a range of digital information sources to libraries. Examples include:

* Macmillan (http://www.macmillan.com) which provides dictionaries and encyclopaedias as well as general science journals such as *Nature* and *Scientific American*.
* Oxford Reference Online (http://www.oxfordreference.com) which has a core collection of 120 of its dictionaries and reference books that are available in a single cross-searchable database.
* Xrefer (http://www.xrefer.com) which was set up in the UK in 1999 with the aim of building a unique aggregated and integrated reference resource and which uses a unique proprietary technology to generate cross-references across titles.

Many international organizations are also making the full texts of their reports and books available online, sometimes on a subscription basis. For instance, the World Bank, one of the world's largest sources of development assistance with its primary focus on helping the poorest people and the poorest countries, launched its e-Library service in 2003 and provides a cross-searchable collection of over 1,200 World Bank books, reports and other documents (http://www.worldbank.org/elibrary).

3.6.4 *Abstracting and indexing databases*

The choice of which abstracting and indexing databases any particular organization will make available to its users will depend on the needs of those users. There are many to choose from and examples include:

- ABI/Inform – business (http://www.proquest.com/products/pt-product-ABI.shtml)
- BIOSIS – biosciences (http://www.biosis.org)
- Chemical Abstracts – chemistry (http://www.cas.org)
- COMPENDEX – engineering (http://www.ei.org)
- EMBASE – biomedicine and pharmacy (http://www.embase.com)
- ERIC – education (http://www.eric.ed.gov)
- INSPEC – physics, electrical engineering, ICT (http://www.iee.org/Publish/INSPEC/)
- Medline – medicine (http://www.nlm.nih.gov/)
- PsycInfo – psychology (http://www.apa.org/psycinfo/)
- Science Citation Index – science (http://www.isinet.com/isi/products/citation/sci/)

Just as there are many databases to choose from, so too are there many ways of making them available ... and options change as technologies develop and companies come and go. In the 1970s companies such as Lockheed Dialog offered online access to a large number of abstracting and indexing databases. Dialog (now part of the Thompson Corporation) has evolved over the years and now offers access to 1.4 billion records covering full-text sources, business data, and images as well as abstracting and indexing databases searched by users in over 100 countries (http://www.dialog.com). Other examples of search services include:

- CSA – Cambridge Scientific Abstracts (http://www.csa.com) has been publishing abstracts and indexes to the scientific and technical research literature since the 1970s and offers an Internet database service to search 70 databases.
- OCLC FirstSearch (http://www.oclc.org/firstsearch/) provides access to 72 databases, including OCLC's WORLDCAT database of some 52 million records of books held by member libraries in 68 countries and territories. OCLC is a nonprofit membership organization which has been providing a variety of services to libraries throughout the world since the 1970s.
- Ovid (http://www.ovid.org) provides a range of digital information sources covering medical information. It is owned by Wolters Kluwer and in 2001 merged with SilverPlatter, an early supplier of bibliographic databases on CD-ROM and then its Electronic Reference Library (ERL) service linking to about 30 databases.

Figure 3.12 shows some of the Chinese abstracting, indexing and full-text databases that are available on CD-ROM, or a local area network, at Shanghai Library. Shanghai Library is the largest public library in China and, as noted

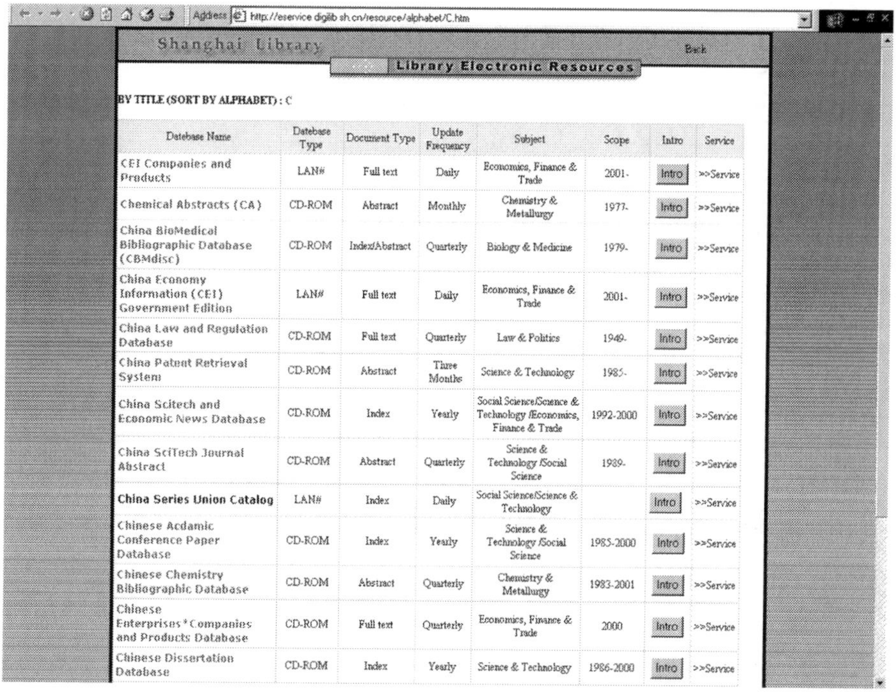

Datebase Name	Datebase Type	Document Type	Update Frequency	Subject	Scope	Intro	Service
CEI Companies and Products	LAN#	Full text	Daily	Economics, Finance & Trade	2001-	Intro	>>Service
Chemical Abstracts (CA)	CD-ROM	Abstract	Monthly	Chemistry & Metallurgy	1977-	Intro	>>Service
China BioMedical Bibliographic Database (CBMdisc)	CD-ROM	Index/Abstract	Quarterly	Biology & Medicine	1979-	Intro	>>Service
China Economy Information (CEI) Government Edition	LAN#	Full text	Daily	Economics, Finance & Trade	2001-	Intro	>>Service
China Law and Regulation Database	CD-ROM	Full text	Quarterly	Law & Politics	1949-	Intro	>>Service
China Patent Retrieval System	CD-ROM	Abstract	Three Months	Science & Technology	1985-	Intro	>>Service
China Scitech and Economic News Database	CD-ROM	Index	Yearly	Social Science/Science & Technology /Economics, Finance & Trade	1992-2000	Intro	>>Service
China SciTech Journal Abstract	CD-ROM	Abstract	Quarterly	Science & Technology /Social Science	1989-	Intro	>>Service
China Series Union Catalog	LAN#	Index	Daily	Social Science/Science & Technology		Intro	>>Service
Chinese Acdamic Conference Paper Database	CD-ROM	Index	Yearly	Science & Technology /Social Science	1985-2000	Intro	>>Service
Chinese Chemistry Bibliographic Database	CD-ROM	Abstract	Quarterly	Chemistry & Metallurgy	1983-2001	Intro	>>Service
Chinese Enterprises* Companies and Products Database	CD-ROM	Full text	Quarterly	Economics, Finance & Trade	2000	Intro	>>Service
Chinese Dissertation Database	CD-ROM	Index	Yearly	Science & Technology	1986-2000	Intro	>>Service

Figure 3.12 Extract of alphabetic listing of abstracting and indexing sources, Shanghai Library, China (reproduced courtesy of Shanghai Library)

in Chapter Two, is an active member of the InterCity Digital Library project in the Asia Pacific region (Miao, 2002). The Library also provides access to a range of digital information sources including ebooks (from netLibrary), English-language databases from sources such as CSA and Emerald, and Chinese-language databases, as well as providing a virtual reference desk (http://eservice.digilib.sh.cn/resource/index.asp).

3.7 Creating Digitized Sources

The digitization of local information sources (be they rare manuscripts, archives, student texts, examination papers, minutes of previous committee meetings, photographs, museum artefacts, or works of art) is an activity undertaken by many developers of digital libraries.

In the Chapter on creating content in the *International Yearbook of Library and Information Management 2002–2003*, Dawson (2003) draws on his work at Re:Source: the Council for Museums, Archives and Libraries in London, and the so-called 'nof-digitise' projects of The People's Network. The People's Network provided £50 million (about 73 million euros) through the New Opportunities Fund (hence the acronym nof) to fund a number of projects related to the digitization of information resources in British public libraries according to three main themes:

- cultural enrichment;
- re-skilling the nation;
- active citizenship.

The resultant EnrichUK website (http://www.enrichuk.net) provides links to these digitization projects; Figure 3.13 shows an example of some digitized material from Gwynedd Archive Service in North Wales in a bilingual (English/Welsh) website covering image and text material on the slate industry.

The importance of adherence to technical standards (as described further in Chapter Four) is emphasized in the 'nof-digitise' projects. These are seen as being linked to the lifecycle model of a digital information source as developed by the UK's Office for Library and information Networking (UKOLN) which, by 2003, was in its fifth revision (http://www.peoplesnetwork. gov.uk/content/ts_index.asp). The stages of this lifecycle comprise:

- Creation of the digital information source – including guidance on the standards for the file formats, methods of data capture, metadata and preservation.

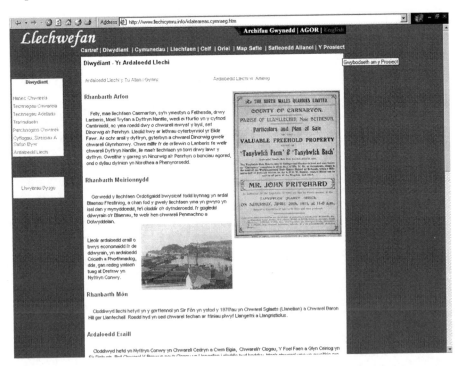

Figure 3.13 Digitized material, Gwynedd Archives, UK (reproduced courtesy of Gwynedd Archive Service)

- Management – preservation of the data, copyright issues, security, intellectual property rights and relevant metadata.
- Collection development – linking the digital information source with others to create a critical mass of digital information sources.
- Access – making information sources available in accessible, usable, secure and responsible ways such as taking into account needs of visually impaired users and adopting appropriate metadata for resource discovery.
- Re-use – digital information sources should be usable in more than one way. For instance, a digitized local history photograph generated for a special online exhibition should be capable of being 'repackaged' into a learning resource for primary school children.

These guidelines have been followed in other countries. In Canada, for instance, the Canadian Culture Online/Culture Canadienne En Ligne project is part of the Department of Canadian Heritage's strategy to encourage a uniquely Canadian presence on the Internet through funding appropriate projects (http://www.pch.gc.ca/progs/pcce-ccop/index_e.cfm). Being a bilingual country, half the funds are ear-marked for the creation of French-language material. The editors of the guidelines for digitization projects acknowledge the work of UKOLN and nof-digitise in compiling their recommendations (Alexander and Kuny, 2002).

A technical advisory service for those in UK public libraries involved in applying this model is offered by UKOLN (http://www.ukoln.ac.uk/nof/support). This service provides information on latest standards, relevant workshops and courses as well as information papers covering key areas. One information paper, produced in conjunction with the UK's Higher Education Digitization Service (HEDS), describes the essential issues a digital project should address during the project planning stage and includes:

- Know your originals. The physical processes required to create a digitized version of an original item depend on various factors (type of item (text, audio, video, image), size, condition, colour (and how important is this?))
- Know, or have a good estimate of, the costs involved. HEDS has produced a matrix of cost factors (http://heds.herts.ac.uk/resources/matrix.html) that takes into account issues such as type of material (printed text, bound text, microfilm, slides, photographs, glass plates etc.) and resolution (no. of dots per inch), preparation time, handling time, skills/experience of staff; this is reproduced in Table 3.1.

In addition a brief technical overview of creating a digital master is included and key management guidelines/decision points include:

- Scan once for all purposes so as to ensure that the complex and expensive preparation work will only need to be done once. The digital master should form the 'archival' copy and surrogates can be generated for easier access over the Web.
- Determine appropriate resolution requirement (dependent on type of original, its size, likely use and so on). For example, digitizing a 35mm.

HEDS Matrix	Materials								Post-Scan Processes	
Cost Factors	Printed A4 Paper (B&W)	Bound A4 Volumes (B&W)	35mm Microfilm (B&W)	Photo prints 5"x4" (Colour)	35mm slides (Colour)	Negative photo film unmounted (B&W)	Glass plates 5"x4" (B&W)	OCR for search & retrieval	Double Rekeying
Typical Specification:	300 dpi 1-bit B&W	400 dpi 1-bit B&W	400 dpi 8-bit greyscale	600 dpi 24-bit colour	2700 dpi 24-bit colour	2700 dpi 8-bit greyscale	600 dpi 8-bit greyscale	Accuracy >80% expected	Accuracy >99.99% expected
Preparation time	LOW	HIGH	LOW	MEDIUM	MEDIUM	HIGH	MEDIUM	LOW	LOW
Handling	LOW	HIGH	MEDIUM	HIGH	LOW	HIGH	VERY HIGH	VERY LOW	VERY LOW
Automated Processing	YES	NO	YES	YES	YES / NO	NO	NO	YES	YES
Skills / Experience rating	LOW	MEDIUM	MEDIUM	HIGH	HIGH	HIGH	MEDIUM	LOW	LOW
Optimisation Costs	LOW	LOW	MEDIUM	HIGH	HIGH	MEDIUM	MEDIUM	HIGH	MEDIUM
Resource Costs	LOW	MEDIUM	VERY HIGH	MEDIUM / HIGH	MEDIUM / HIGH	MEDIUM / HIGH	MEDIUM	LOW	MEDIUM
QA costs	LOW	LOW	MEDIUM	HIGH	HIGH	HIGH	MEDIUM	LOW	MEDIUM
Filesizes	LOW	LOW / MEDIUM	MEDIUM	HIGH	HIGH	MEDIUM	MEDIUM	LOW	LOW
Overall Ratings	LOWER	MEDIUM	LOWER / MEDIUM	HIGHER	MEDIUM / HIGHER	HIGHER	HIGHER	LOWER	MEDIUM / HIGHER

Overall Ratings:

Lower: approx. £0.05 – £0.20 per unit item
Medium: approx. £0.20 – £1.50 per unit item
Higher: approx. £1.50 – £6.00 per unit item
Very High: approx. £6.00 upwards per unit item
Checked and Updated: April 2002

The HEDS Matrix Explained

Table 3.1 HEDS matrix of costs for digitizing materials (reproduced courtesy of the University of Hertfordshire)

transparency will require more dots per inch (dpi) than a 5x4 print because it is smaller and more detailed.

- Decide whether to do the scanning inhouse or use a bureau. If it is decided to do the scanning inhouse then appropriate equipment needs to be acquired and staff trained. Contact or flatbed scanners are required for photographs and some text materials, whereas non-contact or digital cameras are needed for bound copies and oversize flat materials such as maps, plans, and 3D objects (http://www.ukoln.ac.uk/nof/support/ help/papers/digitization_process/).

Increasingly reports appear in print and on the Web of experiences with projects to create local digital information sources. For instance, a 23-step report by staff at the University of Cape Town Libraries on the digitization of a collection of early twentieth- century black and white photographs taken by Dorothea Bleek during her many expeditions to identify and record the San (Bushman) languages of Southern Africa won the Best Poster award at the 2002 IFLA conference. The final piece of advice given in the report was to "teach the process to others and to advise other local projects" (Murray et al, 2002).

Within the UK JISC has set up the Technical Advisory Service for Images (TASI) for those involved in developing collections of digitized images. On its website (http://www.tasi.ac.uk) TASI provides much information (freely) on managing digitization projects as well as creating, delivering and using digital images. In addition a series of case studies describing image digitization projects with which TASI has been involved are provided. These include:

- SCRAN – the Scottish Cultural Resources Access Network began in 1996 and provides access to a range of digitized information sources including sound, images, moving pictures and text to be used for teaching about history and cultural developments in Scotland. It contains over 1.25 million records from museums, art galleries and archives (http://www.scran.ac.uk).
- Bristol Biomedical Image Archive – this collection of almost 9000 images has been assembled by educators in different countries to assist in e-learning programmes for dental, medical and veterinary students (http://www.brisbio.ac.uk/).
- Sudan Archive Photographs Database – this comprises some 30,000 digitized photographs with associated text taken in the Sudan during the Anglo-Egypt Condominium Period (1899–1955).

Members of the Digitization Subgroup of the Corporate Management Forum Information Technology Working Group at the Australian Department of Communications, Information Technology and the Arts also have experience in implementing a number of projects involving the digitization of cultural heritage materials in national museums, galleries and libraries. They have developed a set of principles for any institution embarking on a digitization programme (http://www.nla.gov.au/libraries/digitization/citwg_princ.html). The first two fundamental principles they suggest are:

a) *Have clear goals.* Decisions will need to be taken about the quality of the images as well as the number of items in a collection to be digitized. Digitizing a collection costs money and the number of items to be digitized will depend on the monies available.
b) *Be driven by the policy of the institution.* A digitization programme should reflect the strategic and operational goals of the institution and obey relevant policies. Also, it should reflect internal policies regarding collection access, preservation, collection management and marketing.

In addition this subgroup noted a number of other principles to be adopted, as appropriate, based on the goals of the project:

- Think about the long term requirements, as cheap short-term solutions are not cost-effective in the long term.
- Undertake regular re-evaluation of the technology adopted and processes undertaken in order to optimize the effectiveness and efficiency of the digitization programme.
- Minimize risks – particularly from loss or damage of originals, or from using technological solutions that do not meet the required standards.

- Integrate digitization procedures into institutional activities – for instance, acquisitions processes, ensuring proper documentation and storage facilities, recording information about copyright restrictions and permissions, conserving/preserving and tracking movement of the original, including information about digitized objects in collection management (or other) databases.
- Eliminate duplication – such as manipulating originals twice for different digitization projects.
- Acknowledge provenance – if a digitized copy is being made of an original that has been borrowed from another institution (say for a physical exhibition) then take care that ownership of the original is acknowledged.
- Ensure that appropriate intellectual property legislation is adhered to and that cultural protocols are respected.
- Collaborate with other institutions as appropriate.
- Manage the digitized objects appropriately, including the creation of records to describe their content (metadata), and maintenance and preservation of the digital data.
- Manage the originals appropriately as well.
- Be faithful to the original – digital manipulation can be performed if necessary on digital copies . . . but the main digital version should be a faithful reproduction of the original.

Creating digitized versions of back issues of newspapers is a major challenge which is being addressed by some. For instance, Gale (part of the Thomson Corporation), under an agreement with *The Times* of London has planned and implemented a digital edition covering 200 years of this, the oldest continuously published daily newspaper in the English language. The following principles were adopted during the digitization process:

- Making the complete newspaper, including display and classified advertising, easily retrievable;
- Ensuring the most accurate and comprehensive search results possible;
- Adding a subject category to the metadata of every article, so that the results could be limited to particular areas of enquiry;
- Making use as attractive and as easy as possible;
- Keeping the delivery times of results to a minimum;
- Indicating the context of publication; alongside every search result a full-page thumbnail image appears in which the position of an article or advertisement and the relationship between editorial and advertising content is highlighted;
- Offering seamless navigation from an individual article to its related full page;
- In the browse function, hotlinking all article headings from a page of the paper alongside a large thumbnail page image allowing users to see the article's position on a page (Readings and Holland, 2003).

There are very many examples around the world of digitization projects and several examples were given earlier in this Chapter of Unesco-funded projects covering a range of materials in different countries. A major digitization project in the US is American Memory. The Library of Congress has created some seven million digital items from over 100 historical collections in a variety of formats (written materials, manuscripts, sheet music, maps, motion pictures, photographs and prints and sound recordings) to form American Memory (http://memory.loc.gov/ammem/amhome.html) for its National Digital Library. Figure 3.14 shows a screenshot from the 'Today in History' feature for November 22nd. This digital library started in 1995 and has been built using technical standards as described in Chapter Four and was an early adopter of OAI-PMH (Arms, 2003).

In Europe, the Digital Heritage and Cultural Content (Digicult) programme of the European Union involves various image databases (http://www. cordis.lu/ist/ka3/digicult/projects_a_g.htm). Since 1999 some 100 projects have been funded under this initiative according to the online publication *Cultivate Interactive* (http://www.cultivate-int.org). One project, TRIS (Trials Support), brought together the results of some 25 different European projects and as stated on its website:

> The projects have been experimenting with existing technologies to find novel ways of creating, managing and presenting new classes of digital cultural objects, held by memory institutions across Europe.

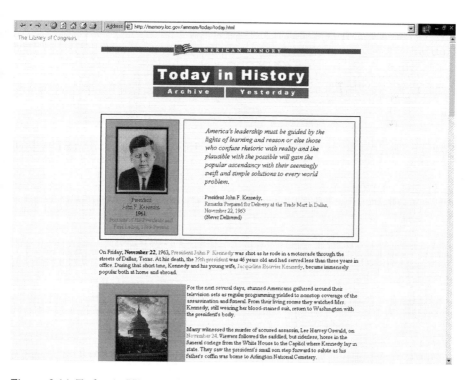

Figure 3.14 Today in History, American Memory, Library of Congress, US (reproduced courtesy of the Library of Congress)

Their goal was to enhance the user experience, by providing innovative means of exploration, learning and entertainment. To this purpose, the projects focused on the user, in particular, on user interaction and models for interactivity with high-quality virtual representations of valuable cultural objects, and the creation and navigation of virtual cultural and scientific landscapes. The trial projects addressed a wide range of cultural heritage themes, and therefore different user communities including tourists, teachers, young people, SMEs (Small and Medium Enterprises), historians, scholars, curators, scientists as well as the individual citizen. (http://www.trisweb.org/tris/trisportalpro/tris/tris_project_sum.asp).

This Chapter has provided an overview of some of the digital information sources that might be included in a digital library. The actual range to be made available within any individual digital library will depend on the needs of the users. Some of the sources will be publicly available and acquired, usually through licences. Other sources will be developed 'locally' and examples shown ranged from a bilingual archive collection in North Wales to a huge archive at the Library of Congress in the US. There is now a fair amount of experience in managing digitization projects within the digital library community and much advice is freely available on the Web, as well as in printed form (Lee, 2001; Tanner, 2001) for those embarking on such a project.

References

Alexander, M. and Kuny, T. (ed.) (2002) *Canadian Heritage: Standards and Guidelines for Digitization Projects*. Hull, Quebec: Canadian Culture Online Programme. Available at: http://www.pch.gc.ca/progs/pcce-ccop/pubs/ccop-pcceguide_e.pdf

Arms, C. R. (2003) Available and useful: OAI at the Library of Congress. *Library Hi Tech*, **21** (2),129–139

Atkinson, J. (2001) Developments in networked moving images for UK higher education. *Program*, **35** (2), 109–118

Chan, L. and Kirsop, B. (2002) Open archiving opportunities for developing countries: towards equitable distribution of global knowledge. *Ariadne*, **30**. Available at: http://www.ariadne.ac.uk/issue30/oai-chan/

Cooke, A. (2001) *A Guide to Finding Quality Information on the Internet: Selection and Evaluation Strategies*. 2nd.ed. London: Facet Publishing

Dawson, D. (2002) Creating content together: an international perspective on digitization programmes. In G.E. Gorman (ed.) *International Yearbook of Library and Information Management 2002–2003. The Digital Factor in Library and Information Services*. London: Facet Publishing, 282–301

Harnad, S. (2003) Online archives for peer-reviewed journal publications. In J. Feather and P. Sturges (eds.) *International Encyclopedia of Library and Information Science*. 2nd ed. London: Taylor and Francis

Lambert, J. (2003) Developments in electronic publishing in the biomedical sciences. *Program*, **37** (1), 6–15

Lee, S.D. (2001) *Digital Imaging: a Practical Handbook*. London: Library Association Publishing

Marcondes, C. H. and Sayão, L. F. (2003) The SciELO Brazilian scientific gateway and open archives. *D-Lib Magazine*, **9** (3). Available at: http://www.dlib.org/dlib/march03/marcondes/03marcondes.html

Matoria, R.K., Upadhyay, P.K. and Mishra, A. (2003) NewsNIC: a Web-based, full-text news clipping service from the National Informatics Centre Library in India. *Program*, **37** (3), 181–189

Mattison, D. (2002) The past in your pocket: digital heritage print collections in Canada and abroad. *Searcher*, **10** (8), 54–67

Miao, Q. (2002) Promoting the regional development of information technology: the InterCity Digital Library Initiative. Paper presented at the World Library Summit 2002, Singapore. Available at: http://www.library.sh.cn/english/events/lectures/03.htm

Muir, A. and Oppenheim, C. (2002) National information policy developments worldwide.1: electronic government. *Journal of Information Science*, **28** (3), 173–186

Murray, K., Hart, L., Dunlop, J. and Struthers, M. (2002) The managerial process of digital imaging projects at the University of Cape Town Libraries. Available at: http://www.ifla.org/IV/ifla68/papers/ps30.jpg

Mutula, S.M. (2002) Africa's web content: current analysis. *Malaysian Journal of Librarianship and Information Science*, **7** (2), 35–55

Pew Research Center (2002) *Counting the Internet* Washington, DC.: Pew Internet and American Life Project. Available at: http://www.pewinternet.org/reports/reports.asp?Report=80&Section=ReportLevel1&Field=Level1ID&ID=350

Prosser, D. (2003) On the transition of journals to open access. *ARL Bimonthly Report* **227**. Available at: http://www.arl.org/newsltr/227/openaccess.html

Readings, R. and Holland, M. (2003) The Times digital archive 1785–1985: 'The Thunderer' on the Web. *Library and Information Update* **2** (7) 38–41. Available at: http://www.cilip.org.uk/update/issues/jul03/article2july.html

Saunders, P. (2002) From the library, any e-time. Paper presented at the Victorian Association of Library Automation, Melbourne, 2002. Available at: http://www.vala.org.au/vala2002/2002pdf/33Saunds.pdf

Tanner, S. (2001) Librarians in the digital age: planning digitization projects. *Program*, **35** (4), 327–337

Chapter 4

Standards and Interoperability

4.1 Introduction

Libraries are no strangers either to standards or to interoperability. Without standards such as the second edition of the Anglo-American Cataloguing Rules (AACR2), or the interoperability afforded, for example, by the Machine-Readable Cataloguing (MARC) record format, libraries would function very differently than at present. If standards and interoperability traditionally have been important for libraries, this importance is further emphasized in the digital library environment. As Chowdhury and Chowdhury (1999) comment, the need for standards and strict adherence to them is much more important in a digital than a traditional library environment. For Rowlands and Bawden (1999), interoperability "permeates almost all aspects of the digital library" and is a fundamental goal in constructing digital libraries out of independently developed collections "that rely on each other to accomplish larger tasks". Although this book has no pretensions as a technical manual, it is impossible to consider digital libraries without at least dipping into the critical waters of standards and the interoperability they facilitate.

4.2 Standards

In his book on standards for librarians, Crawford (1991) considers a standard (or a technical standard as he calls it) to be "an explicit definition that can be communicated, that is not subject to unilateral change without notice, and that, if properly followed, will yield predictable and consistent results." Standards support cooperative relationships and "provide the common bases from which individual developments may emerge". They make it possible to share across institutional and political boundaries. They may also, it is true, retard innovation by maintaining outworn technology and safeguarding established practices. Furthermore, rival standards may do much to undermine the point of having any standard at all. A good example is provided by the numerous rival and incompatible standards by which bibliographic references are to be cited in a book or article: the American Psychological Association, the Modern Language Association, the Chicago Manual of Style, and several other well-known standards, including ANSI Z39.29 – the American National Standard for Bibliographic References – can be chosen by editors or publishers as *their* standard (authors often wittingly or unwittingly create their own schemes, only adding to the confusion).

Standards are supported by a range of national and international organizations, including professional associations such as the Institute of Electrical and Electronics Engineers (IEEE), national standard institutions such as the American National Standards Institute (ANSI) or the British Standards Institution (BSI), and international bodies such as the International Organization for Standardization (ISO). Of particular note for libraries is the US National Information Standards Organization (NISO), accredited by ANSI to prepare standards for library and information science.

A number of important institutions and organizations are actively involved in the development and promotion of standards relevant to digital libraries. For example, the Digital Library Federation (DLF), a consortium of libraries and related agencies such as archives, has as one of its objectives to identify standards for digital collections and network access (http://www.diglib.org). The DLF operates under the administrative umbrella of the Council of Library and Information Resources (http://www.clir.org) located in Washington, DC. The Library of Congress (http://www.loc.gov), also in the US capital, plays an important role in maintaining several key standards such as MARC, and the development of MARC within an XML environment, that will be discussed below. The Consortium for the Computer Interchange of Museum Intelligence (CIMI), until its demise in December 2003, was an international grouping of cultural heritage institutions and organizations that encouraged the use of standards in the museum community. Some of its activities have now been taken over by MDA (formerly the Museum Documentation Association) (http://www.mda.org.uk), an organization that supports information management within the cultural sector. The International Federation of Library Associations and Institutions (IFLA) maintains a gateway – IFLANET Digital Libraries – to resources about a variety of relevant standards (http://www.ifla.org/II/metadata.htm).

4.3 Interoperability

Interoperability, as defined by the IEEE (1990), is "the ability of two or more systems or components to exchange information and to use the information that has been exchanged." The Web Services Interoperability Organization (WS-I), an organization "chartered to promote web services interoperability across platforms, operating systems and programming languages", defines the term 'interoperable' as "suitable for and capable of being implemented in a neutral manner on multiple operating systems and in multiple programming languages" (http://www.ws-i.org). In the specific context of digital libraries, Arms (2000) defines interoperability as the "task of building coherent services for users when the individual components are technically different and managed by different organizations", and he sees as a fundamental challenge to all aspects of digital libraries the problem of getting a wide variety of computing systems to work together. In its most complete form, interoperability would indicate seamless integration of disparate collections held by different organizations.

Borgman (2000) identifies three main aspects relating to interoperability:

- getting systems to work with one another in real time;
- enabling software to work on different systems (portability);
- enabling data to be exchanged among different systems.

As she says, all three are relevant to digital libraries.

Miller (2000) goes further in his definition: to be operable, "one should actively be engaged in the ongoing process of ensuring that the systems, procedures and culture of an organization are managed in such a way as to maximize opportunities for exchange and re-use of information, whether internally or externally." For him, while ensuring compatible hardware and software is important, interoperability also is related to the ways in which organizations work, and especially their attitudes to information. He breaks down interoperability into six aspects:

- Technical interoperability, including the continued development of communication, transport, storage and representation standards (what some have called the plumbing aspects).
- Semantic interoperability, concerned with naming things – for example, in different contexts the terms author, creator, and composer might be used to describe the same, or at least a very similar, concept.
- Political/human interoperability – the decision to make resources more widely available has implications for the organizations concerned (a perceived loss of control or ownership), their staff (who may not possess the skills required to support more complex systems and a newly dispersed user community), and users.
- Inter-community interoperability between institutions and disciplines, as a consequence of researchers requiring access to information from a wide range of sources, both within and without their own subject area.
- Legal interoperability between the requirements of access and privacy legislation in different countries.
- International interoperability – all these issues are magnified when considered on an international scale, where differences in technical approach, working practice, and organization have been enshrined over many years. Other international problem areas related to language and cultural differences are discussed in Chapters Six and Seven.

Arms (2000) discusses the challenges in achieving interoperability in various areas that affect the implementation of digital libraries:

- common user interfaces;
- uniform naming and identification systems;
- standard formats for information resources;
- standard metadata formats;
- standard network protocols;
- standard information retrieval protocols;
- standard measures for authentication, security and so on.

Interoperability increasingly has been viewed as important by a wide range of organizations, including universities, museums and publishing houses. To this list must be added, without doubt, libraries. How can interoperability be achieved by digital libraries? Well, the solution may seem obvious: by everyone adopting common standards for representing text, images, sounds, languages, and so on. Alas, both practical and political reasons make this much easier said than done, although, as Borgman (2000) comments, the trend in information infrastructure development is towards open systems that do support interoperability. In other words, interoperability and standardization are inter-related.

4.4 Metadata

Metadata is a term that crops up throughout this book. You may recall that the term figured prominently in the definition of digital libraries given in Chapter One: ". . . the content of digital libraries includes data, metadata that describe various aspects of the data . . . and metadata that consist of links or relationships to other data or metadata, whether internal or external to the digital library" (Borgman, 2000). Examples of metadata types were given in Chapter Three. We must now take a closer look at what is meant by metadata and their significance for digital libraries.

Metadata, or literally "data about data," is a term interpreted in various ways by the diverse communities that design, create, preserve and use information systems and resources. It is normally understood to mean structured data about resources that can be used to help support a wide range of operations, including resource description and discovery, the management of information resources and their long-term preservation (Day, 2001). Until the mid-1990s, it was a term mainly used by communities involved with data management and systems design, and referred to a set of standards necessary to identify, represent, exchange, manage and use data in an information system (Gilliland-Swetland, 2000). In the library community, a different term was (and is) used to describe this concept: bibliographic data. The definition of the term now has been broadened to include any kind of standardized descriptive information about resources, including non-digital ones: library catalogues, abstracting and indexing services, archival finding aids and museum documentation, for example, might all be seen as containing metadata (Day, 2001). This has allowed librarians, archivists and museum documentation specialists to cooperate across professional boundaries as well as to communicate with other professionals who hold an interest in metadata such as software developers and publishers.

Following Dempsey and Heery (1998), metadata is defined as:

> data associated with objects which relieves their potential users of having to have full advance knowledge of their existence or characteristics. It supports a variety of operations. A user could be either a program or a person.

A fuller definition is provided by Gorman (2004) in the introduction to a book with chapters covering many aspects of metadata: "metadata are structured, encoded data that describe characteristics of information-bearing entities to aid in the identification, discovery, assessment, and management of the described entitities."

Librarians use the term metadata (or bibliographic data) to mean the value-added information that they create to describe documents. Library metadata primarily have been intended to provide intellectual and physical access to content, and use a series of elaborate standards to ensure that documents are described consistently and that these descriptions easily can be exchanged between libraries. Documents are physically described using detailed cataloguing rules such as AACR2, while subject access schemes such as the Library of Congress Subject Headings (LCSH), Medical Subject Headings (MeSH) or the Dewey Decimal Classification (DDC) specify documents' intellectual content. The MARC format is used to encode and exchange these bibliographic records, and individual intellectual documents are uniquely identified by an International Standard Book Number (ISBN) or an International Standard Serial Number (ISSN). Bibliographic metadata have been cooperatively created and exchanged between libraries since the 1960s through national agencies such as the British Library (or its forerunner responsible for bibliographic data – the British National Bibliography) and the Library of Congress as well as cooperative cataloguing services such as OCLC.

In contrast to libraries, both archives and museums traditionally have focused on context to organize and retrieve documents. Their metadata include accession records and finding aids as well as catalogue records. Standardized descriptions to facilitate data exchange have been slower to emerge in the museum than the library or archive communities, where the benefits are less apparent. Nevertheless, the MARC Archival and Manuscript Control (AMC) format was published by the Library of Congress back in 1984 (and now is integrated into the MARC format for bibliographic description).

The distinction between metadata and data is not clear-cut, but depends on the specific context. A bibliographic record, as discussed, above, is a type of metadata that describes certain aspects of a document such as a monograph or a dissertation, and acts as a surrogate for it; the actual monographs and dissertations constitute the data. When a user searches in an OPAC for descriptive and subject information about books, however, in a sense the bibliographic records have become data themselves, and the OPAC is treated as a digital information source as discussed in Chapter Three.

Metadata can significantly enhance information retrieval and also make it possible to search across multiple collections or to create virtual collections from materials that are distributed across several repositories. Digital information systems and emerging metadata standards developed by different professional communities but incorporating some common data elements, such as the Encoded Archival Description (EAD), the Text Encoding Initiative (TEI) and the Dublin Core (see below), are making it easier for users to negotiate between descriptive surrogates of documents and digitized versions of the documents themselves, and to search at both the item and collection level within and across information systems. At the same time, different schemes can introduce inconsistencies that inhibit successful interoperability. To take an example, library catalogues may contain metadata on biographies about, say, the architect Frank Lloyd Wright, reproductions of his designs, critical analyses of his work; museums may have metadata describing his designs in their collection; and archives may have letters written by him that are described in metadata comprising finding aids. One problem likely to be encountered in this example is the different terminology used by these disparate communities: Frank Lloyd Wright might variously be described by them in their metadata as being architect, designer, and author or creator.

Museum, archival, and library repositories do not simply hold individual documents: they maintain collections of documents. In the digital world it is not difficult for a single document within a collection to be digitized, and then to become separated from both its own cataloguing information and its relationship to the other documents in the same collection. Metadata play a critical role in documenting and maintaining those relationships, as well as in indicating the authenticity, structural and procedural integrity, and degree of completeness of documents. Metadata also allow repositories to track rights and reproduction information that may relate to the documents and their multiple versions. Intellectual property issues relating to the self-archiving of research papers in institutional repositories was investigated in the Rights Metadata for Open Archiving (RoMEO) Project in the UK, where a key issue is the role that metadata can play in protecting such documents (Gadd, Oppenheim and Probets, 2003).

If digitized documents that currently are being created are to survive migrations through successive generations of computer hardware and software, or removal to entirely new delivery systems, they will need metadata that enable them to exist independently of the system that is currently being used to store and retrieve them. Technical, descriptive, and preservation metadata that track how a document was created and maintained, how it behaves, and how it relates to other documents all are essential. Examples of such extended metadata are the Australian Recordkeeping Metadata Schema (RKMS), the Multimedia Content Description Interface standard for audio-visual resources, and the NISO draft definition of technical metadata for digital still images (Day, 2001).

Metadata, then, are critical to the continued physical and intellectual accessibility and utility of digital documents. In this sense, to quote Gilliland-Swetland (2000), "metadata provides us with the Rosetta Stone that will make it possible to decode information objects and their transformation into knowledge in the cultural heritage information systems of the twenty-first century". Many metadata standards are used in digital libraries; descriptions of the main ones follow.

4.4.1 MARC

The MARC format was developed by the Library of Congress and released in 1968 as a standard structure for exchanging library cataloguing records. MARC is a specific implementation of ANSI/NISO Z39.2, the standard that specifies a record structure to accommodate bibliographic information. While MARC was developed for books, it can also be used for other print-based formats such as serials and sheet music, as well as audiovisual and digital resources. It was widely adopted around the world, although national variants such as USMARC in the US, CAN/MARC in Canada, UKMARC in Britain and INDOMARC in Indonesia emerged whose paths diverged because of different national cataloguing practices and requirements. In order to facilitate international exchange of bibliographic data between national bibliographic agencies, and as a result of this proliferation of national formats, an international MARC format was developed which in principle would accept records in any MARC format and act as a common conversion format. This Universal MARC Format (UNIMARC) was established (in 1977) and maintained by the IFLA Permanent UNIMARC Committee (PUC); (more information on it can be found at http://www.ukoln.ac.uk/metadata/desire/overview/rev_17.htm). More recently, in 1999 USMARC and CAN/MARC merged to create MARC21, to which UKMARC will adhere in 2004. This harmonization of MARC formats in MARC21 offers new possibilities for a *de facto* international standard for cataloguing records.

Information in a MARC record is stored in fields and sub-fields, each identified by its own tag (or code). Each record includes a description of the item (based, for example, upon AACR2) together with the main and added entries under which it can be sought in the catalogue (again determined by rules in AACR2), subject headings (such as LCSH), and a classification or call number (such as DDC or LC classification number). Figure 4.1 shows one such record in the Library of Congress Online Catalog (http://catalog.loc.gov) describing Borgman's book, *From Gutenberg to the Global Information Structure*. So, for example, the field designated by tag 100 contains the "personal name main entry", in other words, the book's author; field 245, its title; field 300 the physical description, and so on. In field 300 two sub-fields can be seen: one for pagination (sub-field a) and one for the book's height in centimeters (sub-field c); had the book contained illustrations, this would have been noted in sub-field b. Those seeking a brief but more detailed description of the MARC record format can consult Furrie (2003).

The Network Development and MARC Standards Office at the Library of Congress is developing a framework for working with MARC data in

Figure 4.1 MARC record, Library of Congress, US

an XML environment. This framework is intended to be flexible and extensible so as to allow users to work with MARC data in ways specific to their needs (http://www.loc.gov/standards/marcxml//).

4.4.2 Dublin Core

Dublin Core (http://dublincore.org/documents/dces) is a metadata standard comprising a set of data elements that can be used to describe digital documents. So far it has proven to be the most successful generic metadata set for digital libraries, being used for many different applications and by many different communities. It originated in a series of workshops involving representatives from all over the world, starting in 1995, that set out to define and develop metadata requirements for use on the Internet as well as in local applications, so that digital libraries, amongst others, could achieve interoperability in data exchange (the name comes from Dublin, Ohio, where the first workshop was held).

Dublin Core identifies 15 basic elements that all electronic documents should have to support interoperability:

- Title – the name given to the document
- Creator – the entity primarily responsible for making the content

- Subject – the topic of the content, typically keywords or classification codes taken from a controlled vocabulary or formal classification scheme
- Description – an account of the content, such as an abstract or table of contents
- Publisher – an entity responsible for making the resource available
- Contributor – an entity responsible for making contributions to the content
- Date – a date of an event in the lifecycle of the document
- Type – the nature or genre of the content
- Format – the physical or digital manifestation of the document
- Identifier – an unambiguous reference to the document within a given context, such as a Uniform Resource Locator (URL) or ISBN
- Source – a reference to a resource from which the document is derived
- Language – a language of the intellectual content of the document
- Relation – a reference to a related document
- Coverage – the extent or scope of the content, typically a spatial, temporal or jurisdictional location
- Rights – information about rights held in and over the document.

In the case of the Frank Lloyd Wright example cited above, Dublin Core provides just one element, called the creator, by which is to be designated individuals such as the author, designer or architect.

Dublin Core, adopted as a standard by NISO in September 2001 and by ISO in February 2003, is intended for use by people untrained in the arcane ways of library cataloguing. Nevertheless, it is widely used in digital libraries (Witten and Bainbridge, 2003). Its simplicity is both a strength and a weakness. It is much more straightforward for someone to create Dublin Core metadata than, for example, MARC metadata, but this is achieved at the price of a loss in the precision with which a document is described. In contrast to typical bibliographic practices in libraries, Dublin Core does not impose any specific vocabulary control scheme to indicate subject content (although it does recommend use of such schemes), nor any authority control to ensure that the same 'thing' always goes by the same name (for example, any variants on an author's name are standardized to just one of these forms). As a consequence, two people quite legitimately might produce using Dublin Core different descriptions of the same document. Some librarians are sceptical about its virtues. Gorman (1999), for example, describes Dublin Core as essentially a sub-set of MARC that offers "a choice between an inexpensive and ineffective form of cataloguing in which 15 elements ... are filled with unqualified and uncontrolled free text" and an expensive but effective form of cataloguing undertaken by professionals and based on controlled data.

DC-dot, a Dublin Core Metadata Editor (http://www.ukoln.ac.uk/metadata/dcdot), can be used automatically to generate metadata directly from a web page, though it may not be able to find data for all 15 Core elements. DC-dot was developed by staff at UKOLN: the UK Office for Library and information Networking which, amongst many other activities, acts as a focal point within the UK for research on metadata issues. When tried with an article from *D-Lib Magazine*, DC-dot was able to assign many of the 15 elements (see Figure 4.2). Automatic generation of the far more complex

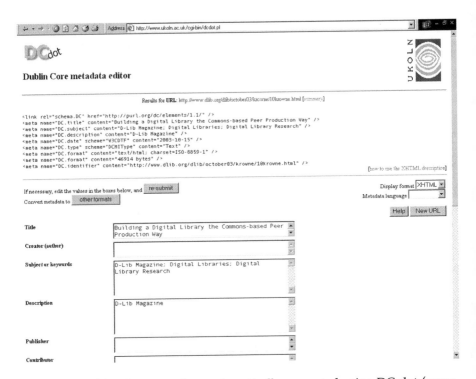

Figure 4.2 Dublin Core metadata automatically generated using DC-dot (reproduced courtesy of the University of Bath)

MARC records, in contrast, is a different matter altogether, and no editor exists to accomplish this task.

Dublin Core has a part to play in cross-language interoperability as it has been translated into many other languages: a list can be found on the Dublin Core Metadata Institute site (http://dublincore.org/resources/translations). Its simple structure makes it relatively straightforward to translate, although for certain languages some new terminology must be developed. Baker (1998) cites as an example the term 'creator' that is usually translated into Bahasa Indonesia as 'pencipta', but to many people this evokes a deity (of course, so can the term 'creator' in English); the committee responsible for translation opted for a loanword, 'kreator', that conveyed the proper scope of the English term without the distracting cultural association. A possible obstacle to Dublin Core acting as a successful metadata interlingua is the risk of instability in the original English-language version: any modifications in this version would necessitate re-translation of all other language versions, or risk the emergence of different language dialects of Dublin Core, an unhelpful development for interoperability.

Dublin Core provides the necessary interoperability between the digitized images in the National Library of Australia's PictureAustralia (http://www. pictureaustralia.org) service that provides a single web entry point to a distributed collection of digitized pictures held in 22 cultural agencies throughout the country (Campbell, 2002). Each of the agencies contributing to PictureAustralia manages its own image collection, but the original descriptive cataloguing information (or metadata) is 'mapped' into a standard PictureAustralia metadata format based on Dublin Core. This metadata is collected (or 'harvested') periodically by the National Library of Australia to build a searchable central index.

4.4.3 The International Standard Archival Description (General)

The International Standard Archival Description (General) or ISAD(G), developed by a committee of the International Council on Archives, provides general guidance on the preparation of archival descriptions in order to identify and explain the context and content of archival materials and to promote their accessibility. The standard, which first appeared in 1996, contains 26 elements that can be combined to constitute the description of an archival entity, but only six are considered essential for international exchange of descriptive archive information: Reference code, Title, Creator, Dates, Extent and medium of the unit of description, and Level of description. It should be seen as an approach to cataloguing rather than a detailed cataloguing standard; it has deliberately been left at a general level to reflect the national, cultural, regional and organizational variations in archival practices. As such, it needs to be used with existing local and national standards.

4.4.4 Encoded Archival Description (EAD)

The EAD is widely used by archives, museums and manuscript libraries as a standard to encode archival finding aids, guides, handlists or catalogues. It is administered jointly by the Society of American Archivists and the Library of Congress (http://www.loc.gov/ead). Its objective is to enable archives and libraries easily to share information about related but different records and collections, and to include information beyond that accommodated by MARC (Pitti, 1999). Its early developers at the University of California Berkeley looked initially at the possibility of using or extending MARC tagging, but instead opted to base a new standard on the Standardized Generalized Markup Language (SGML). Specifically EAD:

- enables archives to communicate and share information about related but different materials, and dispersed materials;
- provides consistent and intelligible descriptions across different repositories;
- offers universal access to distributed collections.

4.4.5 Text Encoding Initiative (TEI)

TEI is an international and interdisciplinary standard to represent those features of a text that need to be identified explicitly to facilitate computerized text processing and the sharing of electronic texts. It comprises a set of tags that can be inserted in a text to mark its structure. Although the impetus for TEI came from the humanities computing community and it was initially intended for literary and linguistic texts, its scope has been broadened and it can now be used with any type of text in any language. Further details can be found at the TEI website (http://www.tei-c.org).

4.4.6 Resource Description Framework (RDF)

The RDF was developed by the World Wide Web Consortium (W3C) and provides a foundation for metadata interoperability across different resource description communities that have adopted incompatible metadata standards. It is designed for use with web resources. Further details can be found at the RDF website (http://www.w3.org/RDF).

4.4.7 Metadata Encoding and Transmission Standard (METS)

METS has the task of encoding descriptive, administrative and structural metadata for objects in a digital library to facilitate the management of such documents within a repository and their exchange between repositories. It is maintained by the Network Development and MARC Standards Office of the Library of Congress (http://www.loc.gov/standards/mets) and is an initiative of the Digital Library Federation, mentioned earlier in the Chapter. The METS format has seven major sections:

- The METS Header contains metadata describing the METS document itself, including such information as creator or editor.
- The Descriptive Metadata section points to descriptive metadata external to the METS document (such as a MARC record in an OPAC or an EAD finding aid on a web server), or contains internally embedded descriptive metadata, or both.
- The Administrative Metadata section provides information about how the files were created and stored, intellectual property rights, the original source from which the digital library object document derives, and information regarding the provenance of the files comprising the digital library object (that is master/derivative file relationships, and migration/transformation information). As with Descriptive Metadata, Administrative Metadata may be either external to the METS document, or encoded internally.
- The File section lists all the files containing content that form part of the digital document.
- The Structural Map provides a hierarchical structure for the digital library document or object, and links the elements of that structure to content files and metadata that pertain to each element.
- The Structural Links section of METS allows METS' creators to record the existence of hyperlinks between nodes in the hierarchy outlined in the Structural Map. This is of particular value when using METS to archive websites.
- The Behaviour section associates executable behaviours with content in the document.

4.4.8 CIMI XML

CIMI was an international consortium with members from cultural heritage institutions and organizations in Australia, Canada, the Netherlands, the UK and the US (http://www.cimi.org). From its inception in 1990 until its termination in December 2003, CIMI actively encouraged open standards-based approaches to creating and sharing digital information. It developed a schema based on XML (described later in the Chapter) that enables museums to encode information relating to museum objects, including associated information about people, places, and events surrounding the history of the objects, as well as information about their management and use. The CIMI XML schema is useful for sharing information between applications and as an interchange format for the Open Archives Initiative-Protocol for Metadata Harvesting (OAI-PMH), discussed below. MDA has taken over the role from CIMI of supporting the XML schema.

The wide range of metadata standards relevant to digital libraries reflects the diverse types of collections and institutions involved, differing philosophies concerning the levels of detail, effort and costs that should be involved in their generation, and technological development that both creates new problems and offers new solutions.

4.5 Presentation Standards

Many standards of various kinds have been developed to regulate how information is presented on the computer screen and to permit it to be exchanged between applications and systems. A short discussion of the most important ones for digital libraries follows.

4.5.1 Character encoding

Character encoding represents the bottom layer in text presentation; it is just a set of character codes that represent plain text with no formatting information such as font size or style. Textual documents are made up of individual characters that in digital form must be recognized by computers and their peripherals. The American Standard Code for Information Interchange (ASCII) for many years was the dominant means of encoding such characters – letters in the Roman alphabet (upper and lower case), numbers from 0 to 9, punctuation marks and other symbols found in text – so that they could be stored, manipulated and retrieved using computers. ASCII uses seven bits to represent any particular character (the capital letter A, for example, is code 1000001). This standard enabled computer processors, keyboards, display screens and printers to recognize and handle digitized text regardless of where or by whom it was originally generated. Unfortunately, the seven-bit ASCII code only provides 128 unique combinations, which is sufficient to accommodate the symbols found in most English-language texts, but not necessarily those found in other versions of the Roman alphabet, let alone those in the many different writing systems found around the world. Even the Extended ASCII, based on a byte of eight bits (and therefore offering 256 unique combinations) proved quite inadequate in this respect. The ISO 8859 eight-bit character set can handle Cyrillic, Arabic, Greek and Hebrew as well as Roman scripts, but for the numerous other scripts the only answer was to develop individual encoding schemes. To further complicate matters, in some cases more than one such scheme is available: for Chinese we have Traditional (Big5) that is popular in Taiwan, Simplified (GB2312) and Simplified (H2); for Cyrillic, DOS, ISO, KOI8-R, KOI8-U and Windows, and so on. Failure to select the correct character set for the encoded script will result in gobbledygook, as illustrated in Figure 4.3. Here the Russian Children's Libraries Regional Site (http://www.deti.spb.ru) is displayed using the Western European (Windows) character set instead of the Cyrillic (Windows) character set. Note that in some places the Russian words can still be read (assuming you know the language) because the writing has been captured as image files rather than text files. When the correct character set is chosen from the browser's menu (the View menu and the Encoding sub-menu in the case of Microsoft's Internet Explorer, as shown in Figure 4.3), all is well (Figure 4.4). If not available from the browser, it should be possible to download the correct character set

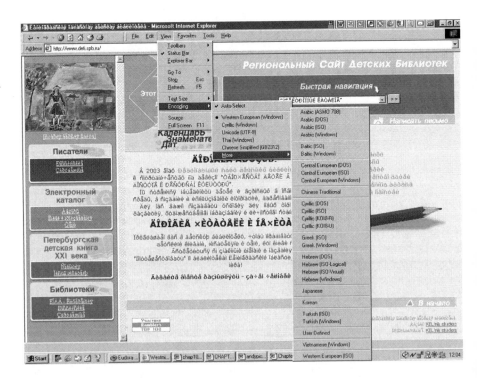

Figure 4.3 The Children's Libraries Regional Site, Russia, displayed in the wrong character encoding set – Western European (Windows) – and the sets available within Microsoft's Internet Explorer

from the Web; a good place to look is Microsoft's MSDN (Microsoft Developer Network) website (http://msdn.microsoft.com/library/default. asp?url=/library/en-us/intl/unicode_6bqr.asp).

Fortunately, there is a solution to this problem of different character-encoding schemes – a scheme that is based on 16-bit encoding, called Unicode, ratified by ISO (ISO 10646) in 1993. Unicode version 4.0 encodes over 96,000 characters. In Unicode each character in a script is allocated a unique number that remains the same in all situations. Unicode saw the light of day in 1988, originally motivated by publishers wanting to design a consistent international standard for text processing. After a slow start it has been adopted with some enthusiasm by the computing industry, and still continues to evolve, though some historical scripts (such as Numidian and Mayan Hieroglyphs) and scripts used by languages with small numbers of speakers who have little political weight are omitted (Anderson, 2003). Major programming languages such as C, Perl and Java support Unicode, it is the default encoding for both HTML and XML, and it is available from web browsers such as Internet Explorer (accessible from the Encoding entry in the View pull-down menu). A good overview of Unicode encoding can be found in Witten and Bainbridge (2003) as well as from the Unicode site (http://www.unicode.org).

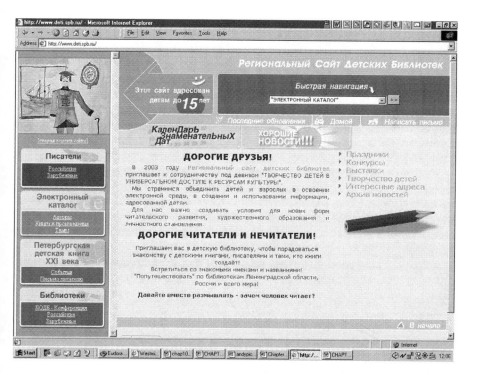

Figure 4.4 The Children's Libraries Regional Site, Russia, displayed correctly using Cyrillic (Windows)

In many instances Unicode is straightforward to incorporate into digital library software. At the same time, it must be conceded that it is not always straightforward to implement, especially for some character sets. In fact, three implementation levels have been defined for Unicode:

- Level 1 gives basic implementation of Unicode that is sufficient for many scripts, but excludes those scripts that raise special problems such as the need to combine characters (as in Arabic or Hebrew).
- Level 2 permits character combination in scripts such as Arabic and Hebrew, but still falls short of a full Unicode implementation.
- Level 3 allows for full implementation of Unicode.

Unicode, though a major step forward for interoperability between documents represented in different scripts, still fails to provide a perfect solution for certain scripts. Witten and Bainbridge (2003) discuss the special problems raised by one group of scripts – Hindi and the ten related Indic scripts used by many languages in the Indian subcontinent. As they say, without a knowledge of these languages it is difficult to explain the complexities encountered by Unicode, and here we shall not even attempt this task!

4.5.2 Formats

A text document comprises characters that are processed in a specific sequence (the actual sequence depends on the language; for example, in English, from left to right and from top to bottom, and in Arabic from right to left and top to bottom). Formatting in such a plain text is limited to such things as line breaks, paragraph demarcation, and indentations. Such presentation has limitations for digital libraries (for example, metadata cannot explicitly be included) but it has one great advantage: the words in the text can be indexed automatically by a computer (probably with the deliberate exclusion of common 'stop words' like articles and conjunctions that are of little use for searching purposes, so as to reduce the size of the index).

Page description languages, in contrast to plain text, allow more sophisticated layout to be achieved while ensuring that documents can still be processed on any computing device. PostScript was the first commercial page description language, and was widely used, but it was not designed for screen displays. Its successor, the Portable Document Format (PDF) does not have that limitation, and is widely used for storing page images. Like PostScript, PDF functions independently of any particular computer or operating system. Documents represented in PDF are very legible, retaining the design characteristics of print, and the files are moderately sized (unless incorporating bit-mapped images). As a consequence, it is often the format chosen to present finished documents online. PostScript and PDF, both developed by Adobe, are widely used as document formats in digital libraries.

Word processors such as Microsoft Word use proprietary software to allow documents to be edited. This can make it difficult to exchange documents between applications, and may prevent users who do not have access to the proprietary software from accessing a digital library collection. Rich Text

Format (RTF) solves this problem, but at the price of requiring far more storage space, and consequently slower download and display times.

Images are represented on a computer screen or printed on paper as a regular matrix of dots called pixels. Picture quality is determined by the number of pixels per square inch. Digital images require a lot of pixels, and therefore can consume a great deal of storage space as well as requiring high bandwidth for satisfactory transmission. This problem is partially remedied by compressing images into a smaller number of bits, using one of the many available image-compression formats. The Tagged Image File Format (TIFF) was developed by Aldus (now Adobe Systems) and Microsoft. This is the format most commonly used by digital libraries to store images, but they may convert them to other formats for display. The most commonly encountered are the Graphics Interchange Format (GIF), originally specified in 1987 and for many years the most widely employed, and the Joint Photographic Experts Group (JPEG) format, now the standard technique for compressing still images, and universally used for photographic images on the Web.

The dominant international compression standard for video and audio is the Moving Picture Experts Group (MPEG) format, a family of standards devised by the ISO Moving Picture Experts Group. As these media must be represented by huge amounts of data – for example, each second of CD-quality sound requires 8000 samples of eight bits per sample – compression is critical for storage and especially transmission.

4.5.3 Markup languages

Markup is used to specify the structure of individual documents and to control how they look when viewed by users (section divisions, headings, enumerated lists, quoted text, and so on). One part of their job is to identify any metadata associated with the document.

SGML, first developed by the publishing industry, is the parent language for most other descriptive tag sets. Tags allow richly structured documents to be created by encoding information such as structural divisions (title page, main body of text, date, author, etc.), or conveying information about presentation and typographical elements (changes in typeface, line breaks, etc). The SGML tags are composed of plain text ASCII characters, so no special software or proprietary code is necessary to create an SGML file. This makes the files easy to deliver across a network. Unlike, say, the code for italic fonts that Word might use, that is specific to that word processor, and that typically will be lost when the text is transferred out of Word and into another format, SGML tags are simply other letters and characters typed in as part of the text, and they travel with the text if it moves from computer system to computer system. SGML itself is not very suitable for digital library applications, however, because complex software is required to process it, and it does not facilitate interoperability (Arms, 2000).

Hypertext Markup Language (HTML) is the underlying document format used to display documents; it focuses upon the appearance of documents. It contains both the document's text and the codes – tags – that describe its format or structure by marking headings, paragraphs, lists, hypertext links etc. HTML is a non-proprietary, simplified version of SGML, and the *lingua franca* for publishing hypertext on the World Wide Web.

Extensible Markup Language (XML) is another variant of SGML, designed specifically for the Web. The development of XML began in 1996, and its use has been a W3C recommendation since 1998 (http://www.w3.org/XML/). XML provides a flexible framework for describing document structure and metadata, and for storing and transmitting documents. XML is designed to be much easier to deliver on the Internet than SGML has proved to be, and much easier for software developers to implement. It is a cross-platform format that is independent of any specific hardware or software, and is ideally suited to digital libraries. Working groups at W3C continue to develop XML, and it is widely used in the digital library world (Witten and Bainbridge, 2003).

A third SGML variant, mentioned earlier in the Chapter, is the EAD, used to encode digitized versions of archival finding aids.

4.6 Digital Object Locators

Uniform Resource Locators (URLs) provide the address system that allows computers to communicate with each other via the Web. The URL indicates whereabouts on which server a digital object is located. One problem here is that the URL only provides the relative location of an object rather than its precise location address. This is equivalent to a traditional library indicating that a book is the fifth volume on a particular shelf and bookcase rather than giving the book its own classification number. If the object is moved elsewhere its URL immediately must change, and it no longer can be found (unless a link is provided from the old to the new URL). Universal Resource Names (URNs) provide permanent names for objects that can then be accessed via their potentially unstable URLs. Several ways have been devised to offer such URNs.

One of particular significance for digital libraries is the Digital Object Identifier (DOI), developed by the Association of American Publishers (AAP), the International Publishers Association, and the International Scientific, Technical and Medical Publishers Association. DOIs are intended to ensure permanent links even if a digital object is moved to another location and therefore its URL changes. In such a case the 'owner' of the object simply updates one central DOI record in a global directory, and from then on the directory re-points all links to that object to its new URL location. Furthermore, by using the multilink feature the DOI can be made to point to all the resources the owner wants it to link to, whether internally within the digital library or to externally located objects.

The DOI itself comprises a prefix and a suffix. The prefix is assigned to any organization that wishes to register DOIs, while the suffix is used to identify the object itself. An existing standard identification number such as an ISBN can be used as the suffix if this is deemed convenient. The DOI for an article by Paloma Diaz (Usability of hypermedia educational e-books) in the March 2003 issue of *D-Lib Magazine*, for example, is: 10.1045/

march2003-diaz (the prefix 10.1045 has been assigned to this particular journal, and the suffix comprises the specific article's month and year of publication together with the author's surname). The overall objective of the DOI, then, is to make the management of digital objects in a networked environment easier and more convenient. Users of the DOI need not be aware of any changes to an object's URL. The International DOI Foundation (http://www.doi.org/welcome.html) manages the development and licensing of the DOI system to registration agencies. DOIs were first applied by the journal publishing industry, but are now widely used in many applications, including digital libraries. By mid-2003 almost ten million DOIs had been assigned. A longer discussion of DOIs can be found in Paskin (2003).

A different approach to the same problem was taken by OCLC in its development of the Persistent URL (PURL). Unlike a URL, a PURL points to an "intermediate resolution service" that associates the PURL with the object's actual URL. This allows a URL for items in a collection to be changed, but a persistent URL nevertheless to be maintained for access to those items.

Yet another option is the OpenURL, developed at Ghent University (Belgium), that can be attached to resources that are used to link one digital object to another (for example, an abstract of an article to that article's full text) even though the two may be stored on different servers (Dahl, 2002).

As Besser (2002) argues, sophisticated persistent naming must include the ability to designate a digital object by its name and not its location, and to distinguish between various instances (versions and editions) of that object and their physical locations. This is a developing area and it is too soon to predict which, if any, of these techniques will offer a long-term solution to this problem.

4.7 Protocols

In order to move information from computer to computer, interoperability is required at the network level. Internet protocols have largely resolved this issue for digital libraries on the Web, although applications demanding continuous streams of data, such as audio or video files, can still create communication problems, as well as inconvenience for users (slow or interrupted signals). An interoperability problem can remain, however, for users who wish simultaneously to search different collections in one digital library, or collections across several digital libraries.

4.7.1 Z39.50

The library community has tried with some success to address the latter issue through use of the Z39.50 protocol, accepted as a standard by ANSI and ISO, and maintained by the Library of Congress (Lynch (1997) discusses the development of the protocol). Z39.50 defines a protocol for information retrieval between a client and a database server. In effect, Z39.50 makes it possible for a user in one library to search and retrieve information from other libraries that have also implemented Z39.50 as if the user has never left the home

system (and even though the other libraries might be using different interfaces and search software than the home library). The power of Z39.50 lies
in its ability to separate the user interface on the client side from the information servers, search engines, and databases on the other side. It provides a
consistent view of information from a wide variety of sources, and it offers
clients the capability to integrate information from a range of databases and
servers. The objective of Z39.50 is to support computer-to-computer communication in standard and mutually understandable terms and support the
transfer of data between systems independently of the structure, content or
format of the data in a particular system. The protocol itself is very complex,
but fortunately digital libraries may not need always to implement all its
parts, and the standard itself specifies a minimal implementation that only
includes the initialization, search and retrieval, and results presentation facilities. In practice the Z39.50 protocol largely is confined to searches on the
metadata stored in library OPACs rather than documents themselves.

The Karlsruhe Virtual Catalogue (http://www.ubka.uni-karlsruhe.de/
hylib/en/kvk.html), for instance, relies upon a Z39.50 implementation.
Figure 4.5 shows the numerous locations that simultaneously can be searched
– in this example, only UC Bavaria, UC Northern Germany and the British
Library have been marked for searching. The Cooperative Academic
Information Retrieval Network for Scotland (CAIRNS) is another example.

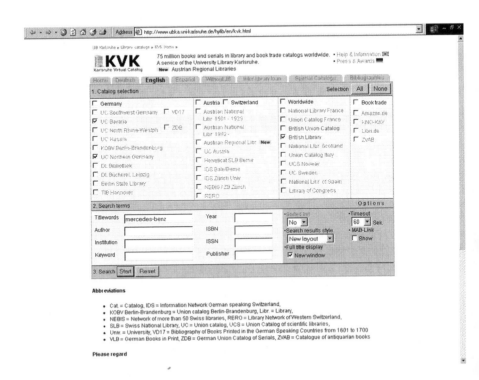

Figure 4.5 The Karlsruhe Virtual Catalogue, Germany (reproduced courtesy of
the University Library Karlsruhe)

It allows the catalogues of several Scottish university and research libraries to be searched as a whole (it can be tried at http://cairns.lib.strath.ac.uk). CAIRNS resulted from research into the integration of Z39.50 compliant catalogues by the University of Strathclyde's Centre for Digital Library Research. More information can be found on this important protocol from the website of the Library of Congress Network Development and MARC Standards Office (http://www.loc.gov/z3950/agency) that maintains it.

4.7.2 Open Archives Initiative-Protocol for Metadata Harvesting

The Open Archives Initiative is intended to develop and promote interoperability standards to facilitate information dissemination. The term 'harvesting' refers to gathering metadata together from multiple distributed repositories into one combined store. The Open Archives Initiative – Protocol for Metadata Harvesting (OAI-PMH) attempts to solve problems of digital library interoperability by enabling metadata to be harvested from OAI-compliant databases and assembled in one central location. It may then be possible to search across the data (although OAI-PMH itself does not provide the actual mechanisms to do such cross-data searching). Institutions that want to share metadata can make it available for harvesting by installing it on an OAI server. OAI-PMH is based upon the Hypertext Transfer Protocol (HTTP) and has focused upon simple protocols that will facilitate metadata exchange. All open archives must be able to use Dublin Core metadata so as to provide at the very least a minimum basis for resource sharing, although the protocol will support a much higher level of interoperability than is provided by Dublin Core – for example, it is assumed that libraries probably will use a form of MARC encoded in XML. Suleman and Fox (2001) argue that OAI has provided digital libraries with a simple but extensible protocol to facilitate interoperability. OCLC provides OAI harvester software to harvest data from other organizations' OAI repositories, and OAI server software to make local data available to harvesters. The OCLC metadata collection for theses and dissertations (the Experimental Thesis Catalog or XTCat) is one of the largest OAI repositories with more than 4.3 million records (Hyatt, 2003).

4.8 Continuity and Change

It might be expected that by definition, a standard is something that remains constant over long periods of time. Such a supposition, however, would only partially be true, at least in the case of standards in the computing and telecommunication fields. The various standards discussed in this Chapter do have a relatively long "shelf life", but as we have seen, even they are prone to adaptation and even obsolescence as technology itself develops. In the library world, standards have a certain durability, as exemplified by MARC, but again they cannot be frozen in time. If only for these reasons, our discussion has been confined to the most important, widely adopted and durable standards. It is hazardous to predict the ways in which standards will evolve. One thing remains certain, however; digital libraries will only achieve a meaningful global presence as a consequence of the further development and adoption of standards to facilitate interoperability on an international scale.

References

Anderson, D. (2003) Unicode and historic scripts. *Ariadne* **37**. Available at: http://www.ariadne.ac.uk/issue37/anderson

Arms, W. Y. (2000) *Digital Libraries*. Cambridge, MASS: MIT Press

Baker, T. (1998) Languages for Dublin Core. *D-Lib Magazine*, **4** (12). Available at: http://www.dlib.org/dlib/december98/12baker.html

Besser, H. (2002) The next stage: moving from isolated digital collections to interoperable digital libraries. *First Monday*, **7** (6). Available at: http://firstmonday.org/issues/issue7_6/besser/index.html

Borgman, C. L. (2000) *From Gutenberg to the Global Information Infrastructure: Access to Information in the Networked World*. Cambridge: MIT Press

Campbell, D. (2002) Federating access to digital objects: PictureAustralia. *Program, **36** (3), 182–187

Chowdhury, G. G. and Chowdhury, S. (1999) Digital library research: major issues and trends. *Journal of Documentation, **55** (4), 409–448

Crawford, W. (1991) *Technical Standards: An Introduction for Librarians*. 2nd ed. Boston: G.K. Hall

Dahl, M. (2002) Open URLs and reference linking: research and practical applications in libraries. *OLA (Oregon Library Association Quarterly)*, **8** (2). Available at: http://www.olaweb.org/quarterly/quar8-2/dahl.shtml

Day, M. (2001). *Metadata in a Nutshell*. Available at: http://www.ukoln.ac.uk/metadata/publications/nutshell

Dempsey, L. and Heery, R. (1998) Metadata: A current view of practice and issues. *Journal of Documentation*, **54** (2), 145–172

Furrie, B. (2003) *Understanding MARC Bibliographic Machine-Readable Cataloguing*. 7th ed. McHenry, ILL: Follett Software. Available at: http://www.loc.gov/marc/umb

Gadd, E., Oppenheim, C. and Probets, S. (2003) The RoMEO Project: protecting metadata in an open access environment. *Ariadne*, **36**. Available at: http://www.ariadne.ac.uk/issue36/romeo

Gilliland-Swetland, A. J. (2000) Setting the stage. In M. Baca, ed. *Introduction to Metadata: Pathways to Digital Information*. Los Angeles: Getty Information Institute. Available at: http://www.getty.edu/research/institute/standards/intrometadata/index.html

Gorman, G.E. (ed.) (2004) *Metadata Applications and Management: International Yearbook of Library and Information Management 2003–2004*. London: Facet Publishing

Gorman, M. (1999) Metadata or cataloguing? A false choice. *Journal of Internet Cataloguing*, **2** (1), 5–22

Hyatt, S. (2004) Developments in cataloguing and metadata. In G. Gorman, ed. *International Yearbook of Library and Information Management 2003–2004: Metadata*. London: Facet Publishing. Available at: http://www.oclc.org/research/publications/archive/2003/hyatt.pdf

IEEE (1990) *Glossary*. Available at: http://www.sei.cmu.edu/str/indexes/glossary/interoperability.html

Lynch, C. (1997) The Z39.50 information retrieval standard. Part I: A strategic view of its past, present and future. *D-Lib Magazine*, **3**(4). Available at: http://www.dlib.org/dlib/april97/04lynch.html

Miller, P. (2000) Interoperability: What is it and why should I want it? *Ariadne*, **24**. Available at: http://www.ariadne.ac.uk/issue24/interoperability

Paskin, N. (2003) DOI: A 2003 progress report. *D-Lib Magazine*, **9** (6). Available at: http://www.dlib.org/dlib/june03/paskin/06paskin.html

Pitti, D. V. (1999) Encoded Archival Description: an introduction and overview. *D-Lib Magazine*, **5** (11). Available at: http://www.dlib.org/dlib/november99/11pitti.html

Rowlands, I. and Bawden, D. (1999) Building the digital library on solid research foundations. *Aslib Proceedings*, **51** (8), 275–282

Suleman, H. and Fox, E. (2001) The Open Archives Initiative: Realizing simple and effective digital library interoperability. *Journal of Library Administration*, **35** (1/2), 125–145

Witten, I. H. and Bainbridge, D. (2003) *How to Build a Digital Library*. San Francisco: Morgan Kaufmann

Chapter 5

Organizing Access to Digital Information Sources

5.1 Introduction

This Chapter provides an overview of the software options for organizing access to digital information sources. For some institutions the development of a digital library is seen as a continuation of the computer-based management system that might have been used for some years to organize the cataloguing, acquisition, circulation, and so on, of printed books, serials, archives or museum objects. Other institutions will, never have used computer systems before, and the implementation of a digital library is a totally new opportunity to provide access to a range of different types of digital information sources and to provide very many more services for their users.

The basic functions of any software which provides access to digital information sources have been referred to by some authors (such as Murray, 2001) as 'discovery to delivery' (or D2D). The use of open standards, as described in Chapter Four, is required to enable these functions to perform appropriately as follows:

- Discovery – searching for information (for example using the Z39.50 protocol).
- Location – identifying an appropriate source which contains the required information (for example using the DOI or the OpenURL).
- Request- ordering or requesting the information from the identified source (for example using HTTP, e-mail or standards for interlibrary loans from ISO).
- Delivery – managing the presentation of the information received following the request by the user.

Experiences in investigating software for the administration and maintenance of libraries of digital objects are provided by Bogen et al. (2001). They recognize the need for those in cultural heritage institutions involved in digitizing original documents and other 'objects' to have appropriate digital library systems, over and above the library management systems which might be in place to provide access to the metadata about those documents or objects. They suggest that the software should have four layers above the digitized objects and their associated metadata:

- A database management system (DBMS). This would include information on the digital objects and their metadata.
- A digital objects server (such as an image server for images, a video server to support video, a 3D server to enable 3D images to be displayed, and so on). This server would handle the requests to/from the DBMS concerning the digital objects.
- 'Middleware', toolkits or 'glue' to link the various 'applications' programs together and which would include directory and security services as well as management facilities.
- Digital library 'clients' that provide the top level of the interface between the user and the digital objects.

Some 70 possible products were investigated by Bogen et al. (2001) and the following features were assessed:

- Background about the product and the supplier.
- Collection management features (including the storage of different qualities/versions of the digital objects and intellectual property rights information).
- Interface issues (including search facilities).
- Support features (including scanning features, indexing).
- Technical requirements (server operating system, use of standards and so on).

In their analysis they divided the software investigated into three categories:

- Library management software.
- Museum management software which provides extra functionality that is of relevance to museums such as collection administration, exhibition management, events and public relations, administration and shipping.
- Digital library software which allows for the manipulation (or retrieval) and delivery of the digital objects.

We have chosen to describe the available software for organizing access to digital information sources in similar, but not quite identical, categories in the next section.

Before that a few descriptions are given of software used in some digital library applications to meet the specific challenge of what is referred to as cross-database searching, federated searching, metasearching, one-stop searching or searching across heterogeneous sources as shown in some of the screenshots in Chapter Seven.

The ability to offer searching facilities across a range of digital information sources is a feature of several digital libraries as described by Tennant (2001), who has been much involved with the California Digital Library (CDL). Within the CDL special software called SearchLight has been developed, in conjunction with staff from the University of California at San Diego, to enable cross-database searching across a range of sources including books, journal indexes, ejournals, e-texts and documents, reference sources, and web directories (http://www.cdlib.org). Cross-database searching is also being investigated and implemented in the University of California at Berkeley Digital Library SunSITE (http://sunsite.berkeley.edu). The mission of the Berkeley Digital Library SunSITE (Sun Software, Information and Technology Exchange) and sponsored by the Library at the University of California Berkeley and Sun Microsystems, is to build digital collections and services as well as providing information and support to digital library developers worldwide. This digital library comprises a large number of discrete collections covering such topics as Catalonian manuscripts, historic topographic maps and nineteenth-century literature. Cross-database searching of this nature is also provided by some commercial software products such as MuseGlobal's MuseSearch and MuseSeek software (http://www.muse-global.com) and WebFeat (http://www.webfeat.org). MuseGlobal's software is used as the underpinning technology in many applications, and Cleveland Public Library is one example of a library that has implemented WebFeat. It is the third largest public library in the US and offers its users a broad range of 100 or more digital information sources. However, users found navigating a range of different interfaces a challenge and so WebFeat was acquired to provide a general interface to all the sources.

5.2 Software Developed from Library Management Systems

The marketplace for library management systems (LMS) software (also called library automation software or integrated library systems or integrated library management systems, and usually comprising a series of modules for cataloguing, acquisitions, circulation control, interlibrary lending and access to the holdings via an OPAC) has changed over the years. An annual review is provided in *Library Journal* and in its 2003 review, Breeding and Roddy (2003) state: "Digital library systems, reference linking products, federated search environments, and enhanced-content web-based OPACs are but a few of the products that increasingly influence the marketplace." They predict a future strong demand for such products, especially in the academic library sector.

The aim of many of the new products from LMS suppliers is to provide for cross-database searching across many digital information sources. This is achieved by using recognized industry standards (as described in Chapter Four) such as:

- Dublin Core, MARC21, TEI, EAD and CIMI for the metadata;
- SGML, HTML, XML for marking up text and searching for structured requests and receipt of information;
- Unicode for character coding;
- TIFF, GIF or JPEG for images;
- Z39.50 for searching various sources that have been enabled with this protocol.

As well as providing for search and discovery, this type of software might also manage 'objects' in the collection, handle licence and rights management, and link between information sources. Linking between items from a range of publishers of digital information sources is made possible by CrossRef – a not-for-profit network of publishers established in 2000 with a mandate to make reference linking throughout online scholarly literature efficient and reliable (http://www.crossref.org). Much of this linking is based on using DOIs or OpenURLs. CrossRef was initially developed by the publishers John Wiley and Sons and Academic Press, and now has hundreds of publishers as members. A variety of other organizations also participate, including libraries, which can use CrossRef as part of their localized linking solutions by enriching online catalogues and databases with links to full-text holdings where appropriate.

Ramsden (2003) provides an overview of the software developed by LMS suppliers to provide access to digital information sources. She lists the features of such software as providing:

- Single search of many disparate databases with a single merged set of results, relevance ranked and with duplicates removed.
- Cross-searching of databases via Z39.50.
- Open linking (possibly using OpenURL) to provide a format for transporting bibliographic metadata about objects.
- A knowledge base about downloadable configurations, linking rules and settings for various digital information sources.
- User profiling for personalization of services.
- Ability to browse digital information sources.
- Systems for authentication and authorization to enable access to sources for *bona fide* users.
- Links to virtual learning environments or other institutional systems and services.
- Support for protocols such as OAI-PMH for metadata harvesting.

Brief descriptions of some of the digital library products on offer are now given; further details of the linking features of the products from Endeavor and Ex Libris are provided by Grogg and Ferguson (2003).

5.2.1 EnCompass from Endeavor (http://www.endinfosys.com)

Endeavor was formed in the US in 1994 and is now a wholly owned subsidiary of Elsevier. Its original LMS, Voyager, is used by about 1,000 academic and research libraries in Australia, Canada, Finland, New Zealand, Sweden, Switzerland, the UK and the US. The WebVoyage module of Voyager allows web browsers to query the Voyager database, which is based on the Oracle relational DBMS. Endeavor has developed a number of other products in its move towards digital library products. Its EnCompass system is intended for managing, searching and linking a range of digital information sources in libraries. The linking function is achieved using another Endeavor product, called LinkFinderPlus, that provides comprehensive linking for all of the library's resources, regardless of the software or information vendor. An interface has also been developed to integrate EnCompass with VLE systems, such as Blackboard and Web CT, so that links can be made from, say, the notes given by a lecturer to a group of students to the full text of specific journal articles in this virtual learning environment. Figure 3.1 showed a screenshot from LEARN at the University of Auckland in New Zealand that provides access to over 350 databases, 13,000 ebooks, over 55,000 ejournals and the library's OPAC. At one point LEARN grew to about 5,000 web pages and the digital library developers found that it was not always intuitive to use, so EnCompass was acquired to improve integrated access to this wide range of digital information sources. The National Library of Scotland and the University of Edinburgh collaborated in the late 1990s to acquire a new library management system and chose Voyager (Cannell and Guy, 2001). In 2003 a decision was made to add the EnCompass module to allow for federated searching of all materials including ejournals and digital collections as well as the OPAC.

5.2.2 Metalib and DigiTool from Ex Libris (http://www.aleph.co.il)

Ex Libris developed its first LMS, the forerunner of its current ALEPH 500, for the Hebrew University in Jerusalem in the 1980s. ALEPH is installed at over 800 sites in 52 countries and the system can be customized for each library's language with some 20 interface languages using a variety of character sets. Ex Libris' pioneering linking technology product, SFX (standing for special effects), was developed in conjunction with researchers at Ghent University in Belgium and is used by customers in many countries. It makes use of the OpenURL standard. Metalib, the cross-database searching module, incorporates SFX to provide context-sensitive linking. So, MetaLib can be seen as a tool which enables libraries to provide a single access point to a variety of digital information sources with simultaneous cross-database searching for those databases supporting Z39.50. SFX complements MetaLib by enabling the searcher to link directly to these digital information sources. The latest Ex Libris product, DigiTool, released in 2003, has been designed to assist in building and managing digital libraries and also incorporates SFX. DigiTool is based on recognized industry standards to ensure that digital data can be acquired, manipulated, shared, searched and distributed. Figure 5.1 shows the result of a browse in the subject category Drama/Theatre Studies of the digital library, incorporating Metalib, at the University of East Anglia in the UK. The information sources such as ejournals, databases, subject gateways and so on that are likely to contain relevant material on this subject are shown.

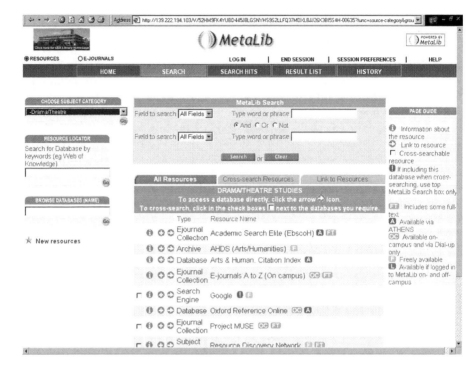

Figure 5.1 MetaLib, University of East Anglia, UK (reproduced courtesy of the University of East Anglia and Ex Libris)

In 2003 Cranfield University, also in the UK, carried out an analysis of the ways in which its staff and students accessed information. The study showed a need for a system to facilitate the management of dynamic areas of its website, particularly those providing access to digital information sources. Cranfield has also chosen MetaLib and SFX to enable cross-database searching and context sensitive linking to full-text sources with a flexible and user-friendly interface. Stubbings (2003) describes the implementation of MetaLib and SFX at Loughborough University and outlines the work involved in ensuring that the digital information sources made available via MetaLib were made 'SFX-compliant' so that users could link in directly to these sources. Beijing Jiaotong University in China has also chosen to use Aleph, MetaLib and SFX for the development of its digital library. The full Unicode support and 'localisation' features of the software were key factors influencing the choice of this system.

5.2.3 Hyperion and Ilink from Sirsi (http://www.sirsi.org)

The Sirsi Corporation of Alabama initially developed an LMS, Unicorn, in the 1980s. By 2003, the company was serving over 10,000 individual libraries (academic, corporate, government, public, school and special) of all sizes around the world. Hyperion is described on the Sirsi website as "an innovative tool for the easy organizing, storing, maintenance, and accessing of non-book holdings in a digital format" and can be used for a range of materials such as historical documents, photographs, artwork, movie clips and engineering drawings.

The Parliamentary Library of New South Wales in Australia has been using Hyperion since the late 1990s, in conjunction with its Unicorn LMS, to provide a news clipping service of Sydney's newspapers for the 1,200 members of Parliament and their staff. The digital archive managed by Hyperion comprises some 80,000 images taken from newspapers. Plans are in hand to add sound recordings of members' appearances on radio. Ilink is a service providing 'portal-type' access to a range of different digital information sources, and cross-database searching is possible using Z39.50.

5.2.4 *Millennium from Innovative Interfaces (http://www.iii.com)*

The American firm Innovative Interfaces was founded in 1978 and now provides services to thousands of libraries in 34 countries. Its LMS, Millennium, includes a number of modules to assist in the development and management of digital collections: Electronic Resource Management; MetaSource (for digital object description, display and storage); Millennium Access Plus (for metasearching, linking and authentication); and the XML server.

In 1998 the Director of the eLib Programme, reporting on a number of individual projects within the programme, noted the wide range of interfaces to different digital information sources (for example, the local OPAC, the regional virtual union catalogue, abstracting and indexing databases, ejournals and ebooks) that a user came across at Warwick University where the eLib Programme directorate was based (Rusbridge, 1998). To overcome this situation and develop an integrated digital library environment to support the university's e-learning strategy, the library staff at Warwick University have acquired Millennium. The library has over 25,000 registered users, a staff of around 150 and its holdings include one million printed volumes, 10 kilometres of archives, about 11,000 journals (of which more than 8,000 are electronic) and more than 200 subscription databases.

5.3 Software Developed from Document/ Information/Museum Management Systems

The LMS software as described above has evolved from systems developed, as the name suggests, specifically for libraries. Separate, but often related, systems have been designed to deal with databases of collections in museums and archives.

5.3.1 CAIRS

CAIRS (Computer Assisted Information Retrieval Software) is used by some institutions for providing access to a range of materials including archives, dissertations, maps and photograph collections (http://www.cairs.co.uk). For instance at the National Library of Wales (NLW), as described further in the case study in Chapter Nine, CAIRS is used to manage a collection of framed works of art and Figure 5.2 shows an example of a CAIRS metadata record and the thumbnail image of a painting by the Welsh artist Kyffin Williams. This early database of digitized objects was developed using the CAIRS software already being used within NLW for the management of non-book materials (http://cairsweb.llgc.org.uk/ffraworks.htm).

The UK company responsible for CAIRS has been producing software for text retrieval and information management since the 1980s. The version of CAIRS used for archives is called CAIRS-ARC.

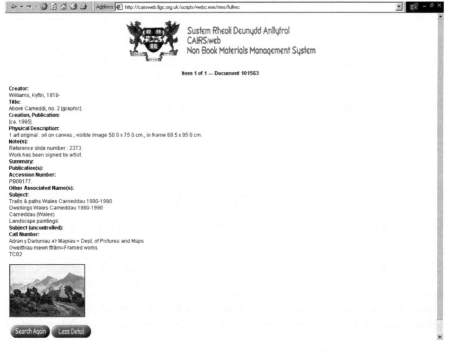

Figure 5.2 Thumbnail image and metadata record in CAIRS, Framed Works of Art Collection, National Library of Wales, UK (reproduced courtesy of Llyfrgell Genedlaethol Cymru / The National Library of Wales)

5.3.2 CALM

The CALM for Archives software is used by many archivists in the UK to provide access to archive records. CALM for Archives comprises a number of modules that have been designed for archival collection management functions such as: hierarchical catalogues, authority files, conservation, and accessions (covering depositors, terms and conditions, insurance and audit requirements). CALM has been developed by the firm DS (http://www.ds. co.uk/calm.html) and there are linked CALM software systems aimed at meeting the needs of museum collections management staff and for those managing local studies collections. Needham (2002), for instance, describes the use of CALM for Archives to provide online access to the archive collections at the University of Birmingham. The ability of the CALM software to deal with records in the ISAD(G) format was a key factor in this university's decision to use CALM. Figure 5.3 shows the metadata of a record from the Austen Chamberlain collection at Birmingham University (http://calm. bham.ac.uk/DServeA/). This collection is part of a collection of 61,000 documents related to the life and works of Joseph Chamberlain, inter alia the first Chancellor of the University of Birmingham, and his sons Austen and Neville who were both politicians. Figure 5.4 shows the record for Figure 5.3 in its hierarchical context.

CALM is also used at the National Archives of Scotland for its catalogue of about one million items (http://www.ds.co.uk/nas.html).

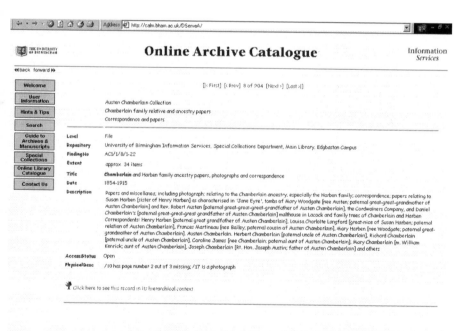

Figure 5.3 Archive record using CALM, University of Birmingham Online Archive Catalogue, UK (reproduced courtesy of the University of Birmingham)

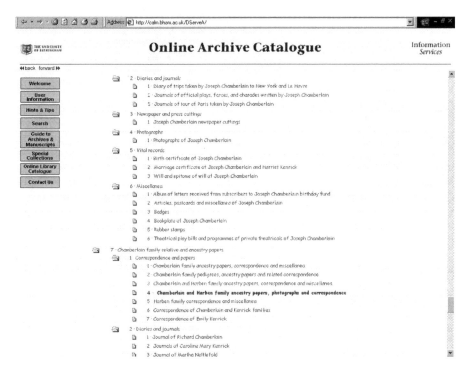

Figure 5.4 Extract from hierarchy of archive records in the Chamberlain Collection, University of Birmingham, UK (reproduced courtesy of the University of Birmingham)

5.3.3 Inmagic

Inmagic is a US company which has been producing information and content management software for many years (http://www.inmagic.com). Glenbow Museum in western Canada, for instance, uses Inmagic for its library and archive collections (http://www.glenbow.org/lasearch/searmenu.htm).

In Figure 5.5 the use of a 'Word Wheel' within Inmagic to select suitable terms or phrases for searching an archive collection of 75,000 photographs covering the people, landscape and development of the Canadian West is shown. By clicking on the Word Wheel a window opens, as shown in Figure 5.5, with an alphabetic listing of the terms used in indexing either the subject, person, year or photographer in the records included in this photographic collection database. Details of the number of 'hits' for each term are shown on the left hand side of the Word Wheel window. In this case an example for terms in the Word Wheel covering the subject of *Lake Louise* are shown.

Two of the 47 records that include Lake Louise, Alberta in the Subject field are shown in Figure 5.6.

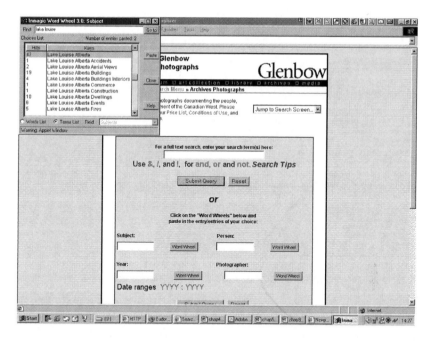

Figure 5.5 Use of Word Wheel to select search terms in Inmagic, Glenbow Museum, Canada (reproduced courtesy of Glenbow Museum)

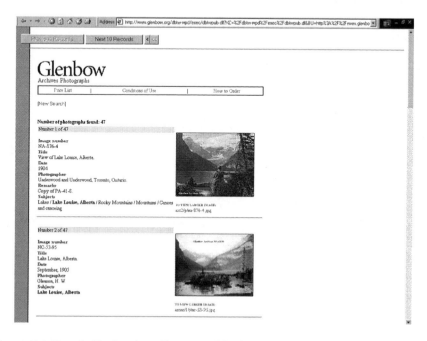

Figure 5.6 Result display from Inmagic, Glenbow Museum, Canada (reproduced courtesy of Glenbow Museum)

5.3.4 KE EMu

KE EMu is an example of collection management software that has been developed specifically for museums, art galleries, herbaria and botanical gardens (http://www.kesoftware.com/emu/). This Electronic Museum (hence the EMu) software has been designed to link a multi-discipline catalogue with interpretive information and multimedia resources. KE EMu is a multilingual system which was developed in 1997 and is used in museums in Australia, Canada, the UK and the US. As indicated in Figure 5.7 Dublin Core metadata are used to describe objects included in KE EMu databases. In addition standards, such as Z39.50 and XML, are supported. One user of KE EMu is the Canadian Museum of Civilization (CMC) Corporation (http://collections.civilization.ca). The CMC is one of the largest Canadian museums, and KE EMu provides access to information on its cultural assets consisting of objects, written, sound or image records of those objects and other museum material, from handwritten manuscripts to electronic documents.

5.3.5 Content management software

A development from document/information/museum management software is content management (CM) software. Boiko (2003) explains many of the concepts of CM which is seen as collecting, managing and making digital

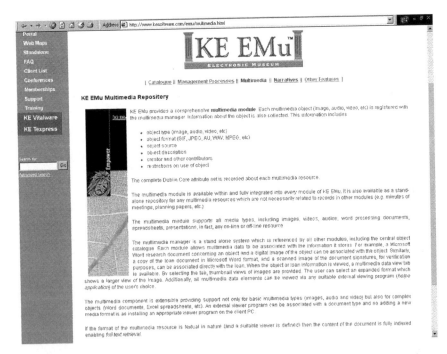

Figure 5.7 Product information about KE EMu electronic museum software (reproduced courtesy of KE EMu)

information available in a form appropriate for its users. In a CM system the information is converted into a master format (perhaps XML) and metadata are created to make the content easier to organize, store and retrieve. Boiko believes that the role of metadata creator is very important in such systems and has coined the term 'metator' and named his company Metatorial Services Inc. (http://www.metatorial.com). Content management software has been developed by various organizations to assist in the process of content management but the field is a developing one; as yet there are no universally accepted standards.

White (2002) provides an overview of the market for CM software and notes that "there are probably around 100 vendors offering some form of content management, most of which are quite small companies operating within their national markets. Some larger companies have evolved from providing solutions for e-commerce websites, but others (Documentum, Gauss and Stellent) have a document management background." A *Technology and Standards Watch Report*, co-authored by the Web Manager at the Natural History Museum in London, looks at CM software and explains how such software can be used for the maintenance of any digital information, including its creation, reviewing, storage, publishing, archiving and possible disposal (Browning and Lowndes, 2001). CM software can be used for any document delivery system involving the Web. In the early days of the Web the management of any website could be carried out manually. Now with very large websites the aim is to have increased integration and automation of the processes so as to support effective and efficient Internet delivery.

The Digital Library software developed by IBM and used in the development of digital library projects at the Hermitage Museum in St. Petersburg in Russia and at the Vatican is now called the DB2 Content Manager (http://www-3.ibm.com/software/data/cm). Mintzner et al. (2001) describe how the digital library of the Hermitage was developed by an international team with technical people from IBM working with museum professionals from Russia. In total some 100 professional staff contributed to this digital library. Standards for the graphical design of pages and the ways in which information could be presented were developed and then the images and descriptive text were added, firstly in English and then in Russian.

A further development of content management software is software to manage the digital assets of a collection. Here the content is seen as having an economic value and intellectual property rights, payment schemes and so on are incorporated into the digital asset management software (DAMS).

5.4 Open Source Software for Digital Library Development

Open source software appeared in the mid-1980s with the creation of the GNU (or GNU's Not Unix) project, aimed at developing a freely available Unix-like operating system. The GNU website provides the following definition of 'free software' which is key to the philosophy of open source software:

'Free software' is a matter of liberty, not price. To understand the concept, you should think of 'free' as in 'free speech' not as in 'free beer'. Free software is a matter of the users' freedom to run, copy, distribute, study, change and improve the software. More precisely it refers to four kinds of freedom for the users of the software:

- The freedom to run the program, for any purpose (freedom 0).
- The freedom to study how the program works, and adapt it to your needs (freedom 1). Access to the source code is a precondition for this.
- The freedom to redistribute copies so you can help your neighbour (freedom 2).
- The freedom to improve the program, and release your improvements to the public, so that the whole community benefits (freedom 3). Access to the source code is a precondition for this.

A program is free software if users have all of these freedoms. Thus, you should be free to redistribute copies, either with or without modifications, either gratis or charging a fee for distribution, to anyone anywhere. Being free to do these things means (among other things) that you do not have to ask or pay for permission. (http://www.gnu.org)

An indication of the worldwide applicability of open source software is provided by the number of languages in which the homepage of the GNU website exists: Albanian, Catalan, Chinese (simplified), Chinese (traditional), Croatian, Czech, Danish, Dutch, English, French, German, Greek, Hungarian, Indonesian, Italian, Japanese, Korean, Norwegian, Polish, Portuguese, Romanian, Serbian, Spanish, Swedish, Thai, Turkish and Vietnamese. A special licence, known as the GNU Licence, is often used for the distribution of open source software. A directory of open source software is available from the Free Software Foundation on the GNU website. The directory was started in 1999 and since 2003 Unesco has been involved in its development. 'Standard' open source software includes:

- Apache – an HTTP-compliant web server
- Linux – an operating system
- MySQL – a relational database management system that supports the query language SQL (Structured Query Language)
- Perl – a general, high-level scripting language.

Open source software is of great benefit in many countries. In using such software it must be realized that a certain amount of expertise is required to enable any particular software to meet the needs of the particular digital library system being developed. Staff with such expertise are likely to be in demand, and may not stay in the institution for a long time. In such cases it will be necessary to ensure that appropriate documentation has been produced so that use of the software and its 'customization' to meet local needs can be understood by successive members of staff. Some LMS suppliers are beginning to be aware of open source software developments: Innovative, for instance supports Linux.

In a special issue of *Information Technology and Libraries* on open source software, Morgan (2002) outlines its possibilities for the development of digital library collections and services. Through funding from the DLI, Morgan was one of the developers of the personalization software MyLibrary@NCState at North Carolina State University (referred to in Chapter Two) and which is now distributed as open source software using the GNU Public Licence. In his paper Morgan emphasizes that open source software is both a "philosophy and a process". The philosophy is described in the quote given above and the process relates to the cooperative approach to software development in which the original developer is assisted by others who are attempting to solve similar problems in a 'two heads are better than one' approach. A list of open source software for libraries is maintained (http://www.oss4lib.org) and details of some relevant to digital library development are given below. Unesco also maintains a directory of 'free software' for digital libraries (http://www.unesco.org/webworld/portal_freesoft/Software/Digital_Library/).

5.4.1 CERN Document Server software

The software used at CERN for managing its documents (and which featured in Figure 2.7) can be used to run an eprint server, a web-based catalogue or document system (http://cdsweb.cern.ch). The software complies with OAI-PMH and uses MARC21 as its underlying bibliographic standard. The interface language can be selected by the user with the following being available: Czech, French, German, Italian, Norwegian, Portuguese, Russian, Spanish, and Swedish. The search engine works with Unicode and so users can type in search terms in any language stored in the database.

5.4.2 DSpace

DSpace, developed by staff at MIT Libraries and the Hewlett Packard Company, refers both to the digital repository of the intellectual output of MIT as well as the software on which the production of this repository is based (http://www.dspace.org). The repository covers a range of material: articles, preprints, conference proceedings, technical reports, books, theses, data sets and computer programs as well as computer simulations and models (Smith et al., 2003). The aim of DSpace is to store, index, preserve and redistribute these materials.

5.4.3 EPrints Archive Software

EPrints Archive Software can be used to create online collections of research papers, preprints, postprints and so on, and was initially developed by staff at the University of Southampton in the UK (http://software.eprints.org/). Staff at the Universities of Edinburgh and Nottingham in the UK have used this software to set up eprint servers for papers published by academic staff in their universities (Pinfield, Gardner and McColl, 2002). There is also a project underway, Eprints UK, which will use this software to develop a series of national, discipline-focused services through which the higher and further education community can access the collective ouput of eprint papers available from OAI-compliant repositories (Martin, 2003). An example of a record (which itself is about the use of open source software for a library application) in the eprint archive at Nottingham University is shown in Figure 5.8.

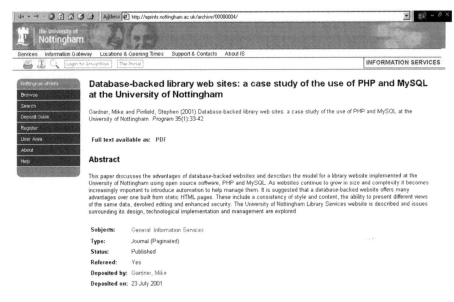

Figure 5.8 Record display, eprint archive, Nottingham University, UK (reproduced courtesy of Nottingham University)

5.4.4 Greenstone

Greenstone, produced by the New Zealand Digital Library (NZDL) Project at the University of Waikato, is a software suite that can be used for building and distributing digital library collections (http://www.greenstone.org*).* Greenstone has been implemented with interfaces in a number of languages and, in addition, the full documentation is available in a number of languages including English, French, Kazak, Russian and Spanish. In Chapter Six there are examples of the Greenstone interface in Arabic (Figure 6.8) and in Czech (Figure 6.9). The aim of the software is to empower users, particularly in universities, libraries, and other public service institutions, to build their own digital libraries. The development and distribution of Greenstone is being carried out by NZDL in conjunction with Unesco and the Human Info NGO (Non-Governmental Organization). The dissemination of educational, scientific and cultural information throughout the world, and particularly its availability in developing countries, is central to Unesco's goals as pursued within its intergovernmental Information for All Programme, and appropriate, accessible ICTs, such as Greenstone, are seen as important tools in this context. The Human Info NGO project is based in Antwerp, Belgium and works with UN agencies and NGOs involved in digitizing documentation of interest to human development and making it widely available, free of charge to developing nations, and on a cost-recovery basis to others.

Greenstone is now used in many countries and organizations including:

- Archives of Indian Labour (http://www.indialabourarchives.org)
- Biblioteca Digital por la Identidad/Human Rights in Argentina (http://conadi.jus.gov.ar/gsdl/cgi-bin/library)
- Digitale Bibliothek Information und Medien at the University of Applied Sciences in Stuttgart, Germany (http://diana.iuk.hdm-stuttgart.de/digbib/gsdl/cgi-bin/library)
- Mirabilie Vicomercate – local history collections in a public library in Italy (http://www.mirabiliavicomercati.org/sezioni/006/index.html)
- Project Gutenberg in the US (http://gutenberg.net)
- Russian Greeenstone Library – material developed by the Elektronnaya Biblioteka Pravitel'stva Respubliki Mariy El (http://gov.mari.ru/gsdl/cgi/library).

An extensive discussion of the Greenstone software can be found in Witten and Bainbridge (2003), and Witten (2003) gives further details of digital libraries around the world that are using the Greenstone software. They emphasize the need for people in developing countries to use open access software, such as Greenstone, to create content for digital libraries and to ensure that intellectual property remains in the hands of those who produce the content.

5.5 Digital Library Architecture

The software used for developing digital libraries, then, can come from a variety of organizations or from an open source collection. Much of the software is based on international (developed and developing) standards that enable functions such as reference linking (that is the ability to click on a reference to an item and then be presented with the item itself on the screen) between many diverse systems and services, as described by Caplan (2001). The interoperable building blocks that can be 'linked' together to develop an application such as a digital library are generally known as 'web services'. Tennant (2002) states that "these can be thought of as a suite of protocols that define how requests and responses between software applications should be encoded (using XML) and transferred (for example over the Web via HTTP or e-mail) and how such services should be described and registered for research discovery and use". Hickey (2003) provides an introduction to the concepts of web services, with examples taken from the digital library world.

In the very first issue of *D-Lib Magazine*, Arms (1995) outlined the key concepts in the architecture of digital library systems which included:

a) The technical framework for a digital library exists within a legal and social framework
Issues such as the needs of users and the intellectual property rights of creators of information sources need to be considered. Any digital library will be developed within a specific economic, legal and social framework.

b) Understanding digital library concepts is hampered by terminology
Since the digital library field is a developing one with systems being implemented as well as being the focus of research, it is probably inevitable that the terminology will evolve. Arms notes that different terms mean different 'things' to different people in different parts of the English-speaking world, depending on their backgrounds. This becomes even more problematic when multiple languages and multiple cultures are involved.

c) The underlying architecture should be separate from the content stored in the library.
Although as we have seen in Chapter Three, various types of information sources (text, audio, image, video and so on) can be included within a digital library, there should be a generic approach to dealing with all sources. For instance, every 'object' within the digital library needs to have a unique name or identifier. However, extensions to the underlying architecture are needed to ensure that different types of material are dealt with in an appropriate manner. This might mean, as indicated at the start of the Chapter, that a 3D server deals with the specifics of 3D objects, a video server supports video and so on.

d) Names and identifiers are the basic building blocks for the digital library
Unique names which are persistent over time are necessary to identify digital objects, to register intellectual property in digital objects, and to record changes of ownership. The solutions being developed for this were described in Chapter Four.

e) Digital library objects are more than collections of bits
Although any item of information stored in a computer is really just a collection of bits (or binary digits) the objects within a digital library comprise the raw content or data as well as the metadata about that data.

f) The digital library object that is used is different from the stored object
Arms notes that the architecture must distinguish carefully between digital objects as they are created by an originator, as they might be stored in a repository, and as they might be disseminated to a user. The user's view of an object retrieved from a digital library will depend on the facilities available to that user for the transmission of data and the local facilities for the display or presentation of information.

g) Repositories must look after the information they hold
The repository, or collection of digital information sources, must be able to 'manage' the sources as well as the metadata.

Although it is a long time ago (in terms of digital library history) that Arms wrote this paper many of his concepts are still valid and need to be considered by those organizing access to digital information sources. Yeates (2002) comments that "the market for computer systems that manage digital content is in turmoil" but adds that " the digital library plays a key role in organizing content and supporting and facilitating access to it". Digital libraries continue to develop and the solutions used within digital libraries to provide access to digital information sources will also develop. Further information on the design of digital libraries is provided by Chowdhury and Chowdhury (2003).

References

Arms, W. Y. (1995) Key concepts in the architecture of the digital library. *D-Lib Magazine*, **1** (1). Available at: http://www.dlib.org/dlib/July95/07arms.html

Bogen, M., Borowski, M., Heisterkamp, S. and Strecker, D. (2001) Requirements and architecture for administration and maintenance of digital object libraries. Paper presented at *Museums and the Web 2001*.Available at: http://www.archimuse.com/mw2001/papers/bogen/bogen.html

Boiko, B. (2002) *Content Management Bible*. New York: Hungry Minds

Breeding, M. and Roddy, C. (2003) The competition heats up: automated systems marketplace 2003. *Library Journal*, **128** (6) 52–64. Available at: http://libraryjournal.reviewsnews.com/index.asp?layout=article&articleid=CA284769&display=FeaturesNewsMore&industry=Features&verticalid=151&starting=9

Browning, P. and Lowndes, M. (2001) *Content Management Systems*. JISC Techwatch Report TSW 01–02. Available at: http://www.jisc.ac.uk/index.cfm?name=techwatch_report_0102

Cannell, S. and Guy, F. (2001) Cross-sectoral collaboration in the choice and implementation of a library management system: the experiences at the University of Edinburgh and the National Library of Scotland. *Program*, **35** (2), 135–156

Caplan, P. (2001) A lesson in linking. *Library Journal NetConnect: Supplement to Library Journal* **126** (17), 16–18 Available at: http://libraryjournal.reviewsnews.com/index.asp?layout=article&articleid=CA177643

Chowdhury, G.G. and Chowdhury, S. (2003) *Introduction to Digital Libraries*. London: Facet Publishing

Grogg, J.E. and Ferguson, C. L. (2003) Linking services unleashed. *Searcher*, **11** (2), 26–31. Available at: http://www.infotoday.com/searcher/feb03/grogg_ferguson.htm

Hickey, T. B. (2003) Web services for digital libraries. Paper presented at *ELAG 2003: Cross Language Applications and the Web. 27th Library Systems Seminar, Bern (Switzerland) 2–4 April 2003*. Available at: http://www.elag2003.ch/pres/pres_hickey.pdf

Martin, R. (2003) Eprints UK: developing a national e-prints archive. *Ariadne*, **35**. Available at: http://www.ariadne.ac.uk/issue35/martin/

Mintzner, F. et al. (2001) Populating the Hermitage Museum's new website. *Communications of the ACM*, **44** (8), 52–60

Morgan, E. L. (2002) Possibilities for Open Source Software in Libraries. *Information Technology and Libraries*, **21** (1), 12–15. Available at: http://www.lita.org/Content/NavigationMenu/LITA/LITA_Publications4/ITAL__Information_Technology_and_Libraries/2101_Morgan.htm

Murray, R. (2001) Better content management for external resources: today's information portals. In Graham, C. (ed.) *Online Information 2001. Proceedings. 4–6 December 2001, London*. Learned Information: Oxford, 57–65

Needham, L. (2002) The development of the Online Archive Catalogue at the University of Birmingham using CALM 2000. *Program,* **36** (1), 23–29

Pinfield, S. Gardner, M. and MacColl, J. (2002) Setting up an institutional e-print archive. *Ariadne,* **31**. Available at: http://www.ariadne.ac.uk/issue31/eprint-archives/

Ramsden, A. (2003) The library portal marketplace. *Vine,* **33** (1), 17–24

Rusbridge, C. (1998) Towards the hybrid library. *D-Lib Magazine,* **4** (7/8). Available at: http://www.dlib.org/dlib/july98/rusbridge/07rusbridge.html

Smith, M., Barton, M., Bass, M., Branschovsky, M., McClellan, G., Stuve, D., Tansley, R., and Walker, J.H. (2003) DSpace: an open source dynamic digital repository. *D-Lib Magazine,* **9** (1). Available at: http://www.dlib.org/dlib/january03/smith/01smith.html

Stubbings, R. (2003) MetaLib and SFX at Loughborough University Library. *Vine,* **33** (1), 25–32.

Tennant, R. (2001) Cross-database search: one stop shopping. *Library Journal,* **126** (17), 29–30

Tennant, R. (2002) Digital libraries- what to know about web services. *Library Journal,* **127** (11) Available at: http://libraryjournal.reviewsnews.com/index.asp?layout=articleArchive&articleId=CA231639&display=searchResults&stt=001&publication=libraryjournal

White, M. (2002) Selecting a content management system. *Vine,* **32** (2), 34–39

Witten, I. H. (2003) Examples of practical digital libraries: collections built internationally using Greenstone. *D-Lib Magazine,* **9** (3). Available at: http://www.dlib.org/dlib/march03/witten/03witten.html

Witten, I.H. and Bainbridge, D. (2003) *How to build a digital library.* San Francisco CA: Morgan Kaufmann

Witten I. H., Loots, M., Trujillo M. F, and Bainbridge, D. (2002). The promise of digital libraries in developing countries *Electronic Library,* **20** (1), 7–13

Yeates, R. (2002) Digital library and information systems: where are we heading? *Vine,* **32** (4), 3–18.

Chapter 6

Interface Design

6.1 Introduction

The interface to a digital library, as the means by which a user interacts with the information collection, has a crucial role to play. As Galitz (2002) defines it, "the user interface is the part of a computer and its software that people can see, hear, touch, talk to, or otherwise understand or direct." It has two components: the input component that governs how a user communicates needs or desires to the computer, and an output component that determines how the computer conveys the results of its computations to that user.

Although this book is not focused upon designing and developing digital libraries, nevertheless it is important to review interface design issues both in general terms and with specific respect to digital library environments. Certainly, the interface will play a vital role in determining whether or not a visit to the digital library is a success or a failure, both in terms of the information retrieved and the user's overall level of satisfaction with the experience. As Arms (2000) puts it, "a digital library is only as good as its interface". Furthermore, some of the software for digital libraries mentioned in Chapter Five enables information professionals to 'customize' the user interface in various ways: this will be more easily and effectively accomplished if a few basic principles are applied.

Dillon (2002) lists five questions he thinks designers of digital library interfaces should be addressing:

- How do we attract users to our resources, and make them stay?
- What will bring a user back to our resources again?
- How do I build an interface that supports a richer comprehension or appreciation of the contents?

- What makes material more learnable by users?
- Can novices learn from viewing an expert's construction of an information space?

When considered from a global perspective, any discussion of interfaces should be extended from basic design criteria to encompass special issues raised by linguistic and cultural diversity. How might digital library users' language and culture affect their perception of its interface, and therefore the kinds of decisions that designers should consider when building it?

6.2 Interface Design Principles: An Overview

Numerous heavy volumes have been dedicated to interface design considerations, and here we can only provide an overview of the principles on which there is general agreement. The starting point should be the users. To quote a major commentator on human-computer interaction (HCI), Shneiderman (1998), "all design should begin with an understanding of the intended users, including population profiles that reflect age, gender, physical abilities, education, cultural or ethnic background, training, motivation, goals and personality." This precept will be more easily followed, obviously, when the digital library's clientele is both straightforward to identify and uniform in its constituency. In practice, often this will not be the case; the interface perforce will have to cope with a diverse user community, when judged by some or all the above personal characteristics. In such instances, the challenge of designing a good interface is greatly intensified. We shall consider later in the Chapter the implications for interface design of different types of user constituencies.

Galitz (2002) has formulated a set of design principles that he argues should be applied to any interface. It should be:

- Aesthetically pleasing and attractive to the eye, as interactions primarily are in the visual realm.
- Visually, conceptually and linguistically clear and unambiguous.
- Compatible with the user and the task, and compatible with any earlier versions of the system, or any other similar kinds of systems (in theory, this would mean that all digital library interfaces would follow a standard design – we have seen enough examples already in earlier chapters to realize that this is not in fact the case).
- Comprehensible, that is, easily learned and understood.
- Configurable, that is, easy to personalize (more of this below), configure and re-configure.
- Consistent in the sense of looking and acting in the same way throughout; the same action should always give the same result.
- Controllable by the user, so that actions result from explicit user requests, are performed quickly, and are interruptible; the user should feel in charge.
- Direct in the ways in which tasks are accomplished; the effect of actions on objects should be visible.

- Efficient, by minimizing eye and hand movements.
- Familiar, by using concepts and language that users should know, using real-world metaphors, and building upon users' existing knowledge.
- Flexible to the differing needs of users (in terms of their knowledge and skills, experience, personal preferences, and habits).
- Forgiving of common and unavoidable human errors; preventing errors whenever possible; and providing constructive messages in case of errors.
- Predictable on the part of users who should be able to anticipate the natural progression of each task.
- Recoverable by allowing reversible actions.
- Responsive to user requests, with visual, textual or auditory acknowledgement.
- Simple.
- Transparent, so that the workings inside the computer remain invisible to users.

Galitz emphasizes that although these principles taken together represent the design ideal, in practice trade-offs will be required between some of the individual principles. The desire to maintain compatibility with earlier versions of the interface, for example, may clash with the desire better to meet many of the other principles; efficiency may clash with flexibility, and so on.

In a nutshell, as Galitz (2002) emphasizes, "the best interface is one that is not noticed, one that permits the user to focus on the information and task at hand, not the mechanisms used to present the information and perform the task." The best digital library interfaces, then, are not the ones that on first encounter impress users with the most vivid colours, the most attention-grabbing icons, or the most intricate screen layout; rather, they are those that unobtrusively allow users, no matter what are their personal characteristics or their task in hand, to find what they are seeking quickly, accurately and with the least effort.

6.3 Interface Design Rules

Interface designers must realize such principles by following more or less well-developed rules relating to such features as screen layout, menu construction, use of fonts, colours, images and sound, and error messages. For example, in the case of colours typically it is recommended that no more than seven should be used in the interface as a whole, and no more than four on any one page. In the case of fonts, often it is recommended that no more than two families, two styles, two weights and three sizes be employed throughout the interface. Heavy use of images, and especially photographs, will slow down transmission rates. In some cases the user is given the option of a low-resolution image or a high-resolution image – an example is the Leonardo Notebook (http://www.bl.uk/collections/treasures/digitisation. html) at the British Library. To view this digital information source special software must be downloaded (for free). The interface designer has helpfully indicated the length of time that it might take to download this software ("as long as 10 minutes if you are using a modem"). User performance tends to decrease with high screen display density, but the answer is not necessarily vertical or especially horizontal scrolling, as this tends to be unpopular with users.

The interface normally is considered to include input and output devices as well as the screen display. Typically a digital library will require both keyboard and mouse as input devices, and display monitor and printer as output devices, but other possibilities such as touch screens for input and storage devices such as CD-ROMs or smart drives as output devices may be encountered.

6.4 Interfaces for Digital Libraries

Computer interfaces are found in many environments, and design principles such as those enunciated above must be adapted to any specific environment. The two most important features of the environment are the task or tasks to be accomplished, and the kinds of users who will be involved. The interface to a digital library must enable users to accomplish certain operations in order to satisfy their task in hand – answering an information need by finding relevant textual, visual or audio sources. Individual digital library interfaces, of course, for several reasons will differ one from another. First, the libraries themselves are far from uniform in content: they vary in such respects as size, subject matter, and linguistic and cultural characteristics (more will be said on these last two characteristics later in this Chapter). Second, they vary in the technology platform on which they are mounted: many are available via the Web, but they may only be accessible from local workstations; and they may wish to be compliant with various PDA (Personal Digital Assistant) devices and mobile telephones. For example, the Stanford Digital Libraries Technologies project has looked at interface design issues for the Palm Pilot, where the small screen and narrow bandwidth require "a radical rethinking of user interfaces to information repositories" (http://www-diglib.stanford.edu/diglib/pub/RetrievingInformation. shtml). Third, the digital library user community or communities will differ in their various characteristics, and the interface will need to take account of them. Finally, digital library interfaces will differ because there is no single way to realize design principles in an interface; there is an art as well as a science to interface design.

In the case of online catalogues, a library can enable users to search on other libraries' catalogues from its own interface using the Z39.50 protocol. Although current versions of Z39.50 can be used with non-bibliographic information formats, unfortunately this remains complicated; in practice such a standardized approach for digital library interfaces is not yet available. Libraries often do not have a seamless interface that links invisibly all of their own collections, let alone collections from disparate digital libraries. And when a common user interface is developed, typically it will function at the lowest common denominator, using the features of the least robust and least flexible of its individual collections (Arant and Payne, 2001).

Although a 'typical' digital library cannot be said to exist, the interface to any digital library normally enables users to undertake a number of common actions. Many screens from digital libraries are reproduced throughout this book (unfortunately, only in monochrome), and all can be studied to identify different design approaches. The following brief discussion considers the major functions that a digital library interface will have to accomplish.

6.4.1 Content overview

It is common to provide an overview of the digital library's content. This can be done in various ways. At Cornell University its various Digital Collections (http://cdl.library.cornell.edu) are displayed using images (Figure 6.1), whereas the Everglades Digital Library (http://everglades.fiu.edu/library) lists its collections in text format (Figure 6.2).

6.4.2 Searching and browsing

Search and browsing are discussed in Chapter Seven, and therefore will not be explored in detail here. There are many ways to provide access to the library's content. These include search boxes, menus of various kinds, and text or image links. For example, Cleveland State University Library in its

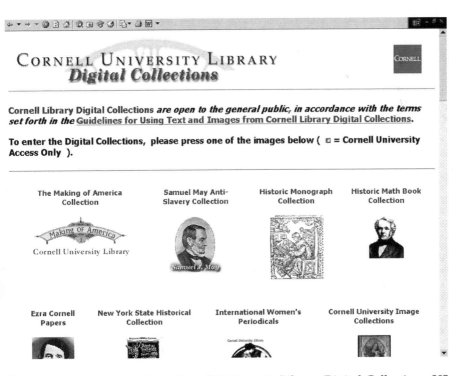

Figure 6.1 Content overview, Cornell University Library Digital Collections, US (reproduced courtesy of Cornell University Library Digital Collections)

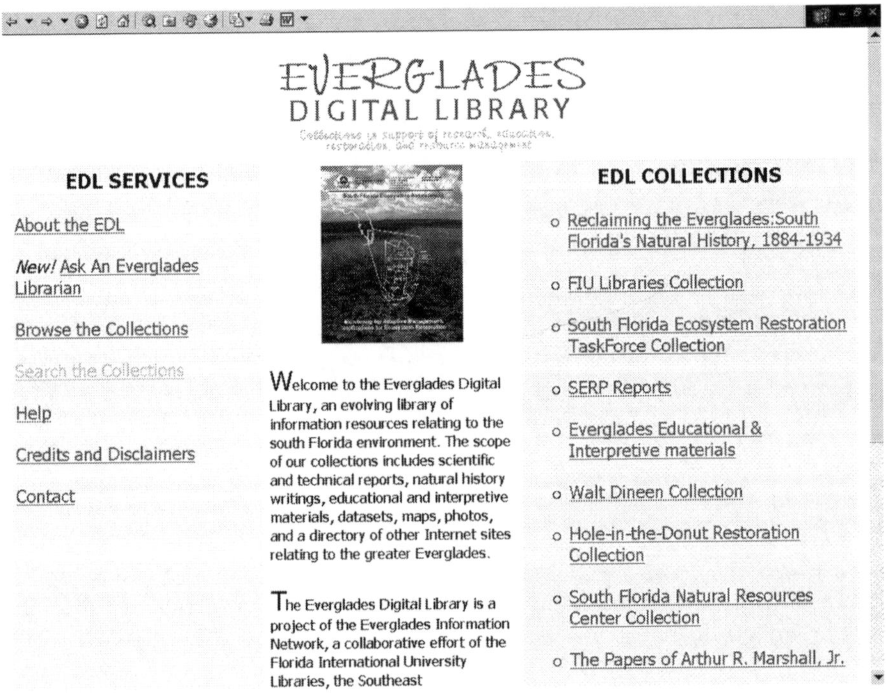

Figure 6.2 Content overview, Everglades Digital Library, US (reproduced courtesy of Florida International University Libraries)

Cleveland Memory Project (http://www.clevelandmemory.org/postcards) provides a pull-down menu of predefined search terms (such as aerial views, bridges, canals, churches) as well as a box for users to enter their own keywords (Figure 6.3). At the University Archives of Virginia Tech (http://spec.lib.vt.edu/archives/blackhistory/timeline) users can browse a timeline to find material on black history (Figure 6.4).

6.4.3 Display of retrieved information

Retrieved information must then be displayed so that users are able to select what is relevant. It is important that relevance decisions can be made as accurately and easily as possible by users, though the way in which this is done will depend considerably on the kind of information involved. In the Everglades Digital Library the titles of retrieved articles are clearly displayed (Figure 6.5). A search of the Postcard collection at the Cleveland Memory Project results in the cards being displayed as images (Figure 6.6).

The ways in which the full text of retrieved items are displayed also varies from library to library. At the New Zealand Digital Library (http://nzdl.org), for example, in its Humanity Development Library collection the title pages and contents of retrieved documents are shown (Figure 6.7). Another way

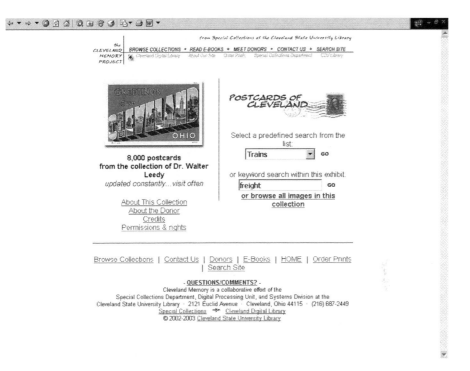

Figure 6.3 Search features at Cleveland Memory Project, Cleveland State University Library, US (reproduced courtesy of Cleveland State University)

to display results is through thumbnail images; in Figure 9.20 the covers of books retrieved in a search on the International Children's Digital Library are displayed so that users can make their selection.

6.4.4 Personalization

We have seen in earlier chapters examples of interface personalization; for example, North Carolina State University's MyLibrary@NCState allows users to create their own personal web interface, and MyGateway at the University of Washington lets users organize frequently used web resources in a similar way to bookmarking but that is independent of the workstation used (see also Section 2.3 of Chapter Two). The New Zealand Digital Library allows users to personalize the interface in several ways (it calls them 'preferences'). For example, a user can opt to display the interface in one of 15 different languages, and in either graphical or textual format. In Figure 6.8 the user has switched the language of the interface from its default English to Arabic, and all succeeding screens will now display the interface (though not, of course, the actual documents retrieved) in Arabic. The character encoding (discussed in Chapter Four) also has been changed from Western to Arabic (Windows) to ensure that the characters in Arabic are correctly displayed

Figure 6.4 Browsing via Timeline of Black History, University Archives, Virginia Tech, US (reproduced courtesy of Virginia Tech)

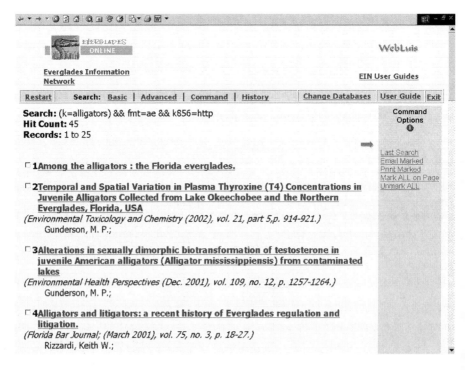

Figure 6.5 Display, Everglades Digital Library, US (reproduced courtesy of the Florida Center for Library Automation)

Figure 6.6 Display, Cleveland Memory Project, Cleveland State University Library, US (reproduced courtesy of Cleveland State University)

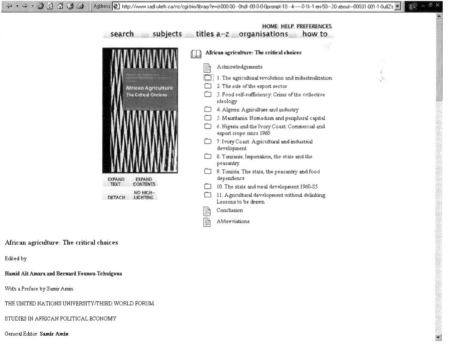

Figure 6.7 Book contents display, Human Development Library, New Zealand Digital Library (reproduced courtesy of Waikato University)

Figure 6.8 Language personalization, New Zealand Digital Library (reproduced courtesy of Waikato University)

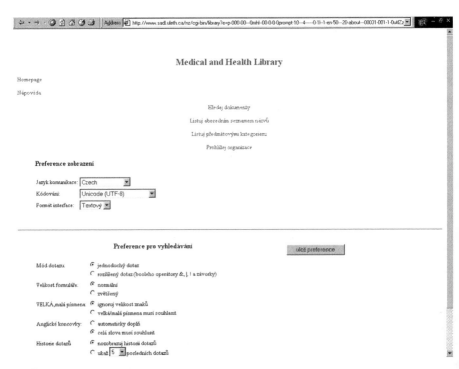

Figure 6.9 Language and presentation personalization, New Zealand Digital Library (reproduced courtesy of Waikato University)

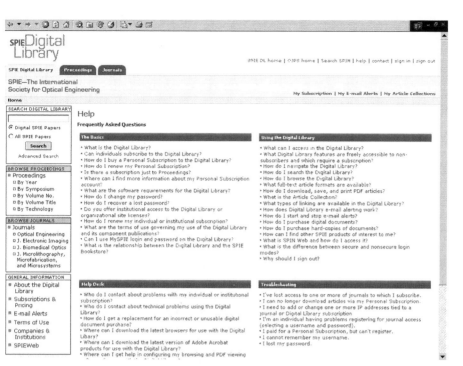

Figure 6.10 Help facilities, The International Society for Optical Engineering Digital Library, US (reproduced courtesy of the International Society for Optical Engineering)

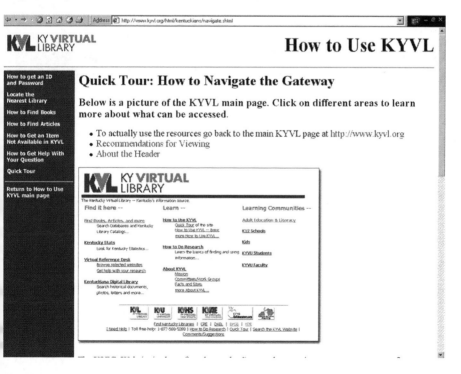

Figure 6.11 Quick Tour, Kentucky Virtual Library, US (reproduced courtesy of the Kentucky Virtual Library)

(and from right to left). In Figure 6.9 the interface has been personalized by selecting this time Czech as the language, and opting for a textual rather than a graphical display.

6.4.5 Help

Normally digital libraries will offer help to users. This can be done in various ways. At the International Society for Optical Engineering Digital Library (http://spiedl.org), for example, a detailed list of Frequently Asked Questions is provided that covers many aspects of using the digital library (Figure 6.10). Some digital libraries provide virtual tours so that users quickly can get a sense of their content and facilities: for example, users can gain an overview of the Kentucky Virtual Library (http://www.kyvl.org/html/kentuckians/ navigate.shtml) by clicking on various areas of the main page image, as shown in Figure 6.11. The California Digital Library (http://californiadigitalli-brary.org) offers advice on a variety of matters including search strategies and technical requirements to access the site (Figure 6.12). Help at the electronic Digital Library Project of the Chicago Public Schools/University of Chicago Internet Project (eCUIP) (http://www.lib.uchicago.edu/ecuip), offers its young users useful tips on how to begin a search for information as well as how to search its collection. The Research Guide asks users whether they are

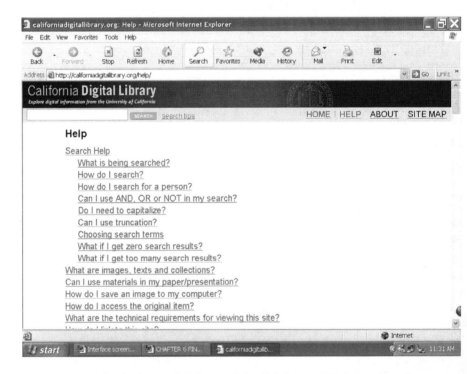

Figure 6.12 Help facilities, California Digital Library, US (reproduced courtesy of the Regents of the University of California)

"researching a topic for a class paper or project", and if so offers several steps to guide them through their research. Its 'Helpful Hints' include advice such as to "write down specific questions and/or topics related to your subject" plus some guidance on how to broaden or narrow a search.

6.5 Interface Developments

Lynch and Garcia-Molina (1995) identified display of information, visualization and navigation of large information collections as key digital library research areas, and these remain at the centre of research attention. It is not our intention here to discuss in any detail the very active research agenda for digital library interfaces. But this topic cannot be overlooked entirely. Many researchers have commented upon the relationship between the way information is arranged on the screen and users' ability to interact with that information. Thong, Hong and Tam (2002), from their interviews with 397 students at the Open University of Hong Kong, found that interface characteristics such as screen design and terminology were significant determinants of perceived ease of use of digital libraries. Inconsistently arranged screens, where like objects are not grouped together, and poorly depicted buttons and icons can create confusion and misunderstanding, whereas a well-organized and carefully designed screen can help users scan and identify relevant information more easily. The terminology employed in an interface should match the users' language, and technical terms and jargon should be avoided. Navigational clarity had a smaller but still significant effect on perceived ease of use. Interface designers, according to this study, should choose broad and shallow structures rather than narrow and deep structures, and redundant screens should be eliminated.

One possible solution to the problems users of digital library interfaces often encounter in processing the potentially large amounts of information retrieved is to adopt visualization techniques of one kind or another. Card, Mackinlay and Shneiderman (1999) define information visualization as "the use of computer-supported, interactive, visual representations of abstract data to amplify cognition", and by cognition they mean the acquisition or use of knowledge. They argue that "visual artifacts aid thought; in fact, they are completely entwined with cognitive action." Information visualization, they say, enhances browsing by presenting more choices in a compact and meaningful overview, and complements searching by helping users to understand the distribution of search results.

Jones (1998) describes a direct manipulation interface that exploits visualization for query specification in a test interface for the New Zealand Digital Library. He suggests the use of Venn Diagrams (overlapping circles) to illustrate sets and their relationships; the circles contain the query terms, and users create complex (Boolean) queries by positioning circles in relation to each other. Users can see the results of query refinements as they make them, and this gives users a sense of control, data patterns quickly can be perceived, and new queries can be generated based on what is discovered through incidental learning. However, when tested, although users commented positively on this dynamic interface and could use it with little or no training, they took significantly longer to form queries and produced more erroneous results than when forming Boolean expressions with textual languages (Jones, McInnes and Staveley, 1999).

An experimental visualization display for cancer journal literature, developed at the Artificial Intelligence Lab, University of Arizona (http://ai.bpa. arizona.edu/go/viz/medicalMap_demo.html), is shown in Figure 6.13. The medical terms on the left of the screen can be scrolled and clicked to move through a hierarchical structure. All the terms related to the highlighted term are presented visually in the topic map. Eventually the user will reach the end of the hierarchy and be presented with the retrieved documents.

Greene et al (2000) also argue that interface designers often fail to provide appropriate views of materials in digital libraries to give an overall sense of their structure and the materials available. For example, they say some museum websites give the impression of having large amounts of digitized art, but in fact only offer exhibit descriptions and links to other sites. Users prefer comprehensible, predictable and controllable environments in which they can rapidly and safely explore and use information. Surrogates are crucial for browsing large distributed collections, and the need to invent new types of surrogates underlies much of the research in digital libraries.

Figure 6.13 Visualization from the Artificial Intelligence Lab, University of Arizona, US (reproduced courtesy of the Artificial Intelligence Lab, University of Arizona)

Greene et al discuss both the preview – a surrogate for a single object of interest, analogous to bibliographic records, and the overview – representing a collection of objects of interest, analogous to library catalogues. Surrogates may need to range from terse, information titles to increasingly detailed surrogates more indicative of primary objects. Greene and his colleagues argue that such surrogates can aid retrieval by acting as a basis for indexing, by helping the user to make quick relevance judgments, by reducing network data transfer (the need to examine the primary object is reduced), and by providing indicators of the scope, size and structure of large information spaces. Surrogates can be literal extracts from primary objects (such as thumbnails, tables of contents, video streamers), or original constructs (such as text abstracts, and controlled vocabulary lists). In the New Zealand Digital Library, surrogates for full documents are provided at several levels of detail (bibliographic data, outline chapter structure and detailed chapter structure). Greene and his colleagues discuss this topic in terms of their experience working in the US with the Library of Congress to develop and test interface designs for its National Digital Library Program.

Computer game enthusiasts are familiar with 3D action games where players walk through virtual worlds and have the illusion of being themselves in those worlds. Christoffel and Schmitt (2002) want to design graphical user interfaces using such real world metaphors so that visitors to the digital library can access the collection in the same way as they would a traditional collection. Their interface is based on an action game called Quake II, but instead of players killing their enemies and ultimately saving the world, they can move around a library, browse its bookshelves, select books from them, and see their contents. The Trials Support (TRIS) initiative of the European Union (EU) coordinated 25 projects experimenting with existing technologies to find new ways of creating, managing and presenting digital cultural objects, with a focus on virtual representations. For example, one project, based on the collection at Wells Cathedral in England, developed a prototype for Web-based historic collections using an interactive 3D model (Tariffi, Morganti and Segbert, 2004).

As for the future, who knows what it holds for digital libraries? Dillon (2002) has risked one prognosis, though as he says, he might be quite off target: "the ideal might be something like an accessible DL that could be voice activated from anywhere, using whatever physical hardware is present to project a screen, offering a personal portal to the online world, shareable on demand and, of course, suffering no download lags or 'out of range' messages."

6.6 Interfaces for Specific User Communities

Several times already in this Chapter the importance of implementing a digital library interface which reflects the needs of the user community has been stressed. A little later in the Chapter, linguistic and cultural factors will be discussed. In this section, however, we shall review the implications for interface designers of working with two specific user communities: young people, and people with visual handicaps.

6.6.1 Interfaces for young users

The information-seeking needs and behaviours of young people have received growing attention since the Web became an important potential source of information for both school and leisure activities (Large, 2004). Nevertheless, Abbas, Norris and Soloway (2002) comment that very few studies have focused upon the use of digital libraries by children or young adults. They discuss the ARTEMIS Digital Library at the University of Michigan (http://hice.org/sciencelaboratory/artemis/tutorial.html) that has been in use since 1997 by science students in grades six through 12 (approximately 12 to 18 years' old). ARTEMIS is organized by topic. It includes a practice area, called the Scavenger Hunt, where students learn how to use the various browse and search features of the interface. The interface also includes 'scaffolding' features that help reduce the cognitive load of the young users: for example, a workplace to save and organize search results and web page links, a means to share with other students resources that are of interest, the opportunity to view results of previous searches, and a dictionary that can be consulted as needed.

Another interesting example in the specific context of digital libraries is provided by the work in the US of Druin at the University of Maryland with the International Children's Digital Library (http://www.icdlbooks.org). Druin and her colleagues (2001) think that young children are being forced to negotiate interfaces that require typing, spelling and reading skills, or necessitate an understanding of abstract concepts or content knowledge, that are beyond their still developing abilities. As an alternative their intergenerational and interdisciplinary design team that includes children alongside adults has designed a graphical direct manipulation interface for searching, browsing and viewing query results (supported by a grant under DLI-2). The International Children's Digital Library (ICDL) was launched in late 2002 and includes books from many countries and in many languages (Druin et al, 2003). The interface screen reproduced in Figure 6.14 shows the use of colourful icons to represent subjects, and the large icons displayed at the top of the screen that are easy for young children to spot and to position the cursor over (as well as a more traditional keyword search box at the foot of the screen). A fuller discussion of the ICDL can be found as a case study in Chapter Nine.

The Children's Digital Library at the Public Library of Charlotte and Mecklenburg County (http://www.storyplace.org) in North Carolina provides a bilingual interface (English and Spanish) and is clearly targeted at young users (Figure 6.15). It offers a variety of services to its young users, including online stories and online activities as well as reading lists (Figure 6.16). Unlike the ICDL, however, the books themselves are not available in full text, although they can be purchased online from this site (http://www.storyplace.org)!

6.6.2 Interfaces for users with visual handicaps

Users with visual handicaps present several kinds of challenges to interface designers, but these can be confronted with a little effort. Users with short sight may find it difficult to read text on a screen if it is too small or uses

Figure 6.14 International Children's Digital Library, US (reproduced courtesy of the International Children's Digital Library)

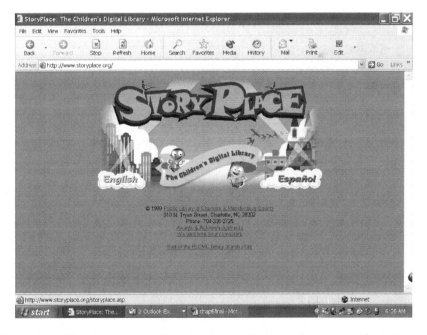

Figure 6.15 The Children's Digital Library, Public Library of Charlotte and Mecklenburg County, US (reproduced courtesy of the Public Library of Charlotte & Mecklenburg County Library)

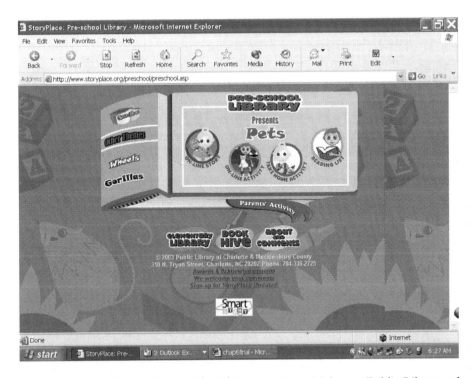

Figure 6.16 Pre-School Library, The Children's Digital Library, Public Library of Charlotte and Mecklenburg County, US (reproduced courtesy of the Public Library of Charlotte & Mecklenburg County)

an intricate font – an italic font, for example, can be difficult to read. The answer here either is to employ larger and regular fonts, or else to provide through personalization the opportunity for users to change the default settings. Certain kinds of fonts such as Arial or Helvetica that use a proportionally spaced sans serif are easier for the visually impaired to read. Non-justified text is easier to track down a page than justified, and a mix of upper and lower case letters is easier to read than upper case only. The interface may also permit users to enlarge text boxes and menus. Figure 2.3 in Chapter Two shows the NIH SeniorHealth interface that is designed for senior citizens and uses large print with short, easy to read segments of information together with a spoken word alternative version.

Users who to varying degrees have colour deficiencies face other challenges. They may find it very difficult to read from screens that have opted for poor foreground and background colour combinations (for example, blue text on a red background), or use together colours like red and green that can look alike to some people. Designers here can minimize problems by careful colour selection – advice can be found in many interface design books such as that by Galitz (2002). Alternatively, they could ensure that all information conveyed with colour is also available in a monochrome version (again, through personalization).

Assistive technologies range from simple magnifying glasses and larger monitor screens to electronic magnifier programs that will display in magnified form a portion of the screen, and work effectively up to about four times magnification (beyond which so little of the original screen is displayed that it becomes difficult to function effectively). Various kinds of Braille devices and speech output systems that convert text into sound can also be employed, though they can be complex to install and operate (see also Section 2.6.1 of Chapter Two). Keyboards can be made easier to use by applying stickers with larger and clearer characters. The interface may allow the mouse-controlled cursor on the screen to be enlarged or coloured for better visibility; alternatively it might be set so that it leaves a trail of multiple images on the screen to highlight its movement. A useful overview of the technology available is provided by the National Library for the Blind's *Library Services for Visually Impaired People: a Manual of Best Practice* (http://bpm.nlb-online.org).

The one snag here is that such techniques can be applied to text but not to images of any kind. The solution to this problem is to provide as an option a textual rather than a graphical presentation. We saw earlier in the Chapter (Figure 6.9) how the New Zealand Digital Library offers such a choice. Another example is provided by the Open University of Hong Kong Electronic Library. The graphical version of this interface is shown in Figure 2.8, but in Figure 6.17 this same homepage is shown in text mode, where images have been replaced by word-based menus. Users can toggle back to the graphical mode from the 'graphic version' button in the upper centre of the screen.

Lewis and Klauber (2002) emphasize the importance of including the visually impaired in any testing of new digital library interfaces, and of selecting software and content from providers that are sensitive to the requirements of visually impaired users.

6.7 Languages and Interface Design

The world is still graced with around 5000 living languages, although their number is in rapid decline. Many of these languages have very small numbers of native speakers, and in some cases they have no written form. Nevertheless, if digital libraries are to offer global access to information, and to serve the needs of a truly global population, they must serve diverse linguistic populations. This applies to the information content of digital libraries, but it equally applies to the interfaces through which such content is accessed. Interfaces certainly must be designed to cope with languages other than English, and writing systems other than the Roman alphabet.

Implementers of a digital library, furthermore, may wish to provide the interface in more than one language. This may be done for several reasons. The interface may be presented in the local language of the user community most directly concerned, but also offered in a second, or third, language (typically including English) that is more accessible to a much wider range of users. For instance, the Biblioteca Virtual em Saùde (the Virtual Health

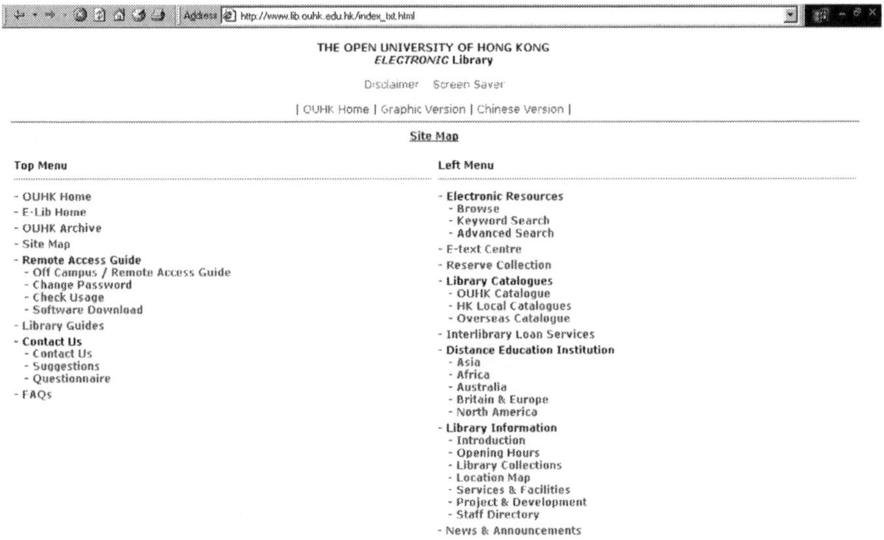

THE OPEN UNIVERSITY OF HONG KONG
ELECTRONIC Library

Disclaimer   Screen Saver

| OUHK Home | Graphic Version | Chinese Version |

Site Map

Top Menu

- OUHK Home
- E-Lib Home
- OUHK Archive
- Site Map
- **Remote Access Guide**
  - Off Campus / Remote Access Guide
  - Change Password
  - Check Usage
  - Software Download
- Library Guides
- **Contact Us**
  - Contact Us
  - Suggestions
  - Questionnaire
- FAQs

Left Menu

- **Electronic Resources**
  - Browse
  - Keyword Search
  - Advanced Search
- E-text Centre
- Reserve Collection
- **Library Catalogues**
  - OUHK Catalogue
  - HK Local Catalogues
  - Overseas Catalogue
- Interlibrary Loan Services
- **Distance Education Institution**
  - Asia
  - Africa
  - Australia
  - Britain & Europe
  - North America
- **Library Information**
  - Introduction
  - Opening Hours
  - Library Collections
  - Location Map
  - Services & Facilities
  - Project & Development
  - Staff Directory
- News & Announcements

Figure 6.17 Homepage in text mode, Electronic Library, Open University of Hong Kong, China (reproduced coutesy of the Open University of Hong Kong)

Library) in Brazil offers its interface in Portuguese, English and Spanish. Alternatively, the primary user community for the digital library might itself be distributed over several languages. An example from Chapter Two is the interface to the Tibetan and Himalayan Digital Library, available in five languages: Tibetan, Chinese, Nepali, Japanese and English (Figure 2.1). In other situations a minority of users may come from a specific language group and so an appropriate language interface may be provided in that language as well as the 'dominant' language. In the UK, the Westminster Libraries' interface (Figure 2.12) is in English, but with Chinese as an alternative where it relates to Chinese digital information sources, reflecting the size of this minority population in the London Borough of Westminster. Some countries have two or more official languages and their digital libraries may reflect this reality. Many digital libraries in Canada, for example, will opt for interfaces in both official languages – English and French.

When an interface is to be made available in more than one language, its developers have three ways to present this choice. They can provide an initial staging page where users are presented with a list of the languages available, and from which one must be chosen. Only after this step has been completed will the user be able to advance. Figure 6.18 shows the home page of the Dubrovnik Museum in Croatia (http://www.mdc.hr/dubrovnik). The museum's name is given in Croatian, English and German (though Croatian is given more typographic prominence), and users must select one of these languages in order to enter the site proper. The page has no other function than to permit language selection.

Alternatively, the designers can select a default language for the interface, but give users from this page the opportunity to switch to any other

Figure 6.18 Trilingual home page, Dubrovački Muzeji, Croatia (reproduced courtesy of the Dubrovnik Museum)

languages in which the interface is available. Figure 6.19 shows the homepage of the Latvian Museum Association (http://www.museji.lv/index.php), in Latvian but offering English and Russian as alternative languages. The page's intricate design structure, however, may obscure the availability of the language alternatives.

Finally, designers can provide the language menu not only on the opening page but on all subsequent pages, as at the National Library of Wales (see for example, Figure 9.35).

The advantage of a staging page is that the interface is language neutral: none of the language alternatives offered is given greater prominence than the others by the designers. In societies where language issues are politically or legally contentious, this may be the best solution. The downside is that the first page of the interface serves no other purpose than to select the interface language. A default language may be preferable when one language can be identified without controversy as being dominant over any other languages offered. In this case the first page can do more than simply offer language choices (as in Figure 6.19). If the language choice can be made from any page in the interface, users are given that much more flexibility as to if and when they opt to switch languages, but then each page must include an additional icon to accomplish this task.

Language choices can be provided within the interface in several ways. The most obvious is simply to list the names of the languages. This begs the issue of the language and the order within such a list. The language options can be presented as they would be written in that language ('Français') or in translation to any 'dominant' language within the interface (if this is

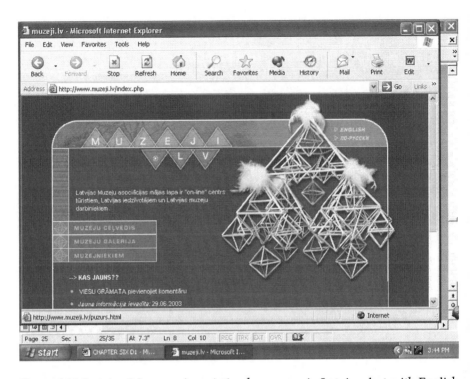

Figure 6.19 Latvian Museum Association homepage in Latvian, but with English and Russian options (reproduced courtesy of the Latvian Museum Association)

English, then 'French'). Nielsen (2000) recommends they be listed in both languages. They can be ranked alphabetically, but only if they share a common writing system and therefore a common alphabetic sequence. If alphabetic order is eschewed, there might be a resulting suggestion that one language is more significant than another. An alternative to naming the languages is to opt for an icon that will represent them visually. National flags are popular icons for this purpose, but languages and nation states do not neatly coincide. Whose national flag should represent the Spanish, English or French languages, for example? Furthermore, not everyone is *au fait* with national flags. Other icons can be tried, such as people in national or some other kind of identifiable costume, but these would raise exactly the same representational and identification problems as do flags, with the additional risk that such national stereotyping might prove offensive.

The decision to provide a bilingual or multilingual interface raises more issues than language selection. Translations between the languages must be accurate, intelligible and free of ambiguity. The interface should be as clear and consistent in one language as in another. This is not always as easy as it may sound. Problems may appear, especially when one of the languages has a more fully developed terminology for interface objects and actions than another. Terminology has the advantage of terseness; in its absence it may be difficult to encapsulate a concept in just one or two words. On a display screen, space is always at a premium, and it may be difficult to accommodate long phrases that term translation from one language to another may produce. Furthermore, some languages make heavier demands upon screen space than others in order to convey the same information. Thai words, for example, tend to be longer than their English equivalents, as illustrated in Figure 6.20 (the Child Institute Digital Library – http://www.childthai.org), where the Thai equivalents of the English 'Search' and "Clear" labels on the search boxes contain considerably more individual characters. This can make it problematic to design an interface in one language, and then simply translate it into other languages – so-called internationalization of the interface. Alternatively, each language version can be designed independently to take account of the particular demands that language imposes – so-called localization of the interface. As we shall see below, similar issues also arise with respect to cultural factors.

Several factors argue in favour of localization. One has just been mentioned: buttons, menus, search boxes and so on, designed for language A may prove to be too big or too small comfortably to accommodate the translation into language B. Interface design issues are further complicated when writing systems opt for different character sequencing. Many languages, like English, are written horizontally from left to right. But Arabic is an example of a language written horizontally from right to left (as we saw in Figure 6.8), and Japanese customarily is written in vertical lines from

Figure 6.20 Contrast in word length between Thai and English, Child Institute Digital Library, Thailand

top to bottom, and from right to left. This clearly has considerable implications for screen layout. Not only must writing run in different directions, but interface objects such as buttons may have to be ordered differently (for example, from right to left in an Arabic interface).

In such cases, a measure at least of localization may be essential. In other cases localization may not be inevitable but may make the interface more efficient and more satisfying for local users. A price might have to be paid, however, for localization. The third maxim from Galitz (2002), cited at the outset of this Chapter, is likely to be transgressed. The interface will look different in each language version, and at least some of the language versions may not follow design conventions that are typically observed in digital library interfaces. In other words, there will be a trade-off between adaptability and conventionality.

The ideal might be neither localization nor internationalization, but globalization – the application of a linguistically neutral approach. Icons were mentioned briefly above as a way of representing language choices. Potentially they provide a means of circumventing individual languages by representing concepts visually. International airports, for example, often attempt to cater for travellers with different native languages by providing signage via icons rather than text. Icons are widely used in interfaces, though it is interesting to see how often they are accompanied by a textual explanation. Some objects and actions can be represented relatively easily by icons (though as we shall see below, icons can create problems when exposed to users from different cultures). We are used, for example, to a trash can (or should it be dustbin?) representing a storage space for deleted files. Choong and Salvendy (1998) assert that "due to the relatively lower verbal abilities and superior visual discrimination abilities of Chinese, Chinese novice users can be expected to prefer pictorial presentation over alphanumeric presentation in interfaces." In a complicated interface structure such as a typical digital library requires, however, written language will not be easy to eliminate – unless ultimately it can be replaced by spoken instructions in the user's preferred language.

Input and output devices may cause problems in multilingual environments. Keyboard layouts, for example, are not standardized across language communities, and problems are exacerbated when working in a writing system for which the keyboard was not designed (for example, inputting Arabic letters with a Roman keyboard). One solution here is an on-screen keyboard with the correct letters, but it is slow to point and click on them using a mouse. Printers also may be unable to cope with certain writing systems. A longer overview of input and output issues can be found in Large and Moukdad (2000).

Pavani (2001) describes how a multilingual interface has been realized in one institution: the Maxwell Digital Library (Portuguese, Spanish and English) implemented in the Department of Electrical Engineering at Pontifícia Universidade Católica do Rio de Janeiro in Brazil. In this case, all language-dependent information for the interface is grouped in an area divided into three sections, one for each language. When the language control parameter specifying the navigation language for this web-based library is identified, the appropriate language section is displayed.

6.8 Cultures and Interface Design

Cultural influences and sensibilities can affect the ways in which an interface is perceived by its users, and therefore they should be taken into account by designers. The term 'culture' is not easily defined, but we can say generally that it concerns how we go about our everyday life and how we use things, including technology. As individuals we do not necessarily belong to just one cultural group: we can talk of corporate cultures and age cultures, for example, but in this section we are interested in national cultures. Digital libraries can cross national cultural boundaries at three levels: designers, content providers, and users all can have different cultural backgrounds. Although digital libraries in practice often are global in their outreach, their design in many cases has remained local. If a digital library is likely to be accessed by users from different cultural communities then cultural aspects of interface design should be heeded (Duncker, Theng and Mohd-Nasir, 2000).

User interfaces, including digital library interfaces, have tended to be based upon psychological and social models derived from North American and European traditions. The stereotypical interface designer has been the (young) adult, Caucasian, American male, who implicitly or explicitly carries his own cultural baggage to the design table. It should be added that cultural bias is no less problematical for being unintentional. How might this have influenced design principles and practice as concerns digital library interfaces, and what kinds of adjustments might be required to suit an interface for other cultural environments?

Digital library interfaces typically are designed around a unifying metaphor. In many cases the metaphor, not too surprisingly, is a traditional library, with its catalogue and its various rooms in which different parts (by form or subject) of the collection are located. Another common metaphor, especially for digital libraries created by museums, is the gallery. The interface metaphor is critical, as it will determine many other design aspects – layout, colour, icons, etc. It should be appropriate for the content and purpose of the digital library, but it also should take account of cultural factors. As Duncker (2002) says, "whether one disapproves of metaphors in the design of our user interfaces or not, there is hardly any controversy about the fact that metaphors and metaphorical thinking are deeply rooted in culture." A digital library that might be used by people unfamiliar with traditional libraries, for example, is better avoiding this particular metaphor for one more familiar to its user community. Duncker cites as an example Maori students in New Zealand who may lack knowledge of how materials are organized in western libraries and therefore find digital libraries based on such a metaphor difficult to use.

Many digital library interfaces incorporate images. Typically these relate to the collection in some way. They might be used to provide an overview of the collection's content (as in Figure 1.1), to provide a 'feel' for the assembled artefacts. A special use of images, often found in digital libraries, is as icons, where the icon represents an action that the user can perform. Images conjure associations that may differ from culture to culture. For example, the image of a policeman in some cultures might suggest a helping hand in a potentially difficult situation (for example, the Watchfile website that provides guidelines for interface design (http://bobby.watchfire.com/bobby/html/en/index.jsp) suggests the use of a policeman image – a London 'bobby' – to indicate that a site complies with these guidelines), whereas in other cultures it may have more threatening connotations. PictureAustralia (http://www.picture australia.org) provides an example of cultural sensitivity in the face of attitudes towards death; its homepage contains the following warning: "Indigenous Australians are advised that PictureAustralia may include images or names of people now deceased" (Figure 6.21). Icons should be avoided that rely upon metaphor as they may be closely related to synonyms in one particular language. For example, the image of a dining table to represent a data table only makes sense if the two concepts happen to be described by the same word. Icons should also be avoided if they relate to culturally specific concepts that are unlikely to resonate with users from other cultures, such as sport or food.

The temptation should be resisted to employ humorous comments in an interface intended for an international market. It may be difficult for users who are not native speakers of the language to grasp the point being made, and even those who share a language may not share a joke. The informal, friendly style favoured on occasion by interfaces developed in the US may be perceived as childish or even condescending in the UK.

Figure 6.21 Cultural sensitivity, PictureAustralia, National Library of Australia (reproduced courtesy of PictureAustralia)

Colour is an important feature in any interface. We have already mentioned guidelines for the use of colour in interfaces, but it also plays an important role in culture, conveying both psychological and physical associations. Studies do suggest that psychological reactions to colour can be culturally related. For example, researchers in the UK reported that British university students favoured pastel shades with a lot of grey and low contrast; Scandinavia students preferred dark colours, also with low contrast; and Jamaican students liked strong and bright colours with high contrasts (Duncker, Theng and Mohd-Nasir, 2000). Another study (Courtney, 1986) found that Americans were more than twice as likely to associate green with 'go', red with 'hot' or 'stop', and yellow with 'caution', than their Hong Kong Chinese counterparts. Physical associations between interface objects and objects in the real world are also facilitated or retarded by colour. Icons provide good examples here. For example, an icon of a post-box to represent a part of the screen to which a file should be moved for transmission elsewhere will be more easily identified as such by Americans if it is coloured blue (as in the real world), but for Canadians it should be coloured red, and in Greece it would be yellow (the shape of the postbox, of course, is also highly relevant to its identification by different cultural communities).

A few examples can be used to illustrate some of these points. Figure 6.22 shows the first page from a seventeenth-century Arabic poem in praise

Figure 6.22 Cultural aspects of interface design, *Treasures of Islam* CD-ROM (reproduced courtesy of McGill University)

of the Prophet Mohammed, one of the digitized manuscripts in Treasures of Islam (Beheshti, Large and Moukdad, 1999). This CD-ROM contains eight Arabic manuscripts – prayer books, poems and a book on calligraphy – as well as examples of Arabic calligraphic work, a collection of miniature paintings from Arabic manuscripts, and examples of manuscript decorated bindings. The interface has been constructed through its use of colour and design to suggest an Islamic manuscript. On the left-hand side of Figure 6.22 is the poem itself, and on the right-hand side, as well as the poem's title in the upper corner, there is a 'keypad' (used to scroll through the poem's 37 pages), navigational buttons, and a loudspeaker icon that can switch on and off a tape of Arabic traditional music.

Lest any reader think that it is the poetic content rather than the cultural environment that explains this interface, let us take a look at a second interface that also deals with poetry, but in a very different culture. Figure 6.23 shows the interface to a collection of poems in French as well as some other languages that has been created in France. Le club des poètes (http://franceweb.fr/poesie) has an altogether different look. It too relies upon a light wash as background, but its two images and various fonts give it a distinctly western feel.

A third example is provided in Figure 6.24; this presents the interface to the Southern African Freedom Struggles collection of the Digital Imaging

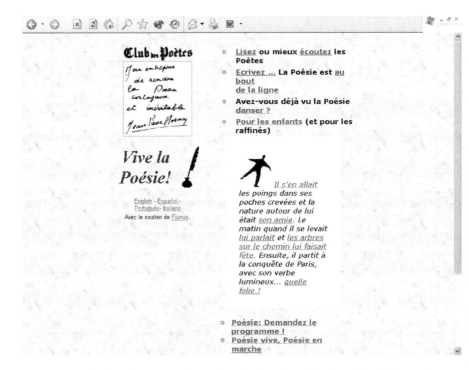

Figure 6.23 Cultural aspects of interface design, Le club des poètes, France (reproduced courtesy of the Club des Poètes)

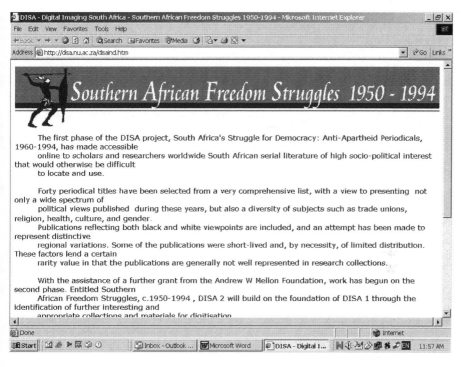

Figure 6.24 The Southern African Freedom Struggles collection, South Africa (reproduced courtesy of the University of Natal)

Project of South Africa (DISA), that provides access to South African material of "high socio-political interest" (http://disa.nu.ac.za). The icon used in the top left of the screen is very appropriate for this particular site, but might be considered culturally as well as politically inappropriate in many other cultural contexts.

The list of other interface features that might create cultural confusion is quite long. Paper sizes are not internationally determined (the two most common sizes are A4 (UK) and US Letter), and therefore default settings might cause problems when printing. It might be assumed that placing an x in a box signifies that the box is to be activated, but the opposite is true in Korea (an x is inserted to de-activate a box). Sequencing or ordering items is commonly required in digital library interfaces, but even the scripts (of which there are many) that employ the Roman alphabet do not use identical letter sequencing (especially if they include accents as well as letters). Likewise, numerical sequencing is far from standardized; in some cultures a point between numbers does not necessarily denote a decimal point. Currencies, times, weights and sizes, all of which differ from culture to culture, are unlikely to be encountered in a digital library interface, but dates may be found. The date on which this paragraph is being written, 16 December 2003, is, for example:

12/16/03 in the US
16/12/03 in the UK

and

16.12.03 in Germany.

At least these are variations within the same Gregorian calendar; in the Middle East, for example, the Islamic calendar would say it is 21/10/1424. Postal addresses and telephone numbers, that might be found in a digital library interface, also are presented according to different conventions.

It should be emphasized that culturalization in interface design is not without its detractors. Some observers point to the difficulty of identifying actual user communities on cultural grounds. For example, members of a cultural community who are frequent users of 'western' software designs may find it counter-productive to be presented with an interface customized supposedly for that community. In this case the rule of conformity between interfaces of similar products will have been broken, and it may prove more difficult to acclimatize to the unfamiliar localized interface than to use the interface from a supposedly alien culture. Others criticize the implicit stereotyping to which culturalization can lead, suspecting it of paternalism. The universalist approach is that if interfaces are designed to support cognitive characteristics, then people will work more easily, efficiently and happily, and because cognitive processes are universal then there should be a single design for everybody. The culturally specific approach, in contrast, argues that the HCI community demonstrates its naivety or ignorance if it refuses to consider factors such as national culture in the belief that it is neutral. As Duncker, Theng and Mohd-Nasir (2000) put it, "in the long term, the consideration of cultural aspects of digital library design and use will prevent industry losses caused by culturally offending and inappropriate technologies."

Readers interested in the relationship between culture and interface design should consult Fernandes (1995) and Nielsen (1990) for a more in-depth discussion.

6.9 Interface Evaluation

It is not the intention in this Chapter to discuss in any detail the interface design process; Shneiderman (1998), and Galitz (2002), for example, can be consulted by those interested in this topic. Briefly, however, Shneiderman cites the Logical User-Centered Interactive Design Methodology and its six stages:

- Develop product concept – create concept, set up design team. Identify user population, identify technical and environmental issues, produce staff plan, schedule and budget.

- Perform research and needs analysis.
- Design prototype and conduct usability tests.
- Complete design into a full system and conduct full-scale usability tests.
- Implement software.
- Provide training and assistance; evaluate.

The fact that an interface has been designed and implemented does not mean that the process is at an end. It must be continuously evaluated to ensure that it is meeting its assigned objectives. Shneiderman (1998) recommends interviews with individual users and focus group discussions to assess the interface's functionality, reliability, clarity and overall satisfaction from the users' perspective. The system itself may generate logging data that can be analyzed to detect problems. Online suggestion boxes (such as employed by the New Zealand Digital Library) enable users to send messages to the designers or maintainers. Online bulletin boards provide users and designers with an opportunity to discuss collaboratively concerns and suggestions.

Five evaluation criteria can be applied to any interface:

- The time it takes to learn how to use the interface properly.
- The speed at which the interface performs actions requested by the user.
- The rate of errors committed by users at the interface.
- The ease with which users can remember the interface and its features from one session to the next session.
- The level of individual satisfaction that users derive from their experience with the interface.

It is difficult, perhaps even impossible, to design an interface that for all users and all tasks on all occasions will function perfectly. But this is no reason not to strive for the ideal.

References

Abbas, J., Norris, C. and Soloway, E. (2002) Middle school children's use of the ARTEMIS digital library. *Proceedings of the 2nd ACM/IEEE-CS Joint Conference on Digital Libraries, Portland, Oregon, 13–17 July 2002.* New York, NY: ACM Press, 98–105. Available at: http://portal.acm.org/citation.cfm?id=544239&jmp=abstract&dl=GUIDE&dl=GUIDE

Arms, W. Y. (2000) *Digital Libraries.* Cambridge, MASS: MIT Press

Arant, W. and Payne, L. (2001) The common user interface in academic libraries: myth or reality? *Library Hi Tech,* **19** (1), 63–76

Beheshti, J., Large, A. and Moukdad, H. (1999) *Treasures of Islam.* CD-ROM. Montreal: McGill University

Card, S. K., Mackinlay, J. D. and Shneiderman, B. (1999) *Readings in Information Visualization: Using Vision to Think.* San Francisco: Morgan Kaufmann

Choong, Y. Y. and Salvendy, G. (1998) Design of icons for use by Chinese in mainland China. *Interacting with Computers,* **9**, 417–430

Christoffel, M. and Schmitt, B. (2002) Accessing libraries as easy as a game. *Second International Workshop on Visual Interfaces to Digital Libraries, July 18, 2002*, Portland, Oregon. Available at: http://vw.indiana.edu/visual02/slides-christoffel.pdf

Courtney, A.J. (1986) Chinese population stereotypes: colour associations. *Human Factors*, **28** (1), 97–99

Dillon, A. (2002) Technologies of information: HCI and the digital library. In J.M. Carroll, ed. *Human-Computer Interaction in the New Millenium*. Boston: ACM Press, 457–474

Druin, A., Bederson, B., Hourcade, J. P., Sherman, L., Revelle, G., Platner, M. and Weng, S. (2001) Designing a digital library for young children: An intergenerational partnership. *Proceedings of the first ACM/IEEE-CS Joint Conference on Digital Libraries*. New York, NY: ACM Press, 398–405

Druin, A., Bederson, B. B., Weeks, A., Farber, A., Grosjean, J., Guha, M. L., Hourcade, J. P., Lee, J., Liao, S., Reuter, K., Rose, A., Takayama, Y. and Zhang, L. (2003) The International Children's Digital Library: description and analysis of first use. *First Monday*, **8** (5) Available at: http://www.firstmonday.dk/issues/issue8_5/druin/index.html

Duncker, E. (2002) Cross-cultural usability of the library metaphor. *Proceedings of the 2nd ACM/IEEE-CS Joint Conference on Digital Libraries, Portland, Oregon, 13–17 July 2002*. New York, NY: ACM Press, 223–230

Duncker, E., Theng, Y. L. and Mohd-Nasir, N. (2000) Cultural usability in digital libraries. *Bulletin of the American Society for Information Science*, **26** (4), 21–22. Available at: http://www.asis.org/Bulletin/May-00/duncker__et_al.html

Fernandes, T. (1995) *Global Interface Design: a Guide to Designing International User Interfaces*. Boston: Academic Press

Galitz, W. O. (2002) *The Essential Guide to User Interface Design*. 2nd ed. New York: Wiley.

Greene, S., Marchionini, G., Plaisant, C. and Shneiderman, B. (2000) Previews and overviews in digital libraries: designing surrogates to support visual information seeking. *Journal of the American Society for Information Science*, **51** (4), 380–393

Jones, S. (1998) Graphical query specification and dynamic result previews for a digital library. *Proceedings of the 11th annual ACM symposium on User Interface Software and Technology* New York: ACM Press, 143–151

Jones, S., McInnes, S. and Staveley, M. S. (1999) A graphical user interface for Boolean query specification. *International Journal of Digital Libraries*, **2** (2–3), 207–223

Large, A. (2004) Information seeking on the Web by elementary school students. In Mary K. Chelton and Colleen Cool, eds. *Youth Information-Seeking Theories, Models, and Approaches*. Lanham, MD: Scarecrow Press, 293–319.

Large, A. and Moukdad, H. (2000) Multilingual access to web resources: an overview. *Program*, **34** (1), 43–58

Lewis, V. and Klauber, J. (2000) [Image] [Image] [Image] [Link] [Link] [Link]: inaccessible web design from the perspective of a blind librarian. *Library Hi-Tech*, 20 (2), 137–140

Lynch, C. and Garcia-Molina, H. (1995) *Interoperability, Scaling, and the Digital Libraries Research Agenda: A Report on the May 18–19, 1995 IITA Digital Libraries Workshop*. Available at: http://www-diglib.stanford.edu/diglib/pub/reports/iita-dlw/main.html

Nielsen, J. (1990) *Designing User Interfaces for International Use*. Amsterdam: Elsevier

Nielsen, J. (2000) *Designing Web Usability*. Indianapolis: New Riders

Pavani, A. M. B. (2001) A model of multilingual digital library. *Ciência da Informação*, **30** (3), 73–81.

Shneiderman, B. (1998) *Designing the User Interface: Strategies for Effective Human-Computer Interaction.* 3rd ed. Reading, MASS: Addison-Wesley.

Tariffi, F., Morganti, B. and Segbert M.(2004) Digital cultural heritage projects in Europe: an overview of TRIS and the takeup trial projects. *Program,* **38** (1), 15–28

Thong, J. Y.L., Hong, W. and Tam, K. (2002) Understanding user acceptance of digital libraries: what are the roles of interface characteristics, organizational context, and individual differences? *International Journal of Human-Computer Studies,* **57** (3), 215–242

Chapter 7
Searching and Browsing

7.1 Libraries and Information Seeking

Libraries have many functions, but since their earliest appearance centuries ago the central task has been clear: to assemble a collection of materials and organize them in such a way that individual items can be located on demand. It does not matter whether these are books, journals, reports, newspapers, CDs, videos or any of the other categories found in libraries, whether they are consulted within the library confines or borrowed for use elsewhere, whether library patrons want to read, view or listen to the entire item or to locate specific elements within it: users of a library must be able quickly and reliably to identify which items are in the collection, to locate them wherever they are stored, and to access their content. This is true of traditional and digital libraries alike. In the case of traditional libraries users typically find items either by searching in the catalogue or by browsing the shelves. In the case of digital libraries, as we have seen, often there are many separate collections of information sources. These can be searched separately, and in some cases can also be searched as if one integrated collection. Material is found by using the features provided in the interface. Normally digital libraries can be both searched and browsed in this way.

7.2 Searching

The objective of any search is to encapsulate a user's information need in one or several words – the query – and display the resulting matched items. In digital libraries this can be accomplished in a variety of ways that in many respects are similar to those encountered in web-based search engines such as Google. One approach is to provide a search box in which users can enter one or more keywords. An example is shown here from the California Digital Library (CDL), a collaborative effort of the various University of California campuses that selects, designs, builds and manages systems for the use and preservation of high-quality digital content (http://www.californiadigitallibrary.org). The CDL provides a single point of access for digital collections – photographs, interviews, sound recordings, maps, historical documents, current articles, videos, sheet music, and more, – produced or managed by the University of California

Figure 7.1 shows the results from a single-term search *Sausalito* for information about that Californian city, with items retrieved from various collections such as the Oliver Family Photograph Collection and the Construction Photographs of the Golden Gate Bridge. The software searches these separate collections as if they are one unified collection. The next step in the search, not shown here, would be to click on one of the titles or entire collections.

This was a simple search using only a single keyword, but more sophisticated searches can also be conducted. Figure 7.2 shows the results of a second search *london not jack* in the CDL to find information about London, the city, but not about Jack London (the CDL contains a collection of writings, correspondence, postcards and so on about this author). Two keywords have been entered in the search box, linked by what is called a Boolean

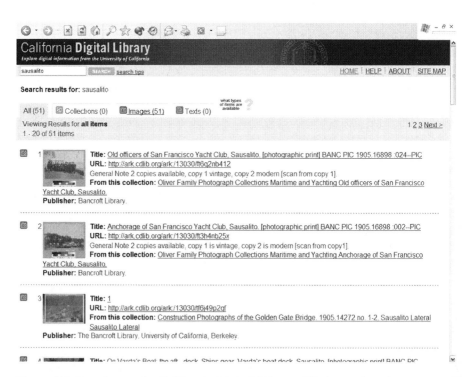

Figure 7.1 Simple search, California Digital Library, US (reproduced courtesy of the Regents of the University of California)

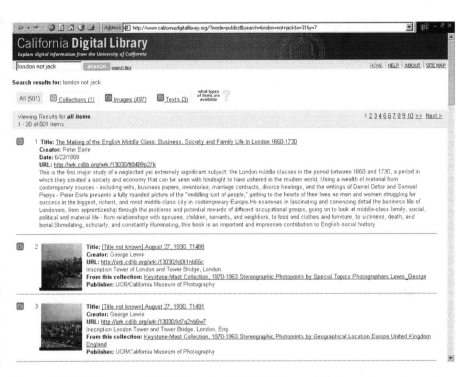

Figure 7.2 Boolean search, California Digital Library, US (reproduced courtesy of the Regents of the University of California)

operator, in this case the NOT operator. This instructs the search engine to find all occurrences of *London* except where the term *Jack* also appears. Again, the results are distributed across three types of text and image collections. Boolean retrieval finds all the items that precisely match the Boolean search statement, and rejects all those that do not precisely match it. As well as the NOT Boolean operator there is the AND operator, which finds items that contain all the keywords entered (for example *Jack* AND *London* would only find items that include both these words and would exclude records only containing the term *London*), and the OR operator which finds items that contain any of the keywords, and is useful to deal with synonyms (for example, *writer* OR *author*). In the Ethnomathematics Digital Library (http://www.ethnomath.org), a resource network and interactive learning community created with support from the National Science Foundation and covering ethnomathematics, with an emphasis on the indigenous mathematics of the Pacific region, multiple search terms (in this case, *culture learning*) are implicitly linked with the AND operator (it is the default operator), although users are not told this on the search screen, as shown in Figure 7.3.

Users can also choose an Advanced Search; in this case they are guided by a series of menus and boxes to specify their search interest more closely – by choosing a subject, geographical area, cultural group, audience level, and so on (Figure 7.4).

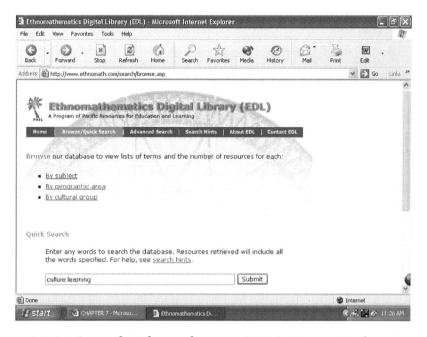

Figure 7.3 Quick search, Ethnomathematics Digital Library, US (reproduced courtesy of Pacific Resources for Education and Learning)

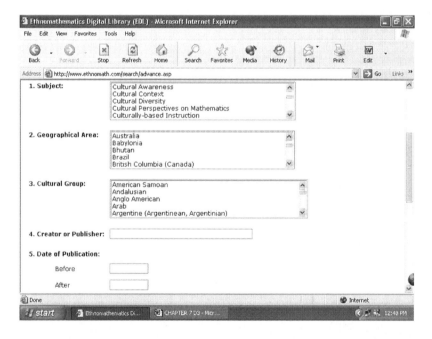

Figure 7.4 Advanced search (extract), Ethnomathematics Digital Library, US (reproduced courtesy of Pacific Resources for Education and Learning)

In the CDL the search engine also has AND as its default setting, but users only discover this if they check on 'Search tips' (see Figure 7.1); they can also opt for the OR and NOT operators. The Perseus Digital Library (http:// www.perseus.tufts.edu), located in the Department of the Classics at Tufts University in the US, offers an 'exact match' (AND) and an 'alternate names' (OR), as well as the options to search only the bibliographic data (metadata) or else the entire full-text contents of the library, and to restrict a search to just one of the collections rather than all the collections (Perseus comprises 12 individual collections relating to the humanities).

The digital library interface may help users accomplish such Boolean searches by providing a separate search box for each keyword, and the option to choose with which operator to link them. The Intellectual Property Digital Library's Structured Search page is shown in Figure 7.5. This Library (http:// pctgazette.wipo.int) contains collections hosted by the World Intellectual Property Organization (WIPO). The interface provides a series of pull-down menu boxes that allow users to look for keywords in a variety of fields such as author, title, and abstract, and offers users five different ways to combine multiple keywords: as well as AND, OR and ANDNOT (the same operator as the NOT operator referred to above), it has XOR (sometimes referred to as exclusive OR where at least one of the words must be present but not both) and NEAR (the keywords must be within five words of each other in the

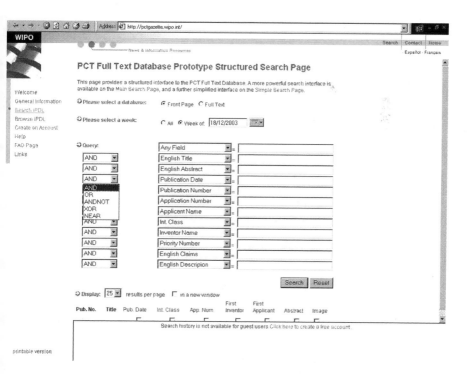

Figure 7.5 Structured search, Intellectual Property Digital Library (reproduced courtesy of the World Intellectual Property Organization)

documents). Words can be right-hand truncated by using the symbol * (for instance, *librar** to match with *library, librarian* and so on), and keywords placed within quotes will be searched as a phrase. Two other search interfaces are also available: a Simple Search Page (shown in Figure 7.6) and an Advanced Search Page: this is an effective way of coping with users who have disparate information-seeking skills and levels of experience. The Simple Search Page offers Boolean searches, but the user need not be familiar with this terminology: the interface instead expresses two of the Boolean operators using phrases ('Any of these words' for the OR operator, and 'All of these words' for the AND). It also allows users to opt for a more restrictive AND search, where the search words must not only all be present in the document, but together as an 'exact phrase'.

An alternative approach is shown in Figure 7.7; here the Early Canadiana Online digital library (http://www.canadiana.org/ECO) has only one search box but radio buttons below it can be clicked to choose the OR operator ('Matches on any word') or the AND operator ('Matches on all words') – the NOT operator is unavailable. The search can be limited to specified elements within the documents, such as the full text (selected in Figure 7.7), or specific parts of the metadata, such as the names of authors or the titles of documents. The three words *Hudson's, Bay* and *Company* have been entered in the search box to find all documents containing this precise phrase: the radio button for 'An exact phrase match' therefore has been clicked (such phrase searching is indicated in many digital library interfaces by enclosing the search terms in quotation marks).

Despite such embellishments as field and phrase searching, Boolean matching is black or white, with no room for ranking in shades of grey documents that the searcher might find more interesting from ones that are likely to be less interesting. Ranking algorithms of various kinds attempt to remedy this drawback; they are used, for example, by web-based search engines such as Google. Here items are ranked in order of importance by assessing their similarity with the query (rather than by a precise match). Ranking can be achieved in several ways: items containing more of the query words can be ranked higher than those with fewer, items containing more of the less common query words (when assessed in terms of all the words in all the items in the database) can be ranked higher; one of the techniques used by Google, PageRank, analyzes links between web pages in order to rank retrieved pages (http://www.google.com/technology/index.html).

The Internet Public Library (http://www.ipl.org) is both a public service organization and a learning/teaching environment at the University of Michigan School of Information in the US. It does not use Boolean operators, but instead relies on 'relevance ranking' of documents (it searches metadata and abstracts, but not the full text of documents). The Internet Public Library (IPL) also provides helpful 'pathfinders' that give tips on search strategies and possible search terms to use in the digital library, or indeed in other libraries or the Web as a whole. The pathfinders provide hotlinks to related sources within the IPL as well as on other websites, but this is taking us away from a discussion of searching into browsing (see below). An extract from the pathfinder provided for patrons searching on Greek mythology is shown in Figure 7.8.

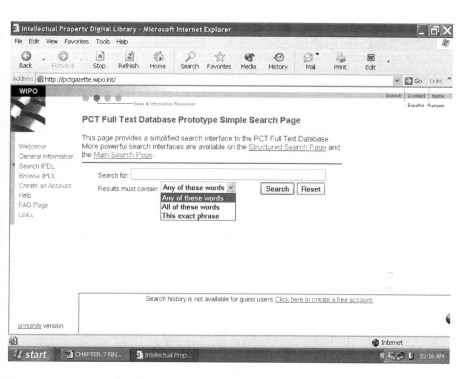

Figure 7.6 Simple search, Intellectual Property Digital Library (reproduced courtesy of the World Intellectual Property Organization)

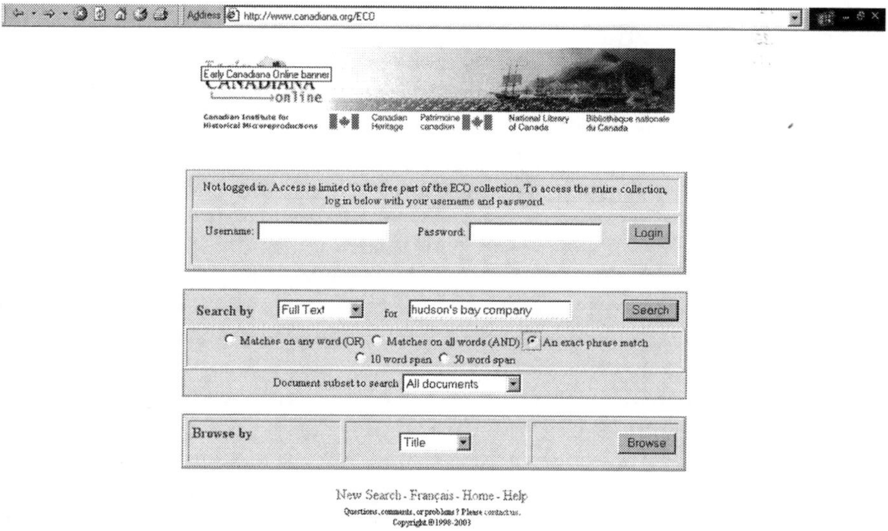

Figure 7.7 Search and browse options, Early Canadiana Online, Canada (reproduced courtesy of the Canadian Institute for Historical Microreproductions)

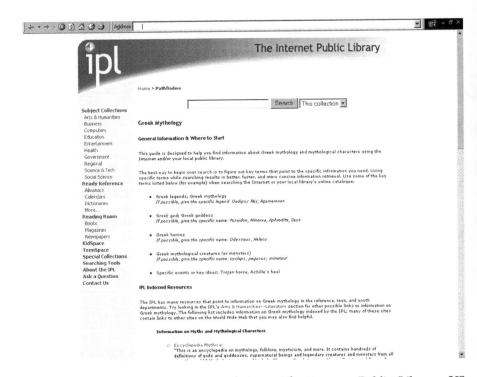

Figure 7.8 Pathfinder for Greek mythology, The Internet Public Library, US (reproduced courtesy of the Regents of the University of Michigan)

As we have already seen, searching in a digital library (unlike a traditional library) is not necessarily confined to metadata. It may be possible to search parts or all of the text in documents, because they have been automatically indexed by a computer. This kind of indexing provides many more entry points to search for a document – the indexing is at a much greater depth than can be achieved by assigning only a few subject headings or class numbers to each document, and this can be done very easily and cheaply (Chinese texts cause some problems, however, because, as Liu and Zhang (2001) explain, it is difficult for computers to identify the individual words included within a Chinese character). The disadvantage of such automatic indexing is that the computer cannot understand the document, decide on its subject content, and then judiciously assign index terms that are consistent with those assigned to other documents in the collection with similar subject content. All terms regardless of importance or consistency are added to the index (probably with the exception of a few 'stop words' that are very common in the language but carry no subject weight, such as definite and indefinite articles, conjunctions and pronouns). Digital libraries have given new life to automatic indexing research that draws upon new approaches such as probabilistic models that retrieve data through weighted word values, or latent semantic indexing where documents are assigned to concepts using mathematical models (Marchionini, 1998). The objective here is to combine the speed and economies of computer indexing with the ability to determine the subject 'aboutness' of a document accurately and consistently that is currently the hallmark of human beings.

7.3 Browsing

Searching presupposes a sharply focused information need. Users must know what it is they want to find, at least to some degree, before they can formulate properly a query. The alternative to searching tolerates a lack of clarity in information need formulation. When browsing, users no longer are required to focus sharply on a search strategy. They can move through a database landscape, glancing around while on the lookout for items of interest. Browsing relies upon users recognizing relevant items when they are displayed, unlike searching that relies upon recalling from their memory information (such as authors, titles or subject descriptions) that might constitute search terms. Browsing prompts serendipitous identification of potentially useful documents, but it can prove slow, especially for those easily distracted by information byways.

Browsing is an important means to find information in digital libraries, and a variety of approaches are offered. Web-based digital libraries make extensive use of hotlinks to navigate through their collections. The various browsing tools must be created by the designers of the digital library, and documents in the collection must be allocated, for example, to entries in a list (indexed, in other words), normally by human indexers rather than computers, in order for browsing to take place.

Many digital libraries make use of lists that can be browsed by users. The American Memory, a part of the Library of Congress (http://memory.loc. gov/ammem/collections/finder.html) is just one example. Its Collection Finder allows users to browse a list of broad subject topics such as Agriculture or Performing Arts (Figure 7.9); once the user has selected a topic, a new screen (not shown here) displays Library of Congress Subject Headings (for the text) and terms from the Thesaurus of Graphic Materials (for the images). The Virtual Library museums pages (VLmp), shown in Figure 2.4, is another example, providing a list of countries, regions and continents that users can browse and then select.

Another common browsing technique is to provide pull-down menus as in the Digital Library collection of the New York Public Library (http://digital.nypl.org). One menu, for example, offers users the opportunity to browse titles, authors or document types – fiction, poetry, biography and autobiography, or essays. Other examples of pull-down menus can be found elsewhere in this book (see, for example, Figure 9.18).

The Canadian Illustrated News (http://www.nlc-bnc.ca/cin/index-e. html) is a service offered by Library and Archives Canada as part of its digital libraries programme. It comprises a selection of almost 4000 images of people, places and events across Canada and around the world taken from this magazine published in Montreal between 1869 and 1883. One approach adopted by this digital library is to provide alphabetical access to its images.

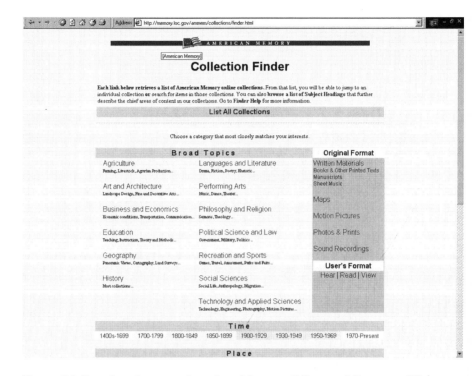

Figure 7.9 Broad topic menu, American Memory, Library of Congress, US (reproduced courtesy of the Library of Congress)

Users can begin browsing by clicking on the first letter of a query word, though of course here they must recall from their memories a suitable word to try with.

An interesting way to find spatial information is via dynamic maps. The Alexandria Digital Library at the University of California, Santa Barbara (http://webclient.alexandria.ucsb.edu/) has a collection of around 15,000 items from the University's Map and Imagery Laboratory. It provides a browser window in which users can reposition a map to a particular location, and use a zoom feature to vary the degree of detail. In Figure 7.10 *New Delhi* has been entered in the Quick Placename Search box; the location of the first hit (the capital city of India) has been indicated on the map browser (it is marked with a cross).

7.4 Information Display

Whether searching or browsing, finding documents or the information within them often involves trial and error: it is an iterative process. A first try may find exactly what is needed, and the session can end. More likely, however, an initial trawl will find nothing at all, or else it will uncover material that

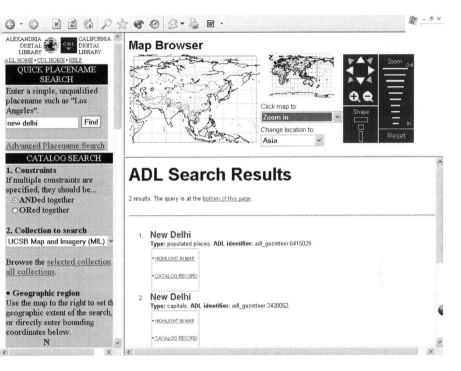

Figure 7.10 Visual browser, Alexandria Digital Library, US (reproduced courtesy of the University of California at Santa Barbara)

does not seem to be exactly what is being sought. In either case, the searching or browsing strategy must be revised (Large, Tedd and Hartley (1999) offer advice on how to do this). In order to make decisions of these kinds, the user must be able quickly to scan any retrieved hits, and this means that information display is an inherent and important part of the information-seeking process.

The standard approach to presenting results is to list them in an abbreviated format (typically the metadata) on screen. Abbreviation allows more records to be displayed on any one page, but it may be more difficult to decide on relevance if the display is too terse. A fuller version can then be accessed by clicking on the short entry. An example is shown in Figure 7.11, taken from the Making of America digital library at the University of Michigan (http://www.hti.umich.edu/m/moagrp/) that contains about 8,500 books and 50,000 journal articles published in the nineteenth century and dealing with American social history. A search on *outlaws* scored 959 hits, but only the metadata records initially are displayed, 25 at a time (Figure 7.11 only shows the first two hits). The records can be displayed in various orders: by author, title, or ascending/ descending date of publication.

Early Canadiana Online (http://www.canadiana.org/eco/english), that includes works published from the arrival of the first European settlers in

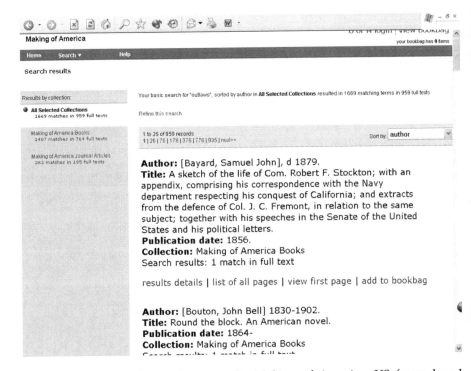

Figure 7.11 Retrieved metadata records, Making of America, US (reproduced courtesy of the University of Michigan University Library)

Canada until the early twentieth century, also displays first the metadata records (Figure 7.12), but it usefully also indicates on which pages of the complete documents are to be found the search terms (in this case a Boolean AND search on the two words *trappers* and *beavers* retrieved 16 hits; the terms themselves appear on 23 separate pages, for example, in the first hit they are on pages 286 and 341).

Other digital libraries display retrieved documents as images. The Cleveland Memory Project is one example (Figure 6.6): retrieved images of postcards are presented to the user for relevance evaluation. More on display techniques, including visualization and 3D techniques, can be found in Chapter Six.

7.5 Searching Multilingual Collections

Many digital libraries include documents in more than one language. And furthermore, even those with monolingual collections may attract users whose language is different from that of the collection. Digital libraries try to cater for such a multilingual environment in various ways.

Metadata can be language independent: they can be assigned in more than one language to items – the Dublin Core, for example, is described and can

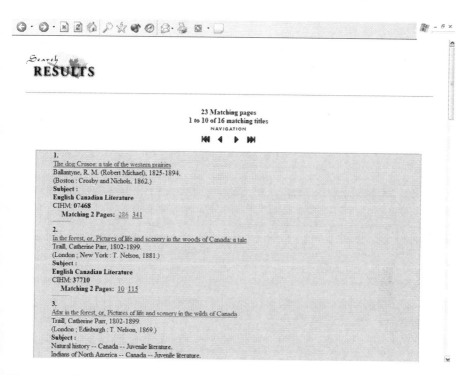

Figure 7.12 Retrieved metadata, Early Canadiana Online, Canada (reproduced courtesy of the Canadian Institute for Historical Microreproductions)

be used in multiple languages. Pavani (2001) explains how 'language dependent' elements in the metadata such as title and abstract are used in all three languages in the digital library at the Department of Electrical Engineering, Pontifícia Universidade Católica do Rio de Janeiro to permit multilingual searching. The International Labour Organization (ILO) in Geneva contains references to all aspects of work and sustainable livelihoods and the work-related aspects of economic and social development and human rights. Its Labordoc database (http://labordoc.ilo.org) includes over 350,000 bibliographic records that have been indexed using the ILO Thesaurus in English, French and German. A search on a subject heading in one language will find all items indexed by that heading in any of the three languages. In Figure 7.13 a search using the French subject heading *blé* has found 92 items; the item displayed, however, is in English rather than French but has been retrieved because it contains the English translation of *blé*, namely *wheat*, in the list of secondary subjects. Davies (2003) describes how this was initially achieved using the MINISIS software and now using the Voyager Endeavor software.

Such approaches that use a bilingual or multilingual thesaurus are very helpful for users who thereby can retrieve documents in multiple languages. Salton (1971) demonstrated many years ago that such a technique could achieve comparable retrieval success to monolingual information retrieval

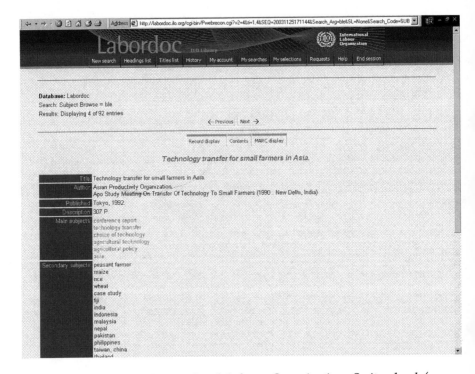

Figure 7.13 Labordoc, International Labour Organization, Switzerland (reproduced courtesy of the International Labour Organization)

systems so long as the bilingual thesaurus was well constructed. This is neither a straightforward nor an inexpensive task, however (Hudon, 1997). Furthermore, it places the onus upon librarians to create more metadata for the items in their collection. Nor will it be of help to users who wish to search the full texts of documents in all available languages rather than merely the metadata.

A digital library may permit users to restrict a search to documents in a particular language. For example, the Google search engine (http://www.google.com) utilized within some digital libraries enables users to select from around 35 languages. This is fine so long as the user is able to formulate a search query in the relevant language. But what if the user cannot do this – and the selection of appropriate search terms in a foreign language is not an easy task? Google again can offer assistance; it provides free translations between 12 language pairs (10 of them involving English either as the language from which or into which the translation will be made). This service can be used to translate search terms from one language into a second language. But what about the resulting hits: how can the user judge their relevance, and decide whether to terminate the search at this point or to revise the search strategy? Google again can provide help as it will try to translate the retrieved web pages from the document language to the user's language. Does this mean that all the problems of such cross-language searching have been eliminated? Unfortunately, the answer is no! Typically there are several drawbacks to such machine translation (MT) services: the quality of the translations cannot be guaranteed; it may be difficult to translate large blocks of text; and translation in all probability will only be available between a limited number of language pairs.

The ideal would be for such cross-language searches to be seamless from the user's perspective: search terms would be entered in, say, English, matched against French records in the digital library, and the resulting hits displayed in English. The ILO digital library could do this, as we saw above, but only when searching subject headings assigned by an indexer and linked through a thesaurus. A different approach is needed to search the titles, abstracts or the full texts of documents that have been automatically indexed.

One solution would be to translate the entire contents of any digital library into all the languages that might be necessary for their user community. Unfortunately, translation is a complex, challenging and slow task for humans to accomplish; it is therefore also very expensive. We have seen already that automatic indexing is faster and cheaper than human indexing, and therefore offers a solution to the problem of indexing large amounts of full-text information; might the computer likewise offer the answer to translation problems?

7.5.1 Machine translation

MT, the term used to describe the automatic translation by a computer of text in one language (the source language or SL) into a second language (the target language or TL), has been around since the 1950s. MT systems today are quite widely used by industry and government as well as by everyday web surfers. Yet for a number of reasons MT systems by themselves cannot provide a practical solution to multilingual access problems in digital libraries.

First, existing MT systems can only handle translations between relatively few language pairs, as we have already seen in the case of Google. MT systems are difficult and expensive to construct, and systems for many language translation pairs have not yet been built. Depending upon their particular design, they may require large digital dictionaries for the languages involved, very sophisticated syntactic and semantic analyses of these languages, or extensive collections (corpora) of reliable, existing translations made by human translators that can form the basis for the translation process. Those desiring more information on how MT works should consult an ageing but still valuable account by Hutchins and Somers (1992).

Second, the translations produced by MT systems are unlikely to be of the highest quality unless human translators have played a part in the process (either by pre-editing the SL or more likely post-editing the TL). Such machine-assisted translation, of course, increases costs and reduces translation speeds. Unfortunately, the long-term MT goal of fully automatic, high quality translation remains elusive; in practice, one or other of these objectives must be compromised. In some cases, of course, digital library users may be content to accept a low-quality translation – for example, where a technical article is required which the subject expert can understand even if the translation employs doubtful syntax and the occasional mistranslated word.

This leads us into the third problem; even the most enthusiastic MT proponents hardly will suggest it be used to translate Shakespeare's Sonnets or the poetry of Goethe, which tax the skills of the most talented human translators. Nor is MT suitable for translating, for example, legal texts where meaning is closely aligned with the precise manner in which it is expressed. MT systems are at their best when literary style is secondary to the task of conveying information content.

Finally, it is inefficient to use MT to translate an entire digital library's collection into all the languages in which users may require it because library user studies clearly demonstrate that while a small percentage of a collection will be heavily consulted, other parts will rarely or never be read in any language by any users. As a consequence, much of the translation effort will be wasted.

7.5.2 Cross-language information retrieval

This is not to say that MT has no significance for digital libraries. In fact, it can play an important ancillary role in cross-language information retrieval (CLIR), a process that most certainly does have relevance to digital libraries. CLIR allows users to input a search query in one language in order to retrieve documents written in a second language. In other words, a user can formulate a query in English but retrieve documents whose metadata or entire content are in, say, Swedish. As a minimum, a CLIR system must be able to:

- Accept a search query in the SL (a language with which the searcher is conversant).
- Translate that query into the TL (the language of the documents to be searched).
- Match the translated query against the TL document collection.
- Display the resulting hits to the user in such a way that the user can make relevance judgments, and decide to modify the search strategy if necessary.
- And perhaps (but not always) translate the retrieved documents – or parts of them – from the TL into the SL.

Translation may take place at the second, fourth and fifth steps. Digital library users may not necessarily require retrieved documents to be translated into their own language; it may be sufficient to translate only their initial search query. To formulate a search query it is necessary to encapsulate an information need into vocabulary that is suitable for the database content, and re-formulate it if initial results prove unsatisfactory. This can be taxing even for users in a monolingual environment, who must cope with the synonyms and homonyms present in all languages, and be ready to select broader or narrower terms in which to express their need. It is that much more difficult to do this in a second language: in some respects it can be likened to doing a crossword in a second language. Users therefore, perhaps ironically, may have the linguistic skills to extract information from retrieved documents in a foreign language, but not to construct the initial query in that language. Alternatively, the retrieved documents may be translated from the TL into the SL by a human rather than a computer.

Relevance judgments on any retrieved documents need not necessarily be made on the basis of their translation (or the translation of their metadata): users may be able to read them in their language of publication (as discussed above). Alternatively, visual rather than linguistic, techniques may be employed to aid user relevance judgments. For example, an experimental interface at the University of New Mexico (called the J24 interface after the 24 July deadline for its completion) employs thumbnail sketches (ten at a time) of retrieved documents to indicate graphically where in the document the query terms (highlighted) appear (Ogden and Davis, 2000). Though searchers cannot read the page (apart from their not being familiar with the language, the display is too small to be able to identify individual words), the number of times the terms appear on the page and their actual position (in the title, in the opening paragraph, and so on) apparently allow users to make quite accurate relevance decisions.

CLIR systems use several techniques to translate query terms into database terms:

- Bilingual or multilingual thesauri (as we have seen in the case of the ILO) through which controlled terms are converted from the query language to their semantic equivalent in the database language.
- Bilingual dictionaries to convert natural-language SL search terms into their TL equivalents in the database language.
- Semantic categorization of terms to help resolve homonyms in the SL (if *light* is a measure of heaviness then it will translate into French as *léger* and not *clair* or *feu*).
- Parallel corpora comprising a text or texts relevant to the contents stored in the CLIR database, that already have been translated (by professional translators) into both the languages of the CLIR system to produce two parallel texts. The search query is matched against the text in its language, in order to find parallel sections in the database-language text, using statistical best-match techniques. These can then be used to extract translation equivalents for the original query terms.

More detail on these techniques can be found in Grefenstette (1998), or in a more recent but briefer account by Savoy (2003).

Many MT systems also include complicated syntactic analysis routines that parse the sentences in a SL text in accordance with the grammatical rules for that language as a prelude to translation. Such analysis has a much less obviously useful role in the case of CLIR systems because typically the SL queries comprise only one or several words or phrases rather than well-formed sentences. MT systems normally are not interactive, but process entire texts, sentence by sentence, at one go. On the other hand, CLIR systems enjoy the advantage that normally users are present during the search. Retrieving information typically is an iterative process in which users respond to system feedback. The CLIR system can exploit this by presenting the user with options from which to choose when, for example, homonyms must be resolved. If the French word *puce* is entered as a keyword, the CLIR system might display two possible English translations: *flea* and *chip*; the French biologist conducting the search may know enough English to choose the first meaning rather than opt for a computer chip.

Despite considerable progress, CLIR faces several major obstacles:

- Although it tends to be simpler to translate individual terms rather than sentences (as MT systems typically must tackle), problems still arise with homonyms and with compound terms – for example, 'spark plug', should not be translated into French as *étincelle* (spark) and *bouchon* (plug) but as *bougie*, itself a homonym in French that can be translated into English as *candle* as well as *spark plug*.
- Dictionaries and thesauri, if used, must be comprehensive (for all relevant subject domains) and kept up-to-date – no easy task.
- The bilingual sets of corpora may be too small or insufficiently focused on the subject domain of the CLIR system to produce good translations. Parallel corpora are hard to come by and produce noisy results outside of the subject domain of the parallel texts.
- Proper names often should not be translated – so, for example, in an English-French CLIR system, the query *June Baker* should not be rendered as *Juin Boulanger*.
- If browsing rather than searching is employed, translation must work quickly enough to enable real-time equivalents of menus, hyperlinks, etc, to be displayed in the user's language

7.6 Searching Visual and Sound Sources

So far discussion of searching and browsing has been confined to digital libraries comprising text-based sources. Digital libraries, however, often contain multimedia collections: still images, videos and sound as well as text. These different media present special challenges for digital library designers and users alike. Responses to such challenges largely are confined to research projects and demonstration software, and in any case it is not possible here to present an extensive discussion of this topic. Nevertheless, it deserves our attention not only for what is currently possible, but for future developments in digital libraries' approaches to opening fully their multimedia collections. Visual content can be browsed, often via reduced-size thumbnail images that maximize the number of images displayed on any one page, thereby facilitating scanning. Sound clips can be browsed via sampling at specific time intervals. Such browsing techniques obviously will be more effective when the collections are relatively small.

In many cases, non-text documents can be described bibliographically, using metadata, without too much difficulty: typically (but not always) it will be relatively straightforward to identify their creator (akin to an author), title, date of creation, and so on. An example of such a metadata description of a collection of postcards at the National Library of Wales (http://www.llgc.org.uk) portraying the disaster in South Wales at the Senghennydd mine in 1901 – is shown in Figure 7.14. Such metadata can be assigned to collections of images (if not always to the individual images themselves), as well as to videos and recorded music. The textual metadata then can be searched in the same way as that for text documents. When we turn to subject indexing the actual images and sounds, however, the situation is rather more complex.

As in the case of text, information professionals can assign index terms to photographs, maps, videos, sound recordings, and so on, which then can be searched (or browsed) as would indexes to textual documents. Such terms can be taken from controlled vocabularies such as the Art and Architecture Thesaurus compiled by the Getty Research Center (http://www.getty.edu/research/tools/vocabulary/aat/about.html). Another example is provided by the Library of Congress (New Delhi office) South Asian Literary Recording Project that can be browsed by author name or country to retrieve sound clips of authors reading excerpts from their own works (http://www.loc.gov/acq/ovop/delhi/salrp/mulkrajanand.html). As we have already seen, indexing of text by information professionals is slow and expensive, and the depth of indexing achieved (the number of index terms assigned)

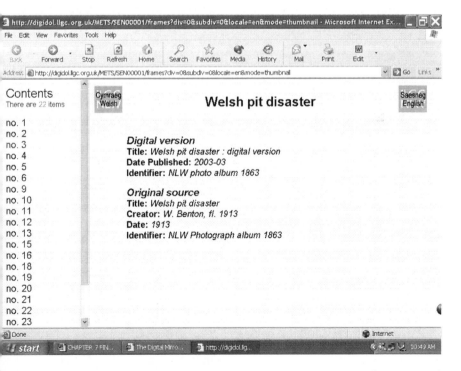

Figure 7.14 Metadata for Postcard Collection, Llyfrgell Genedlaethol Cymru/ National Library of Wales, UK (reproduced courtesy of The National Library of Wales)

typically is shallow. These problems are at least as great with non-textual information content, and may be exacerbated: for example, it is likely to prove more time consuming to verify the content of a documentary video than a printed book – an indexer can quickly scan the contents of a book, whereas a video requires special equipment to view, and cannot so easily be analyzed for subject content.

7.6.1 Automatic indexing of non-text material

The answer to such problems in the case of text, as we saw above, has been indexing by computers rather than human experts. Words in a text can be used to generate indexes that can be searched or browsed. Audio-visual documents may include some textual description – photographs, videos and sound recordings, for example, may be accompanied by titles and captions that can be indexed automatically much as any other text. Unfortunately this offers only a very partial answer to subject indexing problems. It will likely result in a very low specificity of indexing. A video playing for 90 minutes may have an accompanying text of two or three sentences; a collection of 500 photographs may have one generic text caption; a five-minute music clip described by its composer, title and date may contain thousands of notes and perhaps hundreds of spoken or sung words. Yet even a single photograph might require multiple pages of text fully to describe it (hence the adage, a picture is worth a thousand words!).

7.6.2 Automatic image indexing

Content-based image and video retrieval (CBIVR) relying upon indexing visual content – colour, texture, objects, shapes and movement – has attracted attention from researchers (Marques and Furht, 2002). There are search engines already that automatically can retrieve images by their content, but nevertheless the large commercial image systems are still using human indexers to select keywords for their images, even though their databases contain thousands or, in some cases, millions of images. Most successful CBIVR systems can only deal with particular objects that can be represented by precise geometric models, whereas to be really effective they must be able to recognize generic classes of objects and concepts (so that, for example, all images of sports cars can be found, rather than all cars or a specific make and model of car). A limited amount of work has been done in this respect, but no general methodology has yet emerged. Research to date demonstrates that designing a generic computer algorithm that can learn concepts from images and automatically translate their content into linguistic terms is extremely difficult (Li and Wang, 2003). Iqbal and Aggarwal (2003) find no clear consensus among researchers about which precise technique to use for general image retrieval systems. They think the answer depends on many factors, including the number and complexity of objects present in the image, the amount of *a priori* information the searcher has about the scene, and the number of images in the database.

Blobworld, at the University of California Berkeley Digital Library, is a demonstration version of a CBIVR system (http://elib.cs.berkeley.edu/ photos/blobworld). By automatically segmenting each image into regions comprising objects or parts of objects users can search for photographs based on the objects they contain. The example used here is a search for images of tigers. The first step is to select a tiger image from the Blobworld sample database (the selected image and its blob are shown on the top left of Figure 7.15). The user can adjust the blob according to several criteria such as colour, texture, location and shape. The 35,000 images are then ranked according to how well they match the blob, and the hits are displayed 20 at a time. In Figure 7.15 just the first six matches are shown, five of which are on target and show images of tigers. More information about Blobworld can be found in Carson et al (2002).

Another example can be found at the Advanced School for Computing and Imaging, Leiden University, in the Netherlands (http://ind156b.wi.leidenuniv.nl:2000/cgi-bin/FindImage.pl). Its database holds images of 21,094 Dutch portraits dating from 1860 to 1914. Users find portraits by clicking successively on displayed thumbnail images, at each stage choosing the one

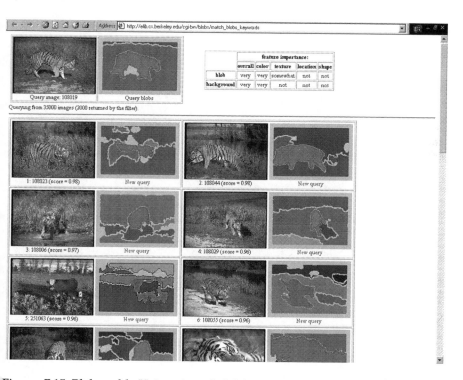

Figure 7.15 Blobworld, University of California Berkeley Digital Library, US (reproduced courtesy of Serge Belongie (University of California, San Diego), Jitendra Malik, Chad Carson and Robert Wilensky (University of California Berkeley))

that seems closest to that sought (thereby providing relevance feedback to the system), until eventually the required portrait is retrieved (Figure 7.16). In the case of video, the problems of retrieving images are compounded by the need to preselect specific shots of interest from the database, and to support the continuous presentation of time-dependent media. Thiel, Everts and Hollfelder (1999) summarize various research projects concerned with browsing and searching mechanisms to extract relevant information from video. One approach, at least in the case of documentary videos, is to utilize the sound track to index the images. Operational speech recognition systems are now encountered in various settings, but they work much better if the vocabulary spoken is limited, the syntactic structures employed are uncomplicated, and the range of speakers (and therefore accents) restricted. These conditions are unlikely to be satisfied with video documentary soundtracks. Fortunately, it seems that relatively high recognition failure rates (as high as 50%) may not greatly reduce recall and precision retrieval rates. Druid (http://parlevink.cs.utwente.nl/Projects/druid.html), developed at the University of Twente in the Netherlands, is an example of a system that utilizes automatic speech recognition, in this case to recognize continuous speech from different speakers of Dutch across a large vocabulary (it also has other video as well as audio applications). It generates transcripts from

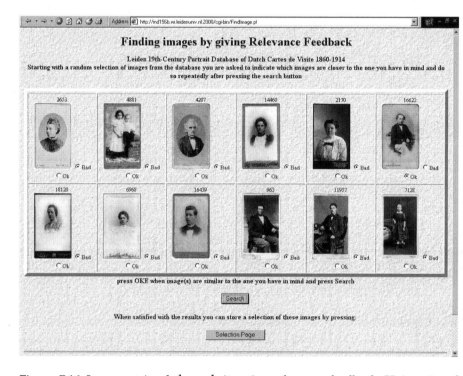

Figure 7.16 Image retrieval through iterative relevance feedback, University of Leiden Portrait Database, Netherlands (reproduced courtesy of the Leiden Institute for Advanced Computer Science)

videos, annotating them with time codes so that their precise location in the video can be established by a searcher. The textual transcripts can then automatically be indexed. Its designers report it has been extremely effective in locating relevant passages in documentaries. Similar text indexing can be undertaken, of course, on videos that have been provided with subtitles (either for various language communities or for the hard of hearing).

7.6.3 Automatic indexing of audio content

This leads us directly into searching and browsing audio content. In the case of speech, the kinds of recognition systems just discussed in the context of video can be applied with varying degrees of accuracy to transcribe and then index content. Music is a little different. Many music search engines also rely on textual retrieval using data such as file names, song titles, composers or performers; they do not make use of the musical content itself. Despite widespread interest from researchers, Byrd and Crawford (2002) in their useful overview remain pessimistic about effective, short-term solutions to the many problems faced in musical content retrieval. They describe music information retrieval as a "very immature field" that is decades behind text. Even when the query and the database are both in audio form and the query is an actual performance of the exact music desired, so much extraneous information is present (related to room acoustics and microphone placement as well as fine details of performance) that Byrd and Crawford believe the problem may be intractible. Music has no units of meaning equivalent to words in text: "the fundamental problem of audio music recognition is simply separating and recognizing the notes." Optical music recognition of printed sheet music is far from straightforward, and mistakes are common; in audio musical recognition "we must assume they will remain common . . . at least for many years to come". Birmingham et al (2002) describe MusArt, a retrieval system they are developing for musical content. The user sings, hums or plays a theme, hook or riff which the system transcribes before searching for related themes in the database, returning the most similar themes. The researchers concede, however, that using a computer to extract major themes from a piece of music is very difficult. More articles can be found on this topic in the Music Information Retrieval Research Bibliography (http://music-ir.org/research_home.html).

7.7 User Feedback on Searching and Browsing

Some feedback about search and browse capabilities is available from users of digital libraries. For example, 159 users of Early Canadiana Online, responded to a web-based questionnaire (this digital library provides access to more than 1,330,000 pages of Canada's printed heritage; a screen is reproduced in Figure 7.12). Almost 75% found the item they were seeking by using the search function, 10% followed a link from another site, and nine percent had used the item before and had bookmarked it. Some respondents commented upon navigability, requesting more links – for example, links from and to the Table of Contents. Respondents especially liked the full-text search capability (Cherry and Duff, 2002).

At the University of Illinois (a site for one of the initial Digital Library Initiative projects – see Chapter One) data from users of the digital library test bed (full-text journal articles) were collected via focus groups, interviews, observations, usability testing, transaction logs and surveys (Bishop et al, 2000). Between November 1997 and August 1998 around 2500 patron sessions were logged; about 30% used the browse facility only, and 70% performed at least one search. Most patrons searched "anywhere in the article" rather than specifying individual fields (the former was the default); a Boolean AND search was only conducted in about 30% of all sessions. About 70% of the searches were subject-based, and 30% were for known items such as an author, editor or title. The survey emphasizes the close relationship between searching and browsing behaviour, on the one hand, and interface design on the other. The researchers say that interface design problems contributed to lack of component use; some people did not use available features because they did not notice them or could not work out how to use them. The advanced search and display features available in the digital library were used only to a limited extent. In fact, the researchers conclude that "the basic convenience (ease of use and reliability) of desktop access to complete journal articles was the strongest motivator of use" of this digital library.

People who are trying to find information from digital libraries seem to exhibit similar search and browse characteristics to those who use other digital databases; rarely do they employ all the sophisticated techniques available to them from the system designers, but they appreciate the opportunity to access the widest possible range of documents (and therefore information) without encountering geographical barriers.

References

Birmingham, W., Pardo, B., Meek, C. and Shifrin, J. (2002) The MusArt music-retrieval system. *D-Lib Magazine* 8 (2). Available at: http://www.dlib.org/dlib/february02/birmingham/02birmingham.html

Bishop, A. P., Neumann, L. J., Star, S. L., Merkel, C., Ignacio, E. and Sandusky, R. J. (2000) Digital libraries: situating use in changing information infrastructure. *Journal of the American Society for Information Science,* **51** (4), 394–413

Byrd, D. and Crawford, T. (2002) Problems of music information retrieval in the real world. *Information Processing and Management,* **38** (2), 249–272

Carson, C., Belongie, S., Greenspan, H. and Malik, J. (2002) Blobworld: color- and texture-based image segmentation using EM and its application to image querying and classification. *IEEE Transactions on Pattern Analysis and Machine Intelligence,* **24** (8), 1026–1038

Cherry, J. M. and Duff, W. M. (2002) Studying digital library users over time: a follow-up survey of Early Canadiana Online. *Information Research* 7 (2). Available at: http://informationr.net/ir/7-2/paper123.html

Davies, R. (2003) Models for multilingual subject access in online library catalogues: the ILO experience. *Cross Language Applications and the Web: 27th Library Systems Seminar, Bern, Switzerland, 2–4 April 2003.* Available at: http://www.elag2003.ch/pres/pres_davies.pdf

Grefenstette, G., ed. (1998) *Cross-Language Information Retrieval.* Boston: Kluwer

Hudon, M. (1997) Multilingual thesaurus construction – integrating the views of different cultures in one gateway to knowledge and concepts. *Information Services and Use*, **17** (2/3), 111–123

Hutchins, W. J. and Somers, H. (1992) *Introduction to Machine Translation*. New York: Academic Press

Iqbal, Q. and Aggarwal, J.K. (2003) Feature integration, multi-image queries and relevance feedback in image retrieval. *6th International Conference on Visual Information Systems*, Miami, 24–26 September 2003. Available at: http://amazon.ece.utexas.edu/~qasim/papers/iqbal_visual03_HDR.pdf

Large, A., Tedd, L. A. and Hartley R.J. (1999) *Information Seeking in the Online Age: Principles and Practice*. London: Bowker

Li, J. and Wang, J. Z. (2003) Automatic linguistic indexing of pictures by a statistical modeling approach. *IEEE Transactions on Pattern Analysis and Machine Intelligence*, **25** (10). Available at: http://www-db.stanford.edu/~wangz/project/imsearch/ALIP/PAMI03

Liu, Y. Q. and Zhang, J. (2001) Digital library infrastructure: A case study on sharing information resources in China. *International Information and Library Review*, **33** (2–3), 205–220

Marchionini, G. (1998) Research and development in digital libraries. *Encyclopedia of Library and Information Science*, Volume 63. New York: Dekker, 259–279

Marques, O. and Furht, B. (2002) *Content-Based Image and Video Retrieval*. Boston: Kluwer

Ogden, W. C. and Davis, M. W. (2000) Improving cross-language text retrieval with human interactions. *Hawaii International Conference on System Sciences, HICSS-33, January 4–7, 2000*. Available at: http://crl.nmsu.edu/Research/Projects/tipster/ursa/Papers/Hawaii.doc

Pavani, A. M. B. (2001) A model of a multilingual digital library. *Ciência da Informação*, **30** (3), 73–81

Salton, G. (1971) Automatic processing of foreign language documents. In G. Salton, ed. *The SMART Retrieval System: Experiments in Automatic Document Processing*. Englewood Cliffs, NJ: Prentice-Hall, 206–219

Savoy, J. (2003) Cross-language information retrieval: experiments based on CLEF 2000 corpora. *Information Processing and Management*, **39** (1), 75–115

Thiel, U., Everts, A. and Hollfelder, S. (1999) *Beyond Similarity Searching: Concept-Based Video Retrieval and Browsing*. Darmstadt: German National Research Center for Information Technology. Available at: http://www.darmstadt.gmd.de/~everts/delos99

Chapter 8

Practical Issues

8.1 The Management of Change

In this Chapter a number of practical issues related to the implementation of digital libraries will be discussed. Anyone involved with implementing a digital library system has to embrace 'change management' as well as the more technical management aspects. Issues covered by the phrase 'change management' include:

- the need to understand change;
- strategic approaches to change;
- flexible structures related to change;
- selecting change strategies;
- planning and implementing change projects
- aspects of the local organizational requirements and the human factors affecting the staff that change managers need to know.

Geyer (2002) provides an overview of how information technology has altered management practices in many organizations. She notes that:

> perhaps no profession has been more enabled to improve service reach and richness than the library profession. Every library has been challenged to meet the increasing demands of an Internet empowered society while maintaining and stabilizing traditional methods.

As an example of an organization that has adopted appropriate change management strategies she cites OCLC in implementing its CORC

(Cooperative Online Resource Catalog) service that enables libraries to select, organize and describe quality websites. Much collaboration was needed between the 489 volunteers in 24 countries, and the Chief Executive Officer of OCLC reported that the change management strategy was based on "common sense, experience and a willingness to experiment and take risks." In dealing with technologically driven change libraries are faced with many challenges including those of decreasing budgets and the availability of information sources in a variety of formats. The key aspect to managing successful digital library systems in this changing global environment is to have a dedicated and skilled set of employees. Indeed this is true of managing any new project or system.

Many of the organizations involved in training staff for working with digital libraries realize the key role that change management has in the development of a digital library environment and include modules on this subject. Examples include:

- the International Summer school on the Digital Library – held annually, since 1996, at the University of Tilburg in the Netherlands and which involves top managers from libraries in various countries sharing their experiences with course participants (http://www.ticer.nl).
- The International Centre for Information Management and Systems (ICIMSS) in Torun, Poland which has provided a range of training opportunities, since 1997, for those involved (mainly in Central and Eastern Europe) in the management of cultural institutions (such as libraries, archives, and museums) with particular attention being devoted to the development of digital libraries (http://www.icimss.edu).

Change management also featured, for example, as one of the modules in the training provided for Slovakian librarians in the European Union (EU)-funded PROLIB project during 1999–2001 (Dahl et al., 2002).

8.2 Users' Needs

Ideally, before the design and implementation of any new system, including a digital library, the needs of potential users should be analyzed. Wright, Marlino and Sumner (2002) describe the development of a community digital library known as the Digital Library for Earth System Education (DLESE) that had a community of users define and guide its development. They note that DLESE enables users to "share, organize and assess their intellectual holdings" and has a mission to "fundamentally change the way students learn, instructors teach and researchers interact by providing new ways of sharing information, tools and services." In order to achieve this a range of users (from the grass-roots) has been involved in the design of the digital library and then in its continued maintenance, initially via a grant from the National Science Foundation (NSF) in the US in 1998. Figure 8.1 shows the DLESE homepage (http://www.dlese.org) and the range of digital information sources for different user groups.

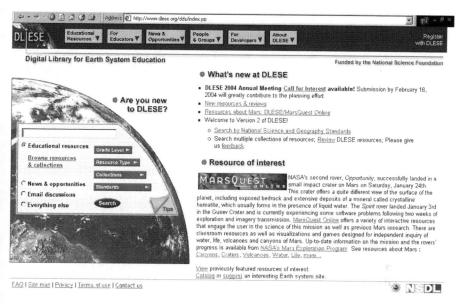

Figure 8.1 Homepage, Digital Library for Earth System Education (reproduced with courtesy of DLESE)

Many staff in libraries and related organizations have experience in assessing users' needs in the context of traditional library services, and developing a digital library should follow along similar lines. In developing a user needs assessment for collection development Biblarz et al. (2002) suggest the following stages:

• Establish the goals – what exact needs of users are to be investigated?
• Assess available resources – who will carry out the analysis and what will it cost?
• Establish the scope of the user needs assessment – what data? what users? over what time?
• Investigate methods of carrying out the assessment.
• Carry out the assessment.
• Analyze the results and prepare a report.

A slightly different approach is described by the University Librarian at Deakin University in Australia (McKnight, 2002). Following a description of the agents for cultural change in academic libraries (including demanding users, ICT developments, budget constraints, changes in scholarly publishing, need to support teaching and curriculum development) as well as broader issues such as the globalization of higher education, she outlines the customer discovery workshops that have been held for various customer groups (undergraduate, postgraduate (taught), postgraduate(research), off-campus students, academic staff). This approach of focusing primarily on user needs has helped in the management of change and restructuring of her staff that, in turn, she believes will provide improved services for her users.

In developing the National electronic Library for Health (NeLH) in the UK a prototyping approach was used to develop a pilot NeLH. This involved assessing user requirements, testing the product, acquiring feedback and refining the product to meet the needs of the users (Turner et al., 2002). One outcome was the development of different portals for different health professional user groups. Figure 8.2 shows the portal for speech therapists with links to key websites (such as *Speech and Language in Practice Magazine*, a database on bilingualism and an autism website) shown on the right hand side of the screen.

There are many ways in which the needs of users may be assessed: questionnaires, interviews, focus groups and so on. However, in carrying out such an assessment it is often a good idea also to find out the needs of non-users – that is those who do not make use of any existing services provided by the library and information unit within an organization – and attempt to discover how a digital library service may be developed to meet their needs.

The general cycle in the implementation of any technology-based system, including a digital library, can be thought of as: planning; requirement specification; selection; installation; running and evaluation and these will be described in the following sections.

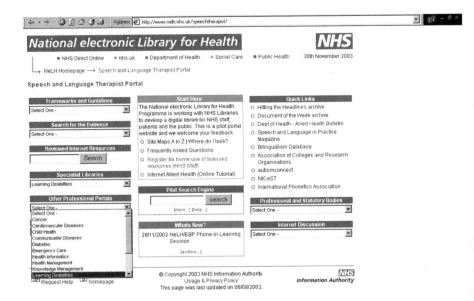

Figure 8.2 Speech and language therapist portal, National electronic Library for Health, UK (reproduced courtesy of the NHS Information Authority)

8.3 Planning

The amount of time spent in planning the implementation of a digital library will vary depending on the type of digital library application and on the parent organization. In developing a digitized collection of existing physical objects the project may well be starting 'from scratch'. In the development of an improved system to control the management of serials and provide online access to the full text of articles, the plans for a new system may impact on other systems and require development of existing systems. The costs involved may also vary greatly and in some circumstances rigorous institutional procedures may have to be followed when acquiring systems. Cohn, Kelsey and Fiels (2001) provide advice for librarians on planning integrated systems and technologies, especially using library management systems (as described briefly in Chapter Five) and explain how these are evolving to enable access to a range of digital information sources.

Formal project planning is a key essential for managing any technology-based project. Tanner (2001) notes that studies of failed technology-based projects (and there have been many) show that about a third are because of inadequate project management and control, a third because of ill-defined objectives and the rest fail because of problems in the communication of ideas between project members; only a minority of projects fail because of the technology itself. One early outcome of the planning of a digital library project usually is a feasibility study. This comprises a formal study to ascertain the advantages, disadvantages, timings and outline costs of the proposed new system so that the appropriate management committee (or person (s)) can schedule the required economic and staff resources. Such a study might be undertaken 'inhouse' or external consultants may carry it out. For instance, the JISC-funded HEDS, referred to in Chapter Three, provides consultancy and production services for digitization and digital resource development and management to a range of organizations including museums, galleries, public and national libraries, archives and other not-for-profit organizations in a number of countries. In particular, HEDS' consultancy services offer feasibility and evaluation studies relating to the design and setting up of digitization units. An example of a feasibility study carried out by HEDS staff for the JISC Image Digitization Initiative is available on its website (http://heds.herts.ac.uk/resources/papers/jidi_fs.html).

8.4 Requirement Specification

Following the feasibility study a full system specification, sometimes also called an operational requirement (OR), will need to be written that will specify in detail the functionality of the digital library system.

The needs of users are taken into account at this stage. Frawley (2003) describes the process of specifying the requirements for the Electronic Library for Northern Ireland (ELFNI) project established to procure, on behalf of five separate public library authorities a system to support and enable the delivery of digital information services to Northern Ireland. The project team took into account the needs of the staff working in the libraries and made a full analysis of all existing services and desired new services. In addition, consultations were also held with representatives from trades unions, library users or potential users, including disability groups, Age Concern (a British support organization for people aged 50 and above) and ethnic minority groups to ensure that the services proposed by ELFNI would pass all equality measures and were in keeping with the expectations of the public. The result, a detailed Output Based Specification, became one of the primary tools informing the negotiations between the project team and prospective service providers.

Many of the digital library systems referred to in this book have bilingual or multilingual interfaces. When planning a digital archive of Russian émigré documents for the Museum of Russian Culture, staff at the Hoover Institution Library and Archives at Stanford University in California were aware that the prime users would be researchers of Russian history worldwide, followed by students working on the history of migration and then members of the public, possibly doing genealogical research. It was therefore decided that the whole website should be bilingual in Russian and English. The designer of the website studied other Russian/English bilingual websites in depth before creating two identical sites in Russian and English (Ilieva, 2003). Her objective was to make the site easy to navigate and search in both Russian and English. Figure 8.3 shows the homepage of this digital archive (http://www.hoover.org/hila/ruscollection/).

The outcome of this requirements specification stage is usually a report detailing the mandatory requirements as well as the desirable features of the digital library system. Such a specification would then be used either for negotiation with external suppliers or with inhouse developers of the new system.

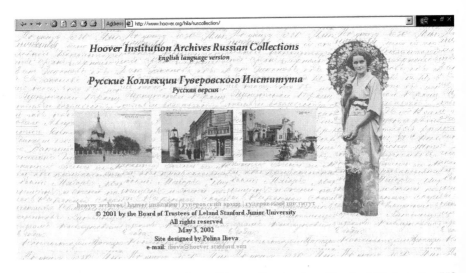

Figure 8.3 Bilingual digital archive, Hoover Institution, Stanford University, US (reproduced courtesy of Hoover Institution Library and Archives and web designer Poliena Ilieva)

8.5 Selection

Details of software options for organizing access to digital information sources and developing digital libraries were given in Chapter Five. Likewise, content providers may offer products that could be considered for use within the digital library as described in Chapter Three. When choosing a particular software system or service provider a number of factors need to be considered. Cost is often a very important criterion, not only the initial costs of setting up the new system/service but also the ongoing costs of maintaining it. Staff time needed to ensure the system is working satisfactorily is also a very important factor to be considered. Other factors include:

- Is the product capable of meeting the mandatory needs specified?
- How many of the desired needs will be met by the product?
- Are the standards used within the product appropriate? (Details of standards for digital libraries were covered in Chapter Four).
- Is the user interface appropriate and easy to use and available in the necessary range of languages? (Details of user interface issues were provided in Chapter Six). If the required language is not available, how challenging would it be to develop the interface in that language. For instance, having decided to acquire Endeavor's Voyager system and needing to have a bilingual (Welsh/English) interface, staff at the University of Wales Aberystwyth developed a Welsh language version of the interface.
- What features are available for searching and browsing the information contained within the digital library? (Details of searching and browsing features were covered in Chapter Seven).
- What have been the experiences of other similar institutions in using this product? In using open source software the extra 'knowledge' needed by staff within the institution to enable that software to be implemented can be considerable. Gaining feedback from other institutions about their experiences can be very helpful.
- What is the reputation of the organization providing the product?
- What is the reputation of the local supplier? In instances where the product is developed by an organization in one country it may be made available in other countries by a regional or national agency.
- What support is available in terms of training, documentation and online help, and is this available in the appropriate language?
- What are the legal implications of using the product? In many cases the legal department of the institution may need to be involved in checking the licence/guarantee of service or other legal documents regarding the acquisition of the product.

In some countries national agencies provide advice and may suggest a similar solution for all libraries within the country. The development of digital libraries has happened speedily and often the range of expertise is limited, so it makes sense to share what expertise is available. Brief details of consortial possibilities are described in a later section.

8.6 Installation

Installing a digital library system can be a lengthy process and it is important not to underestimate the time scales needed for all the tasks. Sometimes the digital library will be implemented in stages and this is exemplified by the case study on the Open University (OU) Library (described in Chapter Nine). Another approach, also exemplified in the OU Library case study, is to 'pilot' a new service with a limited set of users. In that case the MyLibrary software was piloted with students in a limited number of modules. There are a number of other issues, of which the following are probably the most important.

8.6.1 Health and safety issues

The physical aspects relating to the siting of workstations within the library building (cabling, lighting, noise control, suitable ergonomically designed furniture) must be considered during the installation phase as well as specific health and safety issues related to the use of workstations. Different countries will have differing legislation and the US Occupational Safety and Health Administration (http://www.osha.gov/SLTC/etools/computerworkstations/checklist.html) provides a checklist of issues to consider when evaluating the current working environment as well as when purchasing a new workstation. Issues covered include:

- ideal positions for working postures when at workstations (thighs parallel to the floor – no crossed legs);
- seating (there should be support for the lower back);
- input device (the mouse should be easy to activate and of a suitable size);
- work area (the desk should be deep enough to accommodate a monitor placed at least 20″ from the user's eyes).

Those installing a digital library system will need to consider the needs of the full-time employees of the institution as well as members of the public who may make use of services provided by the digital library on the premises of the organization, rather than remotely via a network. Aspects that need to be considered by public libraries in providing Internet access for their users are discussed by Sturges (2002). These include ethical, legal, and policy making issues as well as management aspects. Details of the Council of Europe guidelines on *Public Access and Freedom of Expression in Networked Information*, which Sturges helped to compile, are also included in this text.

8.6.2 Training

Relevant staff will need to receive training in the new system and the services provided. In implementing the People's Network in UK public libraries, money was made available to ensure that all staff (professional and other) undertook training prior to the installation of the public Internet access workstations in all the 4,000 libraries (http://www.peoplesnetwork.gov.uk/training/index.asp). After a study of the ICT needs of public library staff the following topics were covered in the training programme undertaken from 2001 to 2004 by all staff working in UK public libraries:

- a grounding in core ICT fundamentals;
- understanding how ICT can support library staff in their work;
- health and safety and legal issues in the context of ICT;
- knowing how to find things out on behalf of users;
- using ICT to support reader development activities;
- using ICT to support users to ensure effective learning;
- ensuring effective management of ICT resources in libraries;
- knowing how to use ICT to improve their own professional efficiency and to reduce administrative and bureaucratic burdens.

The basic skills were acquired in many cases through training for the ECDL, as described in Chapter Two. More specific library-related matters were covered by specialist training programmes. In addition, more advanced training was undertaken by some staff who were to assume the following roles:

- *Net Navigator* – more advanced searching skills, validating websites and use of alerting services;
- *Information Technology Gatekeeper* – web design skills, mounting and updating information, setting up and managing databases;
- *Information Consultant* – analysis and diagnosis of users' needs, awareness of information sources, building partnerships with other information providers, information design and presentation;
- *Information Manager* – strategic planning, digitization issues, copyright, intellectual property rights;
- *Educator* – design and development of training courses and materials for other staff and users.

Details of how such training was provided for staff in some of the public libraries in Wales, which included the development of bilingual (Welsh/ English) open-learning course packs are described by Tedd (2003).

8.6.3 Documentation and help

Good documentation and help is important both for those involved in running the digital library service and for those using it. This may be in print or, most likely, online and often help is in the form of answers to Frequently Asked Questions (FAQs). For instance, the help provided by the iConn Connecticut Digital Library (http://www.iconn.org/help.html) that provides access to popular and scholarly articles (from 1980 to the present) as well as e-newspapers, business information on over 450,000 companies and health information for students and residents in the US State of Connecticut is in the form of answers to questions:

- How do I use the iCONN databases from my college, school or public library?
- What if I can't access one of the iCONN databases?

The OU in the UK, which is one of the case studies in Chapter Nine, provides a wide range of help for its users including a guided tour of the website, a tutorial on information skills and detailed search guides for specific databases (http://library.open.ac.uk/sitemap.htm#help). Further examples of help screens are shown in Chapter Six: FAQs at the SPIE Digital Library in Fig. 6.10 and the Quick Tour of the Kentucky Virtual Library in Fig. 6.11. It is important that printed help and online documentation is in a language which most of the users can understand.

8.6.4 Authentication, authorization and access

Many digital libraries are freely available and can be used by anyone in the world with the appropriate access technology. Indeed the reasoning behind the development of many of the museum and archive digital collections is to widen the range of users and provide worldwide access. In other cases, however, organizations have acquired (often by paying large amounts of money) the right to license information sources in their digital libraries that can be accessed only by their own users. Here, it is necessary to ensure that a specific user has the necessary identification (authentication); based on this (and possibly other information) it will be necessary to determine what privileges the user has in order to be able to use the resources of the digital library (authorization). One solution is to allow users to access each resource within the digital library via a specific user name and password. Many digital libraries include collections of digital information sources from a range of suppliers and users do not wish to remember a number of different access keys, passwords or usernames. A solution adopted within the UK for students in further and higher education is known as the access management system – ATHENS (http://www.athens.ac.uk). ATHENS was first used in 1996 and enables students who may be registered at a UK university but studying abroad to access the appropriate information resources of the university's digital library. JISC funds research in this area and a programme scheduled to run until late 2004 covers Authentication, Authorization and Accounting issues (http://www.jisc.ac.uk/index.cfm?name=programme_aaa). ATHENS is also used by institutions in the health sector in the UK as well as institutions in Ireland and Scandinavia.

Some institutions have implemented systems where only one log-in procedure is necessary in order to link to all their digital information sources even if the sources physically are located in different institutional homes (all with their own log-in procedures). International standards are being developed that allow for such interoperability. For instance, users in libraries that have implemented the Sirsi Unicorn library management system can, following successful authentication procedures that enable access to basic sources such as the library's catalogue, be linked to other digital information sources such as OCLC FirstSearch's databases. This linkage is possible because both organizations have adopted the NISO Circulation Interchange Protocol (NCIP). NCIP is the approved US National Standard Z39.83–2003 that promotes interoperability of circulation systems and similar applications from different vendors by providing a standardized mechanism for information exchange and communication.

8.6.5 Security issues

The hardware, software and content – either as bought-in materials or inhouse digitized materials – will have cost a lot of money and possibly time and effort to develop. It is therefore necessary to consider security issues – for the physical equipment, the software and the digital information. Antivirus software needs to be installed, kept up-to-date and used to check all incoming files. Firewall software can be used to prevent unauthorized users from accessing and tampering with individual files.

Once the new digital library has been tested and is proved to be working satisfactorily, and some staff are ready to use it, then the next phase of running the system can begin.

8.7 Running

An important process that must be defined and implemented when running the digital library system is backing-up relevant files, databases, websites and software that have been generated within the institution as part of the digital library system. The back-up is a copy of the file, database, website or software that can be used if the original is destroyed by software failure, hardware failure, human error, fire, water, earthquake or vandalism. In many situations the digital library will provide access to digital information sources from organizations outside the institution and in this case the responsibility for keeping appropriate back-up copies lies with the information provider. The back-up system policy needs to be appropriate for the material covered and easy for staff to implement. The back-up policies for the servers at the Digital Library Research Group, Old Dominion University in Norfolk, Virginia in the US (http://dlib.cs.odu.edu/ims/policies.htm) has instructions such as:

- Complete database is backed up from the production server once a week on a Thursday
- All the webpages on the development server are backed up once a week on a Friday

Inevitably while running a digital library system there will be changes as new digital information sources become available from different suppliers, standards may alter, staff may change, new technologies may appear, users' needs may alter, software may be updated or revised, and so on. Knowing how and when to incorporate these changes into the day-to-day running of the digital library can present a challenge for the manager of the digital library. Tanner (2001) notes that risk and resource management is another key essential for any technology-based project and that this involves being able to achieve the project objectives whilst controlling the risk factors that might threaten the project's success.

Users need to be made aware of the facilities available from the digital library and trained in their use. Various techniques can be adopted for marketing the services from a digital library including the production of brochures, announcements on local media (such as television and radio) or broadcast over the institution's intranet, links/information from the institution's website and so on. NeLH (pronounced Nellie), which provides health professionals throughout the UK with access to a wide variety of digital information sources, ran a NeLH awareness week in late 2003 with the aim of helping health professionals and managers to get the most out of health digital libraries. One technique adopted, and which proved to be popular, was free ten-minute phone-in learning sessions where librarians and trainers were able to explain the information sources available and how they might be used to best effect. NeLH is considered to be a success, with some 6,000 individuals accessing it daily. Nevertheless work is in progress in developing an improved search interface (http://www.nelh.nhs.uk/lab/).

The type of training will vary depending on the organization, human and monetary resources available and the type of users. In many academic institutions self-guided tutorials are available for students to find out how to search various digital information sources. The Virtual Training Suite of the Resource Discovery Network in the UK provides tutorials in a range of subjects as shown in Figure 8.4 and incorporates links to appropriate websites for that subject (http://www.vts.rdn.ac.uk). Such tutorials are obviously not linked to a specific digital library but can provide useful general assistance in searching digital information sources.

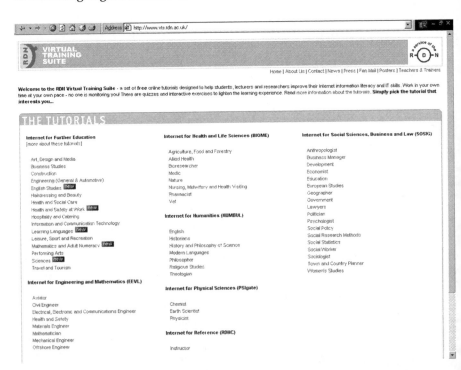

Figure 8.4 Tutorials available, Virtual Training Suite, Resource Discovery Network, UK (reproduced courtesy of Institute for Learning and Research Technology, University of Bristol)

Sometimes workbooks, which might be accessible online for consulting or printing, are produced so that users can work their way through examples from one or more specific digital information source(s). At the University of Leeds in the UK, for instance, a workbook to assist users in searching the ACM Digital Library has been produced (http://www.leeds.ac.uk/library/documents/workbook/acmdl.pdf).

8.8 Evaluation

Evaluation should be an important part of implementing any digital library. However, as with many other technology-based projects in libraries and similar institutions, evaluation is a stage that often has been omitted. There can be various reasons for this:

- no-one asks for an evaluation of the system;
- there were no explicit goals set for the implementation of the system;
- there are no suitable staff to carry out the evaluation and no-one wishes to risk their reputation;
- fear of drawing attention to a system's defects soon after expending great amounts of time, money and collective energy in implementing the system;
- there is no money for an evaluation.

User evaluation techniques adopted for other kinds of library service can be applied to digital libraries. Typically these comprise questionnaires, interviews and, possibly, focus groups. Another approach is to analyse the computer 'logs' of all user transactions within the digital library. Transaction logs, which show exactly how the users communicated instructions to the computer, have the advantage of showing exactly what the users did, rather than what they say they did. Furthermore, all transactions can be fairly easily analyzed for any chosen time period, no matter how many there are. The drawback to the use of transaction logs is that there is, usually, no information about who the users are and what they are trying to do. Researchers have analyzed the user logs of the digital library at the Los Alamos National Research Laboratory in order to study research trends (Bollen et al., 2003).

Chowdhury and Chowdhury (2003) in a chapter on digital library evaluation provide details of some evaluation studies that have been carried out and conclude: "However, since digital library research is at an early stage, and digital libraries themselves are still evolving, not many evaluation studies have taken place so far. Most evaluation studies conducted to date have focused on the usability aspects of digital libraries."

Saracevic (2000) notes that it is recognized that digital library evaluation is an especially difficult and complex undertaking given the recent emergence of digital libraries and their development within both the research community and the practice community. He expands on the general What? How? and Why? questions that are normally asked in any evaluation to provide a more detailed framework of questions to be posed by those carrying out an evaluation of a digital library. These include:

- Construct for the evaluation. What to evaluate? What is actually meant by a digital library? What elements should be involved in the evaluation?
- Context of evaluation. What should be the level of the evaluation?
- Criteria. What parameters of performance should be covered?
- Measures. What specific measures should be used for a specific criterion?
- Methodology. What measuring instrument should be used? What sampling? What processes for data collection? What data analysis?

Work continues on developing strategies for the evaluation of digital libraries. An annual series of workshops has been held (the fifth was in Norway in 2003), funded by the National Science Foundation in the US and the European Union Delos Network of Excellence on Digital Libraries (http://www.delos-noe.org) to investigate the metrics, testbeds and processes for digital library evaluation.

8.9 Consortia

Many of the information sources made available through a digital library will not be owned directly by the organization implementing the digital library but will be licensed for use from the publishers of the information sources. Some organizations form consortia to license one or more digital information sources. As Harris (2002) states, "Consortia may, but do not necessarily, save libraries money on licensing fees, but they can make the same amount of money go much further. They can also benefit libraries by saving time and legal costs in negotiating licences and in sharing negotiating experiences". Consortia can operate on a regional, national or multinational basis.

8.9.1 Regional consortia

One example of a regional consortium is OhioLink – the Ohio Library and Information Network (http://www.ohiolink.edu) – a consortium of Ohio's college and university libraries and the State Library of Ohio in the US. OhioLink started in 1992 as a union catalogue system for its members and now serves about 600,000 students and faculty and staff at 84 institutions by also providing access to some 4,700 ejournals from 34 publishers or providers, 100 abstracting and indexing reference databases and 14,000 ebooks.

8.9.2 National consortia

There are many examples of national consortia for licensing and a brief description of a few are given here.

a) Finland
FinELib (Finnish Electronic Library – http://www.lib.helsinki.fi/finelib/english/index.html) provides consortial services for the acquisition of some 6,000 full-text ejournals and 90 reference databases used in the country's

higher education and research institutions. The wide variety of sources available from this digital library is well illustrated in Figure 8.5 which shows just some of the available titles. The interface to the FinELib website is available in Finnish, English and Swedish.

b) Slovenia
With a population of two million, Slovenia is one of the smallest countries in Europe. All libraries (public, school, academic, special) use the same generic library management system – COBISS (Cooperative Online Bibliographic System and Services). The origins of COBISS go back to 1982 (when Slovenia was part of Yugoslavia) and staff at the Institute of Information Science (IZUM) at the University of Maribor developed a shared cataloguing system which, by the time of the disintegration of Yugoslavia in 1991, was used by 55 institutions. Staff at IZUM have continued to develop COBISS and now organize consortium agreements with publishers so that users within Slovenia can gain access to a number of databases such as those from OCLC FirstSearch, Swets and ProQuest (http://cobiss.izum.si).

c) South Korea
The development, since 1995, of digital libraries in South Korea is described by Choi (2003). The Korean Education Research and Information Service (KERIS) was set up in 1999 to provide a range of education information

Figure 8.5 Information sources, FinELib consortium, Finland

systems to 70 universities and research institutions in the country (http://www.keris.or.kr). In particular, KERIS is involved with nationwide resource sharing of full-text, Korean-language academic journals, theses and dissertations as well as the licensing of material from overseas publishers such as OCLC FirstSearch, netLibrary, CSA and the ACM.

d) UK
JISC has funded specialist centres to host a variety of digital information sources which are made available through consortial agreements. For instance, MIMAS (the Manchester Information and Associated Services) provides British higher education, further education and research communities with networked access to a range of databases to support teaching, learning and research in many disciplines (http://www.mimas.ac.uk).

8.9.3 Multinational consortia

One example of a consortium in this category is eIFL (Electronic Information for Libraries). According to its website eIFL is an independent foundation that:

> strives to lead, negotiate, support and advocate for the wide availability of electronic resources by library users in transition and developing countries. Its main focus is on negotiating affordable subscriptions on a multi-country basis, while supporting the enhancement of emerging national library consortia in member countries (http://www.eifl.net).

eIFL started in 1999 as an initiative of OSI in assisting libraries and their users in Eastern Europe and the former Soviet republics to gain affordable access to scholarly digital information sources. It has negotiated with a number of digital information sources providers (including Blackwell, Cambridge University Press, Ebsco, Highwire Press, the Institute of Physics and ProQuest) for the provision of access to their products.

Multinational consortia can also be formed by organizations involved in a common subject area. For instance, staff in the 16 library and information centres of the Consultative Group on International Agricultural Research (CGIAR) have formed a Library and Information Services Consortium (Ramos, Soeripto and Ali, 2003). The Consortium has implemented a number of initiatives such as exchange of publications, interlibrary lending, and the production of a web-based union catalogue of serials as well as licensing of digital information sources from publishers such as the American Chemical Society, Cambridge University Press, Oxford University Press and the National Research Council of Canada.

8.10 Intellectual Property Rights

Libraries, museums and galleries involved in implementing digital libraries inevitably have to be aware of the relevant intellectual property rights

(IPR) that apply to the creation, storage and dissemination of digital information sources. The World Intellectual Property Organization (WIPO) defines intellectual property as:

> creations of the mind: inventions, literary and artistic works, and symbols, names, images, and designs used in commerce. Intellectual property is divided into two categories: industrial property, which includes inventions(patents), trademarks, industrial designs, and geographic indications of source; and copyright, which includes literary and artistic works such as novels, poems and plays, films, musical works, artistic works such as drawings, paintings, photographs and sculptures, and architectural designs. Rights related to copyright include those of performing artists in their performances, producers of phonograms in their recordings, and those of broadcasters in their radio and television programs. (http://www.wipo.int/about-ip/en/).

Copyright legislation has two main purposes:

* to encourage those who originate creative works to continue to do so by enabling them to earn a revenue from their effort;
* to offer the copyright holder control over how the copyrighted work can be used.

The history of copyright legislation can be traced back to 1662 when the concept of copyright was developed to protect publishers against piracy following the technological advances of the day which enabled cheap and easy printing of books. The world's first copyright legislation was the Statute of Anne in London in 1709 which introduced the concepts of the author being owner of the copyright of created work and there being a fixed term of protection for published works. In addition there was a legal obligation for copies of published books in England to be deposited in certain libraries including those at the universities of Oxford and Cambridge. Later relevant international copyright legislation includes the Berne Convention (http://www.cerebalaw.com/berne.htm) of 1886 with a number of amendments and the Universal Copyright Convention of Unesco of 1952 and its amendment of 1971 (http://www.unesco.org/culture/laws/copyright/html_eng/page1.shtml).
Here is some basic information about copyright:

* Registration is unnecessary – a created work is considered to be protected by copyright as soon as it exists.
* Many countries have their own Copyright Office and Copyright Laws.
* Works become 'out of copyright' after a specific period (often 50 or 70 years but this is country dependent) of either the publication of the work or death of the creator (again this is country dependent).
* A creative work may have more than one copyright holder. For instance, a film has a director, actors, music composers, musicians and so on, all of whom may hold copyright.

- Much copyright legislation is in the process of being updated to deal with digital information sources and access.

Baker and McKenzie (2002) in an overview of IPR legislation in the CONSAL (Congress of South East Asian Librarians) countries include tables showing some of the differences between these countries. Here is an example, taken from Baker and McKenzie, of the variation by country relating to copyright for photographs:

Berne Convention: at least 25 years from making the photograph
Brunei: Life of author plus 50 years
Indonesia: 25 years after publication
Malaysia: Life of author plus 50 years
Myanmar: 50 years from making of original negative
Philippines, Singapore, Thailand: 50 years after publication
Vietnam: Life of author plus 50 years

Implementers of digital libraries have to be aware of copyright legislation with respect to various information sources, including those developed locally as part of the digital library as well as those acquired from other organizations. As Lee (2000) states:

> . . . to the project manager copyright works in both ways: on the one hand, institutions involved in digitization need to be certain that they are operating within the law when it comes to capturing material, but the other side of the coin is that they will also want to feel that there is some attempt being made to safeguard their own rights when the images are eventually delivered.

In dealing with the first question there may be one of several situations:

- the material is out of copyright;
- the material is in copyright and the rights to re-use it are securable;
- the material is in copyright and the rights to re-use it are difficult to obtain or unknown.

The time taken to investigate and secure copyright clearance for items to be digitized can be lengthy and should not be under-estimated, as it could account for a significant cost in a digitization project. Many digitization projects concentrate on material to which the institution owns the rights or on material which is out of copyright according to the legislation of that country. For example at the National Library of Wales, a case study in Chapter Nine, a general policy adopted is that digitization that is likely to lead to IPR difficulties will be avoided. Organizations providing advice on digitization also include advice on copyright issues: for instance TASI provides much information on copyright with respect to digital image collections within the UK. Secker and Plewes (2002) report on research undertaken at University College London on the costs of producing electronic study packs, which included obtaining copyright clearance of items to be placed in the packs. It was generally found to be very advantageous if staff with appropriate knowledge of copyright law and the process of obtaining permissions were involved; otherwise the time taken (and therefore the cost) could be high. Some material was made available free of charge for digitizing whereas one publisher wanted over 900 euros for one digitized article. Figure 8.6 shows the copyright information from the University of Cape Town Library regarding use of photographs from the Dorothy Bleek collection (http://www.lib.uct.ac.za/mss/existing/DBleekXML/website/index.htm#View_agreement).

Another solution adopted by many institutions wishing to protect the rights of material which they have digitized is digital watermarking. This technique enables a digital code to be embedded in audio, image, video or printed items that have been digitized. The digital watermark is imperceptible during normal use but can be detected by special software. The technology for this is available from companies such as Digimarc (http://www.digimarc.com). Royan (2000), for instance, describes the use of digital watermarking in the SCRAN project in Scotland. SCRAN is a not-for-profit company involved in the creation and delivery of the networked learning content, and in the management of the IPR. Royan comments that "perhaps

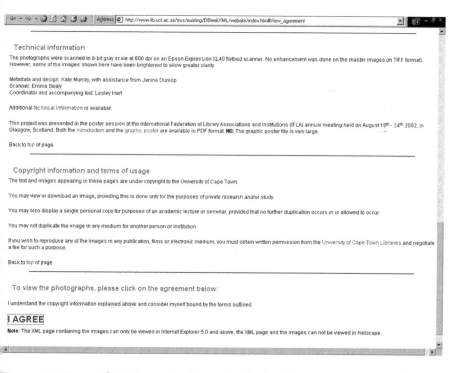

Figure 8.6 Copyright information, Dorothy Bleek collection of photographs from the University of Cape Town Library, South Africa (reproduced courtesy of the University of Cape Town)

the single greatest obstacle to the creation and use of digital content is uncertainty over copyright issues, and in particular a fear that the new technologies may facilitate intellectual property theft". Another example of the use of digital watermarks is at the Digital Islamic Library in Malaysia (http://www.digitalislamiclibrary.com). Ensuring the authenticity and originality of multimedia digital content is of great importance, especially in dealing with material of religious significance.

IPR as related to the development of eprint repositories, described in Chapter Three, was just one of the topics covered within the Focus on Access to Institutional Resources (FAIR) series of 14 projects funded by JISC during 2002–2003. As MacColl and Pinfield (2003) note in a paper describing the Securing a Hybrid Environment for Research Preservation and Access (SHERPA) project within FAIR:

> This programme is inspired by the vision of the Open Archives Initiative (OAI) that digital resources can be shared between organizations based on a simple mechanism allowing metadata about those resources to be harvested into services. ... The model can clearly be extended to include ... learning objects, images, video clips, finding aids, etc. The vision here is of a complex web of resources built by groups with a long term stake in the future of those resources, but made available through service providers to the whole community of learning.

The SHERPA project (http://www.sherpa.ac.uk) aimed to:

- set up 13 institutional open access eprint repositories which comply with OAI-PMH using ePrints software;
- investigate key issues in creating, populating and maintaining eprint collections, including IPR, quality control, collection development policies, business models, scholarly communication cultures, and institutional strategies;
- work with OAI Service Providers to achieve acceptable (technical, metadata and collection management) standards for the effective dissemination of the content;
- investigate digital preservation of eprints using the Open Archival Information System (OAIS) Reference Model;
- disseminate lessons learned and provide advice to others wishing to set up similar services.

The University of Oxford was one of the partners in SHERPA, and Oxford University Press (OUP) provided online access to articles by Oxford University-based authors published in many of the OUP journals from 2002 onwards. The articles will then be searchable via the pilot institutional repository and available free of charge to researchers across the globe.

The Rights Metadata for Open Archiving (ROMEO) project within FAIR investigated the IPR issues related to eprint repositories. The key results from the project are reported by Gadd et al. (2003). Copyright agreements of some

80 publishers were studied and just over 50% allowed self-archiving of some kind by authors. A survey of academic authors was undertaken to elicit their views on institutional repositories: 542 responses were received from 57 countries. As noted in the paper by Gadd et al.

> The majority of respondents (60% or more) were happy for others to display, print, save, excerpt from, and give away their research papers as long as the respondents were attributed as the authors, and that all copies were exact (verbatim) copies of the original work. Most respondents wanted to prohibit sales of their works and 55% wanted to limit usage of their works to certain purposes, e.g., educational or non-commercial. A comparison between these usage limits and those provided by UK copyright law and many electronic journal licences showed that the academics' conditions were far more liberal.

The researchers on this project also proposed to express IPR through metadata which could be communicated to others via the OAI-PMH.

Copyright management is a challenge to be faced by implementers of digital libraries around the world, as highlighted by Jeevan and Bhawan (2002) when describing their experiences in implementing a digital library at the Indian Institute of Technology at Kharagpur. This digital library provides access to a range of digital information sources (including ebooks, online patent information, online theses and dissertations and links to online dictionaries in specialist subjects (for example, aeronautics, architecture, and rubber technology)).

Another IPR challenge is when the digital content of a digital library comprises objects created by, or depicting, indigenous cultures. Sullivan (2002) provides further information on this and suggests that indigenous communities should control the rights management of their IP.

Issues relating to IPR are important and complex and WIPO advises that:

> "... concerning specific matters, it is recommended that you consult a practising lawyer who is specialized in intellectual property in your country."

8.11 Preservation Issues

Digital library developments all over the world have primarily focussed on improving access to information and collections. The management of these digital information sources over time, or their preservation, has only comparatively recently been appreciated and addressed. The following story gives an example of how easy it can be to lose (or almost lose) digital data.

In the 1980s a rich digital archive of life in Britain was compiled by almost one million schoolchildren in conjunction with the BBC (British Broadcasting Corporation) as a way of celebrating the 900th anniversary of the Domesday Book, an archive of land ownership in England compiled in 1086. The BBC used multimedia, interactive videodiscs, a technology thought to be most appropriate at the time (http://www.atsf.co.uk/dottext/domesday.html). However, CD-ROM technology and then web-based technologies soon overtook the videodisc and it became obsolete. Similarly the BBC computers used in the schools became obsolete and so the archive was inaccessible. Ironically, of course, the original Domesday Book, written by monks in the eleventh century, was perfectly readable and is housed at the Public Records Office of the UK's National Archive (http://www.nationalarchives.gov.uk). Fortunately, researchers on a project concerned with preservation issues developed software in 2002 that emulated the obsolete BBC computer and videodisc player and so access to the archive is once again possible. The project, known as CAMiLEON (Creative Archiving at Michigan and Leeds Emulating the Old on the New) is one of a number of US/British projects, jointly funded by JISC and the NSF, studying preservation issues. CAMiLEON has three main objectives:

- to explore the options for long-term retention of the original functionality and 'look and feel' of digital objects;
- to investigate technology emulation as a strategy for long-term preservation and access to digital objects;
- to consider where and how emulation fits into a suite of digital preservation strategies. (http://www.si.umich.edu/CAMILEON/).

Researchers at the University of Leeds had worked, with others, on an earlier project exploring digital preservation issues called CEDARS (CURL Exemplars in Digital Archives), as part of the eLib programme (http://www.leeds.ac.uk/cedars). CEDARS investigated the acquisition, long-term retention, description and access of digital objects. Preservation metadata were one aspect studied by the CEDARS team and that is now recognized as an important factor in any preservation strategy. Preservation metadata are generally defined as being the information necessary to carry out, document, and evaluate the processes that support the long-term retention and accessibility of digital materials. This would include information ranging from a description of the hardware/software environment needed to render a particular class of digital object to a record of the migration of a digital object through successive formats over time. An international working group, under the auspices of OCLC Research and the Research Libraries Group in the US, is investigating implementation strategies for preservation metadata (http://www.oclc.org/research/pmwg/background.shtm). A major development in this area is the OAIS, not to be confused with the OAI described in Chapter Three. The Reference Model for OAIS is an attempt to provide a high-level framework for the development and comparison of digital archives. Initially work related to the need to preserve data from satellites but it has now been developed into a generic model for use in any preservation context. Day (2004) provides further details of OAIS and explains how it is being used in various web archiving projects such as:

- Networked European Deposit Library (NEDLIB) (http://www.kb.nl/coop/nedlib) – a collaborative project of European national libraries.

- Preserving and Accessing Networked Documentary Resources of Australia (PANDORA) (http://pandora.nla.gov.au).

Marcum and Friedlander (2003) of the Council on Library and Information Resources in the US, describe how lessons may be learnt from library history (dealing with brittle books that had been produced on inexpensive paper, microfilming projects, and so on) for the preservation of digital information sources. They note that:

> As we work our way in the twenty-first century toward the library of the digital era, we need new tools that can help us organize expanding kinds of information, enable us to coordinate and share our resources, and bring us together in preserving them. Librarians also bring a history of distributed organizational practices to the table that will be as necessary as tools and technologies. Just as the danger of brittle books spurred work on print preservation, the threat of losing digital information is driving efforts to save electronic resources. It will require us to do things differently but our mission remains constant: to preserve the resources on which research, teaching, and learning so heavily depend.

A number of organizations in different countries are involved in investigating the preservation of digital materials, including:

- The Digital Preservation Coalition (DPC), set up in 2001 with the broad aim of securing the preservation of digital resources in the UK and working with others internationally to secure a global digital memory and knowledge base (http:// www.dpconline.org).
- Preserving Access to Digital Information (PADI), traces its origins to a workshop in 1993 and is now an initiative of the National Library of Australia. It aims to provide mechanisms that will help ensure information in digital form is managed with appropriate consideration for preservation and future access (http://www.nla.gov.au/padi).

A handbook on the preservation management of digital materials provides an internationally authoritative and practical guide to managing digital resources over time and the issues in sustaining access to them (Jones and Beagrie, 2003). Beagrie (2003) also provides an overview of international preservation developments in Australia, France, the Netherlands and the UK in a report commissioned by the National Digital Information Infrastructure and Preservation Program (NDIIPP) in the US (http://www.digitalpreservation.gov/ndiipp/). NDIIPP has the mission to "develop a national strategy to collect, archive and preserve the burgeoning amounts of digital content, especially materials that are created only in digital formats, for current and future generations". Beagrie's report states that:

- Decisions concerning preservation of digital materials must be made relatively quickly – well before their historical importance has been proved.

- Increases in both traditional and digital information are straining national institutions, and these institutions themselves must now evaluate much of the digital material, because the Internet makes publication possible without vetting by established publishers.
- New areas of collecting are growing: film, television, and websites have become important parts of the cultural record.
- Distribution arrangements are changing. Institutions now license access to, rather than purchase, most of their digital information. It is not clear who has responsibility for archiving this licensed material.
- The commercial need to protect intellectual property rights is overshadowing the need of cultural heritage institutions for permission to archive. No country surveyed had enacted comprehensive legal provisions for archiving digital publications.
- Archiving arrangements need to be global, because international publishers deliver digital material globally. Fortunately, international information technology marketing encourages the use of common technologies that increase possibilities for collaboration.

The report concludes that none of the countries surveyed had an ultimate preservation solution and a combination of approaches was likely to be necessary. No national library in the developed countries surveyed had core funding commensurate with the preservation challenge, and funding increases will be necessary. This will be even more the case in developing countries that are now creating many digital information sources and where the necessary infrastructure must be put in place to preserve them.

However, it is not just national libraries in the English-speaking or 'western' world that are developing digital collections for their users now and in the future. Omar (2003), for instance, describes the activities within the National Library of Malaysia to preserve the collection of Malay manuscripts. These important manuscripts, as described in Figure 8.7, were hand-written in the Malay language on palm leaves and date from the fourteenth century. As most of the manuscripts are written in Jawi script (the version of Arabic used to express the Malay language) they are digitized using the Portable Document File (PDF) format and appropriate metadata are created.

The role of national libraries in facing the challenging and daunting task of being custodians of intellectual materials is described by Omar and involves:

- reformatting and preserving the intellectual content of the past for the use of future generations;
- working closely with creators of new technologies to ensure appropriate technological solutions;
- ensuring that intellectual content is accessible in whatever format.

Those involved in preservation of national intellectual content are not only interested in the past – they also have to consider the present. With much information being 'born' in a digital format the task of archiving the web

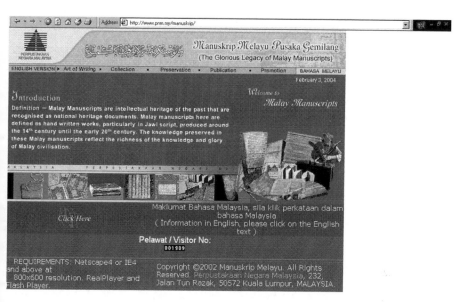

Figure 8.7 Homepage, Glorious Legacy of Malay Manuscripts, National Library
of Malaysia (reproduced courtesy of the National Library of Malaysia)

'space' for any country is a challenge being faced by many national libraries.
In the UK, the Legal Deposit Act of 1911, which ensures that one copy of
each printed book published in the UK is deposited in the British Library
and that the other legal deposit libraries (the National Libraries of Scotland
and Wales and the university libraries of Oxford and Cambridge as well as
Trinity College Dublin) have the right to a free copy, was amended in late
2003 to pave the way for the inclusion of legal deposit of digital information. Other countries, such as Lithuania, already have this. In Sweden the
use of harvester technology to preserve the content of Swedish websites was
first used within the Royal Library in 1996. Since then the Swedish web
'space' has been archived ten times. More information on techniques and
progress on archiving websites can be found on the website of the Internet
Archive (http://www.archive.org).

8.12 Staffing

It is generally recognized that digital library developments around the world
impact greatly on the skills required by the staff involved in developing and
maintaining such libraries. This means that the curricula of academic programmes in library and information science should reflect such changes. Also,
it is necessary that current practitioners are offered appropriate continuing
professional development opportunities so that they become skilled in working within a digital library environment. A training package on ICT for use
by library and information professionals in developing countries has been

published by Unesco (http://www.unescobkk.org/ips/ebooks/documents/ictlip/ictlip.htm). As with other material produced by Unesco the modules are in the public domain and can be freely copied and translated into other languages. Training courses on issues such as copyright and licensing, and national consortial arrangements for accessing digital information sources are regularly run by eIFL. These courses are held in various developing and 'transition' countries and in various languages (http://www.eifl.net).

An indication of changes in skills required by those working in organizations involved with implementing digital libraries can be seen in the nomenclature of some of the posts advertised. Here are some examples:

- E-services and Systems Development Officer – to be involved in the development and improved delivery of an increasing range of electronic resources and services to users.
- Electronic Resources Coordinator – to play a key role in ensuring optimal management of access for all users to the library's electronic resources and to be responsible for licensing, authentication, usage analysis and project management.
- Director of Library Digital Publishing – to develop and lead programmes for digital publishing to make collections available for the advancement of teaching, research and public access, and to conduct publishing projects to convert materials to digital formats and publish newly created electronic information as well as to organize and investigate new ICT, technology standards and new publishing models.
- Assistant Director, Digital Library Initiatives – to provide leadership in the development of systems and projects to support the digital presence of the university and, with the Director, to provide leadership for the development of the digital library infrastructure and implementation of the technical architecture and systems.
- Digital Information Services Coordinator – to develop, enhance and deliver digital collections and services and to coordinate and participate in consortial project teams to identify, track and apply evolving computing trends, and best practices in the digital library field.

In the chapter *Digital librarians: new roles for the information age*, Deegan and Tanner (2002) suggest some of the additional roles that library and information staff are likely to pursue:

- *Knowledge mediator*. This involves the tasks, undertaken currently by many, of providing insights to users about the existing body of knowledge outwith the information sources held within the library and its catalogue and can be summarized as: resource discovery; resource provision and resource delivery.
- *Information architect*. This task involves structuring digital content so as to present it and organize it in a way appropriate for users.
- *Hybrid librarian*. The role here would be to provide integration of services and systems (whether print or digitally based) within the existing organizational framework.

• *Knowledge preserver*. With much emphasis based on digital information sources it will be necessary for library and information staff to have the skills to ensure that digital data are appropriately preserved and maintained.

As well as changing roles for individuals within the organization the development of digital libraries has affected the staffing structures in some organizations. At the National Library of New Zealand, for instance, a holistic approach to the long-term management of its digital assets is being adopted and a Digital Library Transition Team has been established to:

• develop and implement business process workflows;
• specify infrastructure for digital material, for example: storage, access, and data authentication;
• research and develop a range of digital library activities, for example: metadata (resource discovery, preservation, structural) and persistent identifiers;
• pilot web harvesting for the capture and preservation of New Zealand websites;
• implement production processes for bulk digitization of textual materials (Searle and Thompson, 2003).

At Oxford University the Oxford Digital Library (ODL) group was established in 2001, with funds received from the Andrew W. Mellon Foundation, to create the intellectual framework and to develop the technical infrastructure for an enhanced service, providing online access to the vast scholarly library collections of the University. Staff at the ODL are responsible for a range of activities including the provision of access to digital information sources, the central digital conversion of library holdings, and developing and setting standards for digital information sources. By 2003 the ODL group comprised:

• Head (also a senior manager for Oxford University Libraries Imaging Service)
• Administrator
• Metadata strategy coordinator
• Metadata service coordinator
• Digital Imaging Adviser
• Database designer
• Digital image production (http://www.odl.ox.ac.uk/contact.htm).

8.13 Principles for Digital Library Development

Building digital libraries is expensive in real money as well as in staff time. In order to achieve an effective and efficient digital library it is necessary to follow some basic principles. Those suggested by McCray and Gallagher (2001) are:

a) *Expect change.* The digital library world is a fast moving one and change is inevitable. We have had to address change during the writing of this text and anyone implementing a digital library has to expect change and attempt to plan accordingly.

b) *Know your content.* Content is probably the most important feature of a digital library for users. It is therefore necessary to select appropriate information sources for inclusion in the digital library.

c) *Involve the right people.* Individuals from a variety of specialist backgrounds will need to be involved in the implementation of a digital library. The days when staff within the library could expect to have all the necessary skills for providing a service from the library have passed and it is necessary to ensure that suitable people are brought in as appropriate.

d) *Design usable systems.* The user interface issues discussed in Chapter Six need to be implemented in the digital library.

e) *Ensure open access.* One way to ensure open access is to avoid the use of proprietary hardware and software solutions wherever possible.

f) *Be aware of intellectual property rights relating to the content of the digital library.* These aspects were discussed earlier in this Chapter.

g) *Automate wherever possible.* Building a digital library requires a significant amount of intellectual effort by the creators of that library. As more and more content is added to the digital library the task of managing it can become very time consuming and so any software tools that might be available to help in these processes should be used.

h) *Adopt and adhere to standards.* The importance of the use of standards in the implementation of digital libraries was described in Chapter Four.

i) *Ensure quality.* Quality standards need to be applied to the selection of information sources, the creation of metadata, the capture of images (in a digitization project) and the overall usability of the system. The metadata play an important role not only in resource discovery but also in managing the collection and it is very important to ensure quality in the metadata records that are generated within the digital library.

j) *Be concerned about persistence.* Issues relating to the preservation of information sources within a digital library were discussed earlier in this Chapter.

8.14 Further Sources of Information

Throughout this book we have been careful to select relevant references for readers from a range of published sources. The key journals which cover aspects related to digital library development include:

- *Ariadne* (http://www.ariadne.ac.uk)
- *D-Lib Magazine* (http://www.dlib.org)
- *Electronic Library* (http://www.emeraldinsight.com/el.htm)
- *First Monday* (http://www.firstmonday.org)
- *Information Technology and Libraries* (http://www.lita.org/ital/index.htm)
- *Library Hi Tech* (http://www.emeraldinsight.com/lht.htm)

- *Program: electronic library and information systems* (http://www.emeraldinsight.com/prog.htm)
- *Vine: the journal of information and knowledge management systems* (http://www.emeraldinsight.com/vine.htm)

Also there are several books published on digital libraries including those referred to in this chapter (for instance by Chowdhury and Chowdhury (2003), Deegan and Tanner (2002)), as well as those (for instance by Arms (2000), and Witten and Bainbridge (2003)) referred to in several previous chapters. International yearbooks, such as the series *International Yearbook of Library and Information Management,* also cover relevant material that is written by recognised experts and brought together in a concise manner. In addition there are very many conferences held on a regular basis around the world which cover developments related to digital libraries. A selection is included here:

- International Conference of Asian Digital Libraries held in different Asian countries since 1998. For instance the 6th conference was held in Malaysia in 2003 (http://www.ftsm.ukm.my/icadl2003/).
- International Conference on Digital Libraries – the first in this series was in India in 2004 (http://www.teriin.org/events/icdl/background.htm).
- European Conference on Digital Libraries – held in different European locations since 1997 (http://www.ecdl2003.org).
- Joint Conference on Digital Libraries held annually since 1994 in the US and which brings together conferences organized by the Association for Computing Machinery Digital Libraries Group and the Institution for Electrical and Electronic Engineering – Computer Science Advances in Digital Libraries (http://www.jcdl.org).
- Libraries in the Digital Age (LIDA) held in Croatia annually since 2000 (http://knjiga.pedos.hr/lida/).
- Libraries and Associations in the Transient World: New Technologies and New Forms of Cooperation held annually in the Crimea since 1993 (http://www.dl-forum.de/engl/Veranstaltungen/crimea2003.html).
- Museums and the Web held annually in Canada or the US since 1997 (http://www.archimuse.com/conferences/mw.html).

Finally there are a number of sources of funding for digital library-related research projects and the websites of these organizations can provide useful sources of information including:

- National Science Foundation Digital Libraries Initiative in the US (http://www.dli2.nsf.gov/).
- Joint Information Systems Committee in the UK (http://www.jisc.ac.uk).
- Open Society Institute Information Program in Central and Eastern Europe and countries of the former Soviet Republic (http://www.osi.hu/nlp/).

References

Baker and McKenzie (2002), *Guide to Regional Intellectual Property Laws for Librarians.* Singapore: National Library Board

Beagrie, N. (2003) *National Digital Preservation Initiatives: an Overview of Developments in Australia, France, the Netherlands and the United Kingdom and of Related International Activity*. Washington, DC: Council on Library and Information Resources. Available at: http://www.clir.org/pubs/abstract/pub116abst.html

Biblarz, D., Bosch, S. and Sugnet, C. (eds.) (2002), *Guide to Library User Needs Assessment for Integrated Information Resource Management and Collection Development*. London: Scarecrow Press

Bollen, J., Luce, R., Vemulapalli, S.S. and Xu, W. (2003) Usage analysis for the identification of research trends in digital libraries. *D-Lib Magazine*, **9** (5). Available at: http://www.dlib.org/dlib/may03/bollen/05bollen.html

Choi, W. (2003) The development of digital libraries in South Korea. *Libri*, **53** (2), 130–141

Chowdhury, G.G. and Chowdhury, S. (2003) *Introduction to Digital Libraries*. London: Facet Publishing

Cohn J.M., Kelsey, A.L. and Fiels, K.M. (2001) *Planning for Integrated Systems and Technologies: a How-To-Do-It Manual for Librarians*. New York: Neal Schuman

Dahl, K., Francis, S., Tedd, L.A., Tetrevova M. and Zihlavnikova E. (2002) Training for professional librarians in Slovakia by distance-learning: an overview of the PROLIB and EDULIB projects. *Library Hi Tech*, **20** (3), 340–351

Day, M. (2004) Preservation metadata. In G. Gorman (ed.) *International Yearbook of Library and Information Management 2003–2004: Metadata Applications and their Management*. London: Facet Publishing. 253–273

Deegan, M. and Tanner, S. (2002) *Digital Futures: Strategies for the Information Age*. London: Library Association Publishing

Frawley, R. (2003) ELFNI (Electronic libraries for Northern Ireland Project): an overview. *Program*, **37** (2), 94–102

Gadd,E., Oppenheim, C. and Probets, S. (2003) The Intellectual Property Rights issues facing self-archiving: key findings from the ROMEO project. *D-Lib Magazine*, **9** (9). Available at: http://www.dlib.org/dlib/september03/gadd/09gadd.html

Geyer, E.M. (2002) IT enabled organizational change: a framework for management. *Journal of Library Administration*, **36** (4), 67–81

Harris, L. E. (2002) *Licensing Digital Content: a Practical Guide for Librarians*. Chicago: American Library Association

Jeevan, V.K.J. and Dhawan, S.M. (2002) Problems in the transition to a digital library: an Indian perspective. *DESIDOC Bulletin of Information Technology*, **22** (6), 13–19

Ilieva, P. E. (2003) Planning for access in multiple languages is an important issue. Designing a bilingual virtual archival experience: the Museum of Russian Culture collections at the Hoover Institution Archives. Paper presented at Museums and the Web 2003. Available at: http://www.archimuse.com/mw2003/papers/ilieva/ilieva.html

Jones, M. and Beagrie, N. (2003) *Preservation Management of Digital Materials: a Handbook*. Available at: http://www.dpconline.org/graphics/handbook/index.html

Lee, S.D. (2000) *Digital Imaging: a Practical Handbook*. London: Library Association Publishing

MacColl J. and Pinfield, S. (2003) Climbing the scholarly publishing mountain with SHERPA. *Ariadne*, **33**. Available at: http://www.ariadne.ac.uk/issue33/sherpa/

Marcum, D. and Friedlander, A. (2003) Keepers of the crumbling culture. What digital preservation can learn from library history. *D-Lib Magazine*, **9** (5). Available at: http://www.dlib.org/dlib/may03/friedlander/05friedlander.html

McCray, A.T. and Gallagher, M.E. (2001) Principles for digital library development. *Communications of the ACM*, **44** (5). 48–54

McKnight, S. (2002) Managing cultural change: the challenge of merging library services, curriculum development and academic professional development. Paper presented at 68th IFLA conference, 18–24 August, 2002. Available at: http://www.ifla.org/IV/ifla68/papers/123-106e.pdf

Omar, M.S.M. (2003) Preservation of intellectual heritage. In *CONSAL XII Information Resources Empowerment Enhancing Knowledge Heritage*. Bandar Seri Begawan: Dewan Bahasa dan Pustaka. 122–130

Ramos, M. M., Soeripto, Y. and Ali, K. M. (2003) Cultivating communities of practice: the CGIAR information management professionals' experience. In *CONSAL XII Information Resources Empowerment Enhancing Knowledge Heritage*. Bandar Seri Begawan: Dewan Bahasa dan Pustaka. 27–37

Royan, B. (2000), Content creation and rights management: experiences of SCRAN (the Scottish Cultural Resources Access Network). *Program*, **34** (2), 131–142

Saracevic T. Digital library evaluation: toward an evolution of concepts. *Library Trends*, **49** (2), 350–369

Searle, S. and Thompson, D. (2003) Preservation metadata: pragmatic first steps at the National library of New Zealand. *D-Lib Magazine*, **9** (4). Available at: http://www.dlib.org/dlib/april03/thompson/04thompson.html

Secker, J. and Plewes, L. (2002) Traditional and electronic study packs: a case study of the production process. *Program*, **36** (2), 99–109

Sullivan, R. (2002) Indigenous cultural and intellectual property rights: a digital library context. *D-Lib Magazine*, **8** (5). Available at: http://www.dlib.org/dlib/may02/sullivan/05sullivan.html

Sturges, P. (2002) *Public internet access in libraries and information services*. London: Facet Publishing

Tanner, S. (2001), Librarians in the digital age: planning digitization projects. *Program*, **35** (4), 327–337

Tedd, L. A. (2003), Training for public librarians in Wales as part of the UK's People's Network: some experiences from Aberystwyth (also available in Catalan). *Biblioteconomia i Documentacio*, **10**. Available at: http://www2.ub.es/bid/consulta_articulos.php?fichero=10tedd.htm

Turner, A., Fraser, V., Muir Gray, J.A. and Toth, B. (2002), A first class knowledge service: developing the National electronic Library for Health. *Health Information and Libraries Journal*, **19** (3), 133–145

Wright, M., Marlino, M. and Sumner, T. (2002), Meta-design of a community digital library. *D-Lib Magazine*, **8** (5). Available at: http://www.dlib.org/dlib/may02/wright/05wright.html

Chapter 9

Case Studies

9.1 Introduction

This chapter contains eight case studies dealing with digital library implementations in a variety of institutions. The case studies have been compiled following visits or face-to-face discussions with staff responsible for their implementation.

9.2 Open Library, Open University, UK

9.2.1 Background to the institution

The Open University (OU) was established in 1969 with a mission to give students with no qualifications a chance to study at university level without having to give up their jobs or other commitments. By 2003, 200,000 students were registered in courses at the OU, and there are 4,000 staff and 7,000 Associate Lecturers spread across the UK. By 2005, it is expected that all students and Associate Lecturers will have online access for teaching, learning and research.

The concept of the OU, which provides for a very flexible learning approach, has been adopted in many other countries and the OU has particular links with some of these such as the Arab Open University, and the Open University of Hong Kong. The OU has always been a world leader in the use of new technologies to improve the quality of education for students and to broaden their access to it. Originally, supporting materials to assist students in their learning included: printed course materials; television and radio programmes; audio and videotapes; and home experiment kits.

However, with the huge advances in ICT the OU has embraced e-learning concepts by including virtual tutorials, e-discussion groups, electronic submission and marking of assignments, and so on.

9.2.2 Background to the library

The Library on the OU's campus at Milton Keynes has always been seen as a key resource for all academic staff charged with developing teaching materials for the 360 or more courses, and students were not expected to visit the library. However, in 1997 a new mission statement emphasized more sharply the library's aim to provide e-support for students in line with the OU's Teaching and Learning Strategy:

> The Library will provide a high quality information service which supports Open University learning, teaching, and research; enable delivery of the University's strategic plan by supporting its business needs and the personal development of all its staff; play a role in the local learning community by working in partnership with other information providers. (http://library.open.ac.uk/aboutus/mission. html)

This major change has impacted both the number of staff in the library and the required physical space. In 1997 there were 35 staff but by 2003 this had increased to about 90 staff (although some were on short-term contracts) and a new library building is being built for 2004.

9.2.3 Digital library implementation and use

Open Library is the digital library service for OU students and staff which has been developed in stages and in consultation with teams of academic teaching staff (http://library.open.ac.uk). Students are made aware of Open Library in various ways, including talks given during the annual residential study schools and at Regional Centres, the production of a printed brochure summarizing the services offered, and via a link on the 'Student Homepage'.

One of the first services developed within Open Library was ROUTES (Resources for Open University Teachers and Students) which provides quality-assured websites of relevance for specific courses (Ramsden and O'Sullivan, 1999). ROUTES was originally developed using the ROADS software (one of the projects funded by the UK's eLib Programme) but now uses commercial software (Index+ from Systems Simulations). The 3,000 or so ROUTES resources can be searched by course code or subject and can also be browsed by course or subject. Over 70% of the courses at the OU now use ROUTES, and Figure 9.1 shows an example of the selected website links for a course on film and television history. Subject specialists work with course teams to integrate resources into course activities. Maintenance of the websites included in ROUTES is an ongoing process with the links being checked automatically, and six-monthly meetings are held with course teams to overview the selection of quality websites.

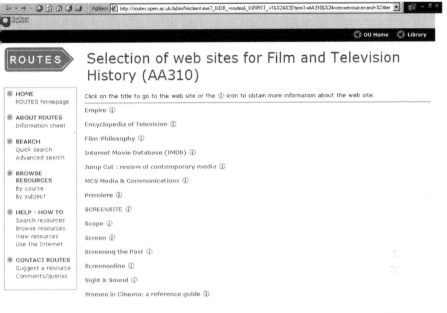

Figure 9.1 ROUTES websites for the course on Film and Television History at the Open University, UK (reproduced courtesy of the Open University)

During 2000 a new library management system was selected and implemented. The resulting system, Voyager, provides access to a range of digital information sources as well as to physical sources (such as books, videos, and journals). The digital resources include:

- ejournals (some 7,000 available from a number of suppliers including ACM Digital Library, Emerald, ingenta, JSTOR, Science Direct, Swetswise);
- ebooks (including a range of reference sources from Oxford Reference Online, engineering handbooks and items from netLibrary);
- databases (access is provided to a wide range of bibliographic databases (for example, the British Education Index), full-text databases, market reports (for example, Reuters Business Insight), and statistical databases;
- image databases (for example, the Grove Dictionary of Art, Ebsco Image collections, SCRAN);
- quick reference sources (for example, xrefer, online newspapers, street maps, telephone directories and links to UK government publications);
- statistical data (for example, Eurostat);
- theses (for example, Digital Dissertations from ProQuest as well as a selection of dissertations by OU students).

A range of specific helpsheets has been developed to assist users of digital information sources (http://library.open.ac.uk/help/helpsheets/helpsheets. html). In addition links are made from specific courses to the digital information sources that would be particularly beneficial for that course. There are

two methods of authentication for accessing resources. The ATHENS authen‐
tication system is used to ensure that only students registered on OU course
have access to the digital information sources. Also the Ezproxy 'proxy serve
is used to enable OU users to sign on to resources using the OU's local authen‐
tication system. Once authenticated, each resource URL accessed is forced
through Ezproxy which does the Internet Protocol authentication. This allow
remote users to access journals and databases by making the external data
base service think that they are viewing the resources on the OU campus.

Enabling users to access the digital information services has been a chal‐
lenge for the OU library staff. An online 'tour' of the sources and service
of Open Library has been developed and its opening page is shown in
Figure 9.2. The tour provides a link to the OU's SAFARI tutorial on informa‐
tion literacy described in Chapter Two.

In line with UK disability legislation, the OU provides a range of service
for its 7,000 or so students who are registered as disabled. In order to ensur
that the facilities of the Open Library are available to disabled users, in 200
a special one-year project was internally funded. The project's aims included
raising awareness of accessibility issues amongst library staff, carrying ou
an accessibility audit of the library's website, and surveying (by question
naire) disabled users. The homepage of the library's website indicates tha
WAI guidelines were adhered to in its production. Another research projec

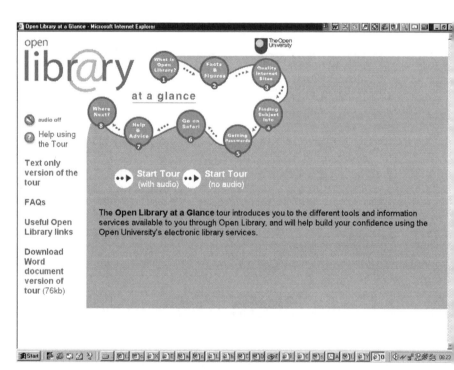

Figure 9.2 Open Library tour, Open University, UK (reproduced courtesy of the
Open University)

hat may result in improvements for students with a hearing impairment is)iVA – Digital Video Applications. This project, which lasts from 2002 to :004, is also investigating the use of digital video in a number of contexts ncluding production (for example, re-use of video clips on the Web or on :D-ROM), resource-based learning, and processing (including the possibility f automatic media analysis tools to assist in cataloguing and indexing).

Another way in which the OU is helping its students in their use of Open ibrary is the development of MyOpenLibrary – a personalized digital library nvironment as described in Chapter Two. In 2002 money was allocated from the OU's eUniversity system which is supporting a range of initiatives elated to e-learning) for a two-year project to investigate, implement and valuate such a system. The software chosen, MyLibrary, was being piloted t the time of the visit on courses in the Faculties of Health and Social Welfare, nd Arts. The MyOpenLibrary website (http://myopenlibrary.open.ac.uk/) rovides more details, including the likely advantages, how it can be accessed nd so on. A personalized library for the A173 – Starting Writing Family listory course is shown in Figure 9.3.

One of the challenges of personalization is making appropriate course naterial available for individual students. One solution being investigated y the Learning and Teaching Solutions section within the OU involves the levelopment of a Content Management System, based on the Tridion

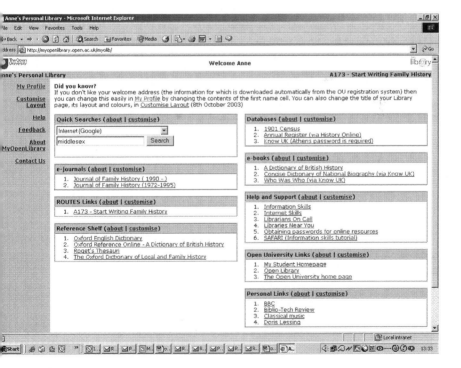

igure 9.3 MyOpenLibrary for A173 course at the Open University, UK (repro- luced courtesy of the Open University)

DialogServer (http://www.tridion.com/com/customers/customersarchive/ oucase.asp). With this XML-based system the initial development of digital course materials has been improved, updating has become easier and the content is more easily accessible for students.

Supporting users by answering their requests for information is an important part of any library service. In the Open Library 'chat' software (Live Person) is used to provide the Librarians on Call service for online help. This was developed following a six-month pilot and operates daily at fixed hours and relies on 'real' people answering the queries. Another project, OPAL (Online Personal Academic Librarian), investigated the use of software to provide automatic answers to common and predictable questions from users on a 24/7 basis (Payne and Bradbury, 2002). OPAL was developed with two other UK universities: the University of Leicester and Birkbeck College, University of London. An early prototype was developed and provided a useful testbed for student feedback. However, the cost benefits of the prototype indicated that another approach was needed. In 2003, a sophisticated search engine (Ultraseek) was implemented to help users find the right resources or page on the website. Ultraseek logs which queries users are submitting, so it is possible to monitor usage and carry out continuous improvements of the website to meet user needs.

The implications of the electronic learning environment are that Associate Lecturers and students work at any time of the day or night, and so need access to support 24 hours a day. The OU students are part-time and so their time is critical. Hence there has been rapid development of online services within the OU. However, greater access to information also generates overload for students and it is necessary to provide direction to relevant digital information sources.

The OU, then, is developing digital library services in a gradual manner and developing and trying out new innovative services before making them available to users throughout the world (Ramsden, 2003).

9.3 Biblioteca Mario Rostoni, Università Carlo Cattaneo, Italy

9.3.1 Background to the institution

The Università Carlo Cattaneo (LIUC) was established in 1991 by the Industrial Association of the province of Varese in north-west Italy. In common with other higher education institutions in Italy and in 29 countries of Europe, LIUC has had to implement reforms resulting from the Bologna Declaration. The basis of this Declaration (signed in Bologna in 1999 by European ministers in charge of higher education) is to work towards the establishment of the European area of higher education by 2010 in which it is intended to:

- adopt a system of easily readable and comparable degrees;
- adopt a system with two main cycles (undergraduate/graduate);

- establish a system of credits;
- promote mobility by overcoming obstacles;
- promote European cooperation in quality assurance;
- promote European dimensions in higher education (http://www.bologna-berlin2003.de/en/basic/index.htm).

Traditionally, undergraduate students in Italian universities have not been great users of libraries and these new reforms have resulted in the need for a change in teaching methods and assessment, and also in library use.

LIUC has some 3,000 students in three faculties: Economics, Engineering and Law. The majority of the courses are held in Italian, although some, involving international students, are held in English. Computing facilities are available in laboratories and classrooms around the university campus as well as in the student residences and it is possible for students from outside the campus to access computing facilities on campus.

9.3.2 Background to the library

The general goals of the library at LIUC are to collect and organize materials in the disciplines studied and researched at LIUC. The library has a staff of eight and is structured to provide the usual range of services. In addition one member of staff is particularly responsible for the computer-based library systems. Seating is available within the library for 350 students and 10 PCs are provided for MS Office applications, Internet access, e-mail and so on. In addition communication points are available for students to link their laptop computers to the campus network. Printed materials comprising 40,000 books and subscriptions to about 700 journals as well as audio, video and CD-ROM products are all on open access. Since 1996 several Italian publishers have presented copies of their books on economics to the LIUC library in return for description, abstracts and table of contents data being made available. This database is maintained and updated each month so that anyone can access the LIUC library website and see details of recently acquired books.

The library is unique as a service department within the university in having its own website. The website is available in English as well as Italian and Figure 9.4 shows the homepage with an icon (the Italian flag) that switches the interface from English to the original Italian version (http://www.biblio.liuc.it).

9.3.3 Digital library implementation and use

The needs of users have predominated in all design aspects relating to the implementation of the digital library system at LIUC. The current LMS at LIUC has been specially designed by a local software company and includes facilities for browsing and searching a range of databases, including a database of theses by LIUC students, and information about companies.

In addition a number of full-text journal articles are available via LIUC's library. These include journals from suppliers such as Ebsco Online and JSTOR as well as Italian initiatives such as:

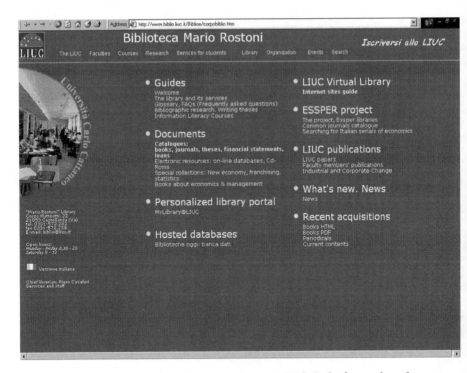

Figure 9.4 Homepage, Mario Rostoni Library, LIUC, Italy (reproduced courtesy of Biblioteca Mario Rostoni)

- CILEA Digital Library. CILEA (Consorzio Interuniversitario Lombardo per l'Elaborazione Automatica) is a consortium formed in the Milan area in the 1970s to support universities and research institutions in joint initiatives aimed at sharing digital information sources. In 1998 the CILEA Digital Library Project (http://cdl.cilea.it) was launched which aims to share the subscription costs to ejournals bought by the consortium from various publishers by hosting them on a project server. Publishers include: Elsevier; ACM; the American Chemical Society; the Institute of Physics; Wiley InterScience; Blackwells Scientific Publishing and Kluwer.
- ESSPER – is a project run from the library at LIUC that provides access to the main Italian-language journals in economics, law and the social sciences. ESSPER receives no funding and is dependent on voluntary input from staff in relevant libraries throughout Italy. The project started in 1995 and now involves some 55 libraries.

There is a general problem (not unique to Italy) that large amounts of the published literature are in English, while most of the students (especially undergraduates) wish to read articles in their native language – in this case Italian. The Italian-language journals typically have annual subscription rates of less than 100 euros and the publishers have not, to date, made the full texts of these journals available online. One exception, however, is *Biblioteche*

Oggi, the main Italian professional library journal. A subject and keyword index to *Biblioteche Oggi* has been developed by staff at LIUC (http://www.biblio.liuc.it/scripts/bibloggi/home.asp). From the index is possible to access the full text of 500 articles from 1998 to date. This full-text collection will be updated on a 'one year old moving wall' basis.

The full text of papers published within LIUC are also made available through the LIUC digital library, and Figure 9.5 shows the abstract (in Italian and English) of one such paper with a link to the full text.

The staff at LIUC started to develop, in 1997, a set of links to quality websites (now about 2500) of likely relevance to their users. This is known as the Virtual Library and includes a dynamic database structure behind a 'static' user interface to enable easy updating. In Figure 9.6 some of the entries under the heading Standards show the metadata, in Italian, for each website included. The language of the website is noted in the description.

The automatic link checker, LinkBot, is used to check actual links every 15 days and the database is updated on a regular basis following recommendations from staff in the library.

In 2000 the Director identified personalization systems (as described in Chapter Two) as a key development, as they provide librarians with the ability to add a 'human' touch in their dealings with users in an increasingly digital world. As with the OU in the previous case study, the chosen

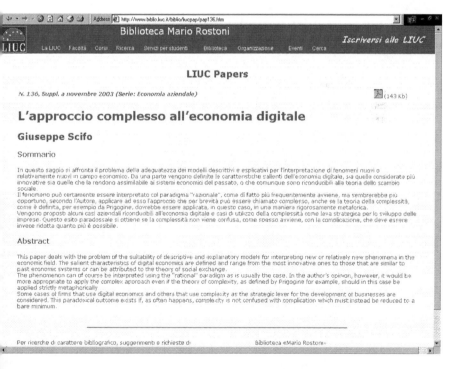

Figure 9.5 Record in LIUC Papers database at Biblioteca Mario Rostoni, LIUC, Italy (reproduced courtesy of Biblioteca Mario Rostoni)

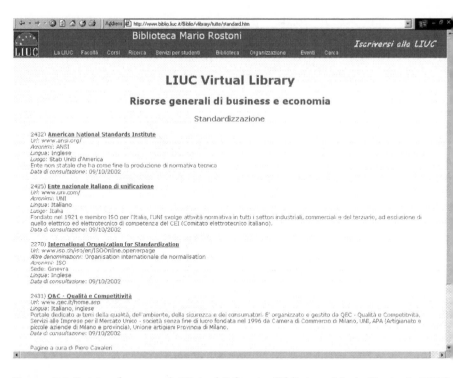

Figure 9.6 Entries for records,Virtual Library, Biblioteca Mario Rostoni, LIUC, Italy (reproduced courtesy of Biblioteca Mario Rostoni)

software was MyLibrary@North Carolina, and this has been used to develop MyLibrary@LIUC which has an Italian-language interface (see Figure 2.9). Some 250 users have set up profiles using this software.

As with any digital library service it is important that users have the necessary information literacy skills to enable them to make the most of all the services offered. LIUC staff have developed a range of courses and solutions to this since 1997 and funding has been available from the European Social Fund to run courses of 15 hours (five sessions of three hours each) for students. These courses have little face-to-face tuition, as much of the teaching is carried out using ebooks and planned exercises.

From the visit and talking with other librarians in economic faculties in Italian universities it is obvious that staff at LIUC were, and continue to be, early adopters of a range of digital library developments which are being implemented to improve services for their users as well as being key developers of relevant services in Italy. In developing the digital library at LIUC staff found that it is necessary to:

- harmonize the digital library developments with the resources (both human and financial) needed to support the 'everyday' needs of their users.

- understand the new technologies very well. Software can be bought, or acquired, but library staff may need to experiment to understand the implications fully before, perhaps, asking for amendments to satisfy particular requirements.
- keep abreast of the latest developments. Library staff need to be very knowledgeable and to adopt an entrepreneurial attitude.

9.4 University of Moratuwa Library, Sri Lanka

9.4.1 Background to the institution

Sri Lanka is a multi-ethnic and multi-religious country with a diverse and rich culture and a total population of 19 million. English is widely spoken and is studied as a compulsory secondary language in schools; the two other main languages are Sinhala (spoken by 74% of the population) and Tamil (spoken by 18%). Many websites in Sri Lanka are in English but there are some examples of trilingual (English, Sinhala and, Tamil) websites. There are 26 universities, postgraduate institutes and higher education institutes funded by the University Grants Committee (UGC) in Sri Lanka. The editorial in the 2002 issue of the *Journal of University Librarians' Association of Sri Lanka* described the digital divide which affects the country (the infrastructure, the language, technology barriers and bureaucracy) and outlined the role that academic librarians can play to bridge the divide by educating and influencing their users and by possessing appropriate information skills, providing digital media resources and re-packaging and disseminating information through digital means.

The University of Moratuwa originated in 1893 as the Ceylon Technical College and became a University in its own right in 1978. The university is structured into three faculties: Architecture, Engineering and Information Technology and has a full-time population of about 5,000 undergraduates, 200 postgraduates and 350 members of staff. English is the main language used within the university. Staff from the University of Moratuwa have been key leaders in Internet-related developments in Sri Lanka. For instance, the first e-mail service for academics was set up in 1990 at Moratuwa in cooperation with volunteers from the University of California, Purdue, and Stanford University in the US. The Lanka Educational Academic and Research Network now interconnects educational and research and development institutions across the country and provides e-mail, dial-up and dedicated Internet connections; its technical operations and training are carried out by staff at the University of Moratuwa.

9.4.2 Background to the library

The Library provides access to some 70,000 printed books, maps, standards, theses and research reports, and 300 printed journals as well as a collection of audiovisual and digital information sources. On the ground floor are some 30 PCs for word processing by students and in addition there are four study carrels also with PCs. All students at the University are registered for Internet access and there are network links from all over the campus. In addition many students also have Internet access from their homes. The UGC provided funds to the universities in Sri Lanka to spend on the provision of ICT facilities for students. The library has a staff of six with academic status and about 33 others.

9.4.3 Digital library implementation and use

Unesco's freely available database software, CDS/ISIS, was used for some years to provide an online search facility for the university's catalogue and this was made available on the Web in 1998. In Sri Lanka, as in many other developing countries, CDS/ISIS (and its newer 'relative' WinIsis) has been used widely as money has not been available to acquire other software. The development of a low-cost web-based library management system for Sri Lanka is described by Seneviratne and Amaraweera (2002).

At the University of Moratuwa, however, funds were available from the Asian Development Bank to purchase a purpose-built library management system, and the LibSys integrated library management system, developed by Info-Tek Consultants in India, (http://www.libsys.co.in/home.html) was chosen. LibSys has an open system architecture and the capability to handle a number of Indian-language scripts including Sinhala. Bibliographic information on a number of sources (including examination papers, undergraduate reports, theses, standards, and conference proceedings as well as books, and audiovisual materials) can be searched using the OPAC module of LibSys. At the time of the visit one librarian at the University of Ruhuna in Sri Lanka was working on a system, using the open source integrated library system, Koha (http://www.koha.org) developed in New Zealand, to catalogue records in Sinhalese. LibSys has search and browse features commonly found in other similar systems and at Moratuwa users can choose from a variety of databases, including books, audiovisual materials, standards, theses and conference proceedings. Gamage describes the modules of LibSys and their use at the University of Moratuwa as well as emphasizing the importance placed on education and training of the library's users in this system. (Gamage, 2002). The homepage for the library (http://www.lib.mrt.ac.lk) is shown in Figure 9.7.

Staff from the library helped in the development of the University's first website in 1998, which had a few pages about the library. The library has had its own website and server since 2000. A number of digital information sources are made available from the website including online journals, and research reports from Moratuwa staff. Figure 9.8 shows details from the list of research reports collection (from UM ResearchDocs option on the menu on the left-hand side of the homepage) with links to the full text of these reports or publications. The possibility of loading course materials on to this website is also being investigated.

Dwindling library budgets and escalating prices of scholarly periodicals have compelled university libraries in many developing countries to cancel valuable periodical subscriptions year after year, to the great detriment of

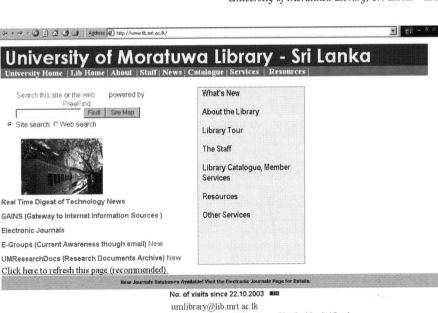

Figure 9.7 Homepage, University of Moratuwa Library, Sri Lanka (reproduced courtesy of the University of Moratuwa)

scholarly research in the universities. Moratuwa has been no exception. However, help for a number of Sri Lankan university libraries has been provided by SIDA – the Swedish International Development cooperation Agency (http://www.nsf.ac.lk/sida/library.htm). More recently some online journals have been made available via a project known as PERI (Programme for the Enhancement of Research Information). PERI operates under the International Network for the Availability of Scientific Publications (INASP), Oxford, UK (http://www.inasp.info/peri) in conjunction with SIDA. Staff at PERI identified Sri Lanka as a beneficiary and for 2003–2005 licence fees for a set of current awareness and full-text online scholarly periodicals databases have been paid by INASP. Some of the sources for the full-text journals are shown in Figure 9.9.

In addition, the library provides links for its users to a number of other freely available ejournals: the *Journal of Artificial Intelligence Research*, and the *Journal of Computer-mediated Communication* are two examples. If a printed copy of an article is needed users must use printers attached to the computers within their departments. Access to these ejournals is available from the Library's homepage, or from an intermediate page describing the sources available.

Another link from these pages provides access to GAINS – Gateway to Internet Information Sources. Staff in the library have compiled a list of links

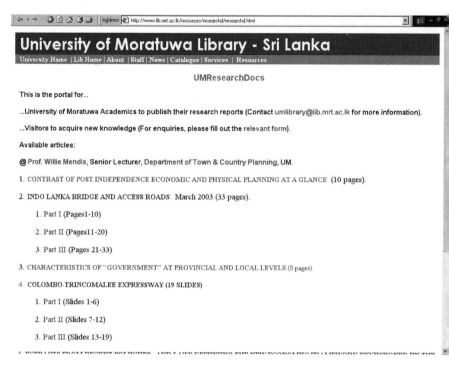

Figure 9.8 Research reports, University of Moratuwa Library, Sri Lanka (reproduced courtesy of the University of Moratuwa)

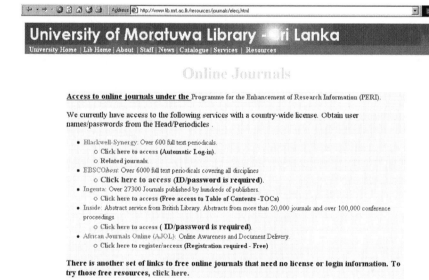

Figure 9.9 Sources for full-text journals, University of Moratuwa Library, Sri Lanka (reproduced courtesy of the University of Moratuwa)

o quality websites or gateways (such as the Edinburgh Engineering Virtual Library (http://www.eevl.ac.uk)) deemed to be of potential relevance to students and researchers at Moratuwa. Further links from the homepage provide access to a real-time digest of technology news from Moreover Technologies. Users can select a particular category of news from a drop-down menu. The categories have been chosen to reflect the interest of academics within the university and cover: Technology (general); Textiles and clothing; Computers and the Internet; Electronics and telecommunications. Each category is then sub-divided into sub-categories for more specific topics. Most of the news sources for this service are based in North America and Figure 9.10 shows how this source can also be used to view how the overseas news media are reporting on news items about Sri Lanka.

As in other institutions, staff at the University of Moratuwa have to work hard to promote the use of this digital library. Sessions have been held for research and faculty staff in different departments and it has been acknowledged that students will only use these digital information sources on the advice and direction of their lecturers. The University is currently considering a credit-bearing course on information skills that would involve the use of the digital information sources. Being a small country, there is much cooperation amongst libraries and librarians, and particularly between university libraries in Sri Lanka. In late 2003 a virtual meeting place for

Figure 9.10 Real-time technology news update, University of Moratuwa Library, Sri Lanka (reproduced courtesy of the University of Moratuwa)

library and information professionals within Sri Lanka was set up on Yahoo at http://asia.groups.yahoo.com/group/library_friends/. The library at the University of Moratuwa is seen as a key developer of digital library applications and the experiences gained are being shared with other professional colleagues.

9.5 Vidyanidhi Digital Library, University of Mysore, India

9.5.1 Background to the institution

The University in Mysore in India was founded in 1916 and became the first university outside the English administration in India and the sixth university to be created in India. The university has about 53,000 students and offers undergraduate and postgraduate courses in a wide range of subjects. The Department of Studies in Library and Information Science (DSLIS) was opened in 1965 with a bachelor's degree programme, a master's programme was established in 1971 and a doctoral programme in 1976. Digital libraries constitute one of the key research areas in the Department.

9.5.2 Background to the Vidyanidhi Digital Library project

Vidyanidhi is a Sanskrit word meaning 'Treasure of knowledge'. The Vidyandhi Digital Library developed from a pilot project in 2000 by staff at the DSLIS. Its aim was to demonstrate the feasibility of developing a digital collection of theses and dissertations in India and was sponsored by the Indian Government, the Department for Scientific and Industrial Research (DSIR) and the National Information System for Science and Technology (NISSAT). In 1999 a number of policy initiatives were identified by the Government of India's National Task Force on Information Technology and Software Development. One decision was to make it mandatory for all universities in India to host every research dissertation and thesis written by students at those universities on a designated website. The development of Viyanidhi was further enhanced by its Director working with staff at the NDLTD at the University of Virginia in the US (described further in Chapter Three) for a period of six months.

9.5.3 Vidyanidhi Digital Library and E-Scholarship Portal

Following the pilot project a more ambitious project was initiated in 2001 ultimately to establish a national repository and a collaborative consortium of participating universities and academic institutions for the creation, submission, archiving and accessing of Indian theses and dissertations. This work is being supported by Microsoft India and The Ford Foundation. The Microsoft India support is particularly involved with the implementation of Unicode for Indian languages and The Ford Foundation support is specifically for focusing on doctoral theses in the Social Sciences and the

Humanities. Vidyanidhi is being implemented and maintained by a team of five or so researchers and software developers working within the DSLIS. Figure 9.11 shows the opening page of Vidyanidhi (http://www.vidyanidhi. org.in).

In particular Vidyanidhi's mission is to:

* develop a repository for Indian doctoral theses;
* digitize, archive and improve access to doctoral theses in India;
* make theses available online (as per the restrictions desired by the doctoral students) and help enhance the visibility of Indian doctoral research;
* offer tools and resources to strengthen and augment the research capacities of doctoral students and universities;
* enhance the quality of doctoral research in India by developing and using standard formats and templates;
* mould 'best practices' in scholarship and scholarly writing among students;
* prepare the doctoral students in e-publishing, e-scholarship and digital libraries by offering training programmes and online tutorials.

Vidyanidhi offers a number of services including the following.

1) Searching the bibliographic database of Indian Theses
A database of some 50,000 bibliographic records of doctoral theses produced by students in Indian universities has been developed and is being updated with new and retrospective records from participating institutions. Figure 9.12 gives an example of the search facilities of this database. Users can choose between a simple search or advanced search which permits searching by specific fields. The default operator for search terms entered is AND and so a search for *women India* will result in records, such as those shown in

Figure 9.11 Homepage, Vidyanidhi Digital Library, University of Mysore, India (reproduced courtesy of Shalini Urs)

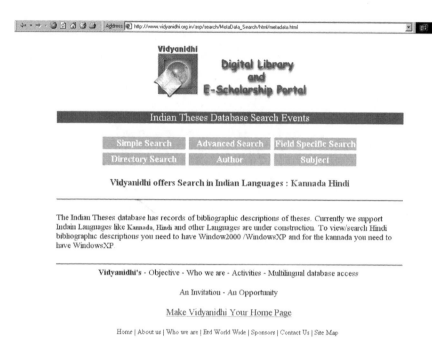

Figure 9.12 Search facilities within Vidyanidhi Digital Library, University of Mysore, India (reproduced courtesy of Shalini Urs)

Figure 9.13 with both women and India included in the metadata record. Vidyanidhi has been developed initially in English, but, to enable access to theses that have been written in Kannada (the language of Karnataka and Southern India) or in Hindi (the national language of India) facilities have been developed, using Unicode, for the storage and retrieval of such records. At the time of writing (late 2003) there were some 15,000 bibliographic records in Hindi and 632 in Kannada. Figure 9.14 shows a display of records in Kannada. There are also plans to expand the database to include dissertations in other Indian languages.

b) Searching the database containing the full text of doctoral Indian dissertations
By late 2003 there were some 500 full-text dissertations included in the Vidyanidhi database. Searching (of the metadata records) is comparable to that of the bibliographic database and the output is similar to that from the bibliographic database but with the addition of a link to the full text.

When making digitized material available intellectual property rights need to be considered. Within Vidyanidhi copyright restrictions have resulted in three forms of access to the theses and dissertations being possible:

- No restrictions – open access for anyone.
- Access/download only the first 25 pages, Table of Contents, and full abstracts.
- Access/download after payment.

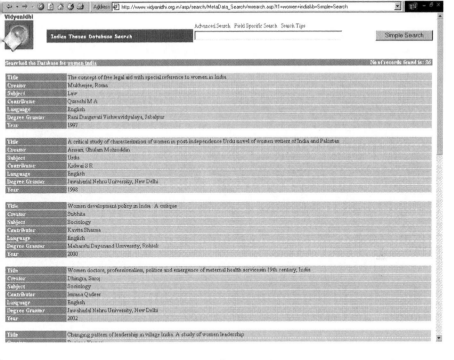

Figure 9.13 Retrieved records, Vidyanidhi Digital Library, University of Mysore, India (reproduced courtesy of Shalini Urs)

Issues of copyright in doctoral theses, as described by Urs (2003), can be very 'murky' as:

- the research which results in the thesis is often supported by public funds;
- the research can be seen as a collaboration between the researcher (and author of the final thesis) and the supervisor(s) as well as the academic support system within the university;
- the thesis, as such, is unpublished but has the potential for being published in some form;
- the thesis can be considered as part of the intellectual heritage of the concerned university or academic institution.

Such considerations have resulted in Urs' suggestion that copyright issues for scholarly works should be considered in a very different way from those for 'entertainment'.

c) E-scholarship portal
To complement the Vidyanidhi Digital Library an E-Scholarship Portal has been developed to assist all doctoral students with a variety of relevant tools and resources such as reference management software, tutorials and templates and style sheets.

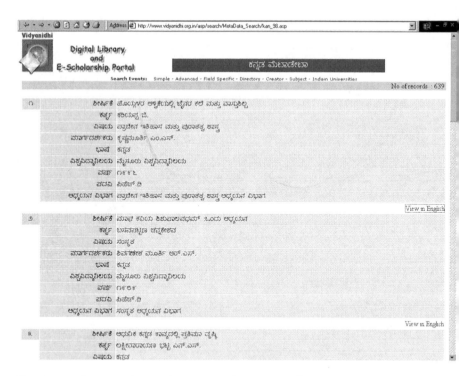

Figure 9.14   Retrieved records in Kannada, Vidyanidhi Digital Library, University of Mysore, India (reproduced courtesy of Shalini Urs)

The Vidyanidhi project is considered an important digital library development within India. Staff from the project have made links with many other similar projects worldwide and the 4th International Conference of Asian Digital Libraries was organized by the University of Mysore and the Indian Institute of Information Technology in Bangalore in 2001. Staff from Vidyanidhi have successfully followed Unesco's mandate to promote free and universal exchange of scientific information and the transfer of advanced digital library and publishing technologies to developing countries by the promotion of ETD initiatives (http://www.unesco.org/webworld/etd).

9.6 ElibraryHub and Digital Library, National Library Board, Singapore

9.6.1 Background to the institution

The National Library in Singapore, from its formation in 1958, has been directly responsible for both the national library itself and public library functions. In 1995, following a comprehensive review of public library services, the National Library Board (NLB) was established with a core function of providing reference and information services to the general public, researchers, professionals and other information seekers, and a mission to "expand the learning capacity of the nation so as to enhance national competitiveness and to promote a gracious society". (http://www.nlb.gov.sg/fr_abtUs_overview.html).

This aim is achieved via a multi-tier public library system comprising the main National Reference Library, two regional libraries, 20 community libraries (nine of which are located in shopping malls), 33 community children's libraries plus libraries belonging to government agencies, schools, and private institutions. PCs began to be installed in some of the public libraries in 1995. This move was much welcomed as at that time not many Singaporeans had Internet access from home. In addition users, from within the physical boundaries of the libraries could access a variety of digital information sources such as databases and ejournals. In the late 1990s the NLB implemented an integrated library management system from the CARL Corporation in the US (http://www.carl.org) and this is used to provide integrated access to the holdings of the NLB libraries. Particular features of this implementation include:

- ability to search for items published in each of Singapore's four national languages (Chinese, English, Malay and Tamil);
- self-service circulation stations which make use of radio frequency identification systems that employ a chip embedded in the library material;
- a multilingual phone circulation system which allows users to place holds and renew items via the telephone in any one of Singapore's four national languages;
- borrower enquiry workstations which allow users to consult their records and pay fines and fees using cash card technology.

Another digital service offered by NLB in the late 1990s was TiARA – Timely Information for all Relevant and Affordable. TiARA was a web-based online information service which provided access to a range of subscription information sources including:

- Dialog – access to a range of databases (http://www.dialog.com)
- The Engineering Information Village (http://www.ei.org)
- Faulkner Information Services – in depth information for technology professionals (http://www.faulkner.com)
- Gartner Interactive Services – a research and advisory firm to help clients use technology for business (http://www.gartner.com).

In addition staff at NLB compiled a list of relevant, quality websites for TiARA users as well as a separate list of handy websites for children covering broad subject categories such as History, Geography, Mathematics, Science and General Knowledge.

9.6.2 ELibraryHub and the Digital Library

The ELibraryHub service (http://www.elibraryhub.com) was launched by the NLB in April 2002. A description of the services offered to a new user by eLibraryHub is shown on its website and in Figure 9.15. A virtual tour is also available to inform users of the digital sources and services available

The NLB's Digital Library, which forms part of the eLibraryHub, is designed around the metaphor of a physical library and comprises the following sections:

a) *an atrium* – which provides basic information for users

b) *a public library* – which comprises a range of digital information sources as shown in Figure 9.16 and includes:

- 10,000 ebooks from netLibrary including popular topics such as gardening, cookery, travel and self-help;
- links to websites of relevance for travel in and around Singapore;
- fairly detailed summaries of about 1000 new books;
- a wide collection of digital reference sources such as dictionaries, encyclopaedias, and thesauri.

In addition there are links to specialist websites for students in Singapore and to government services.

c) *a reference library* – where real people help users in their information seeking activities. The reference service is a collaborative venture between the NLB and the Shanghai Library in China and also includes document delivery services and a Chinese-English translation service.

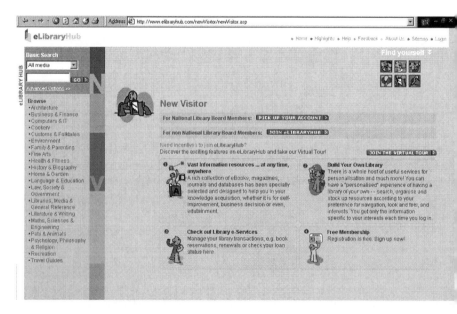

Figure 9.15 Information for the new user, eLibraryHub, National Library Board of Singapore (reproduced courtesy of the National Library Board, Singapore)

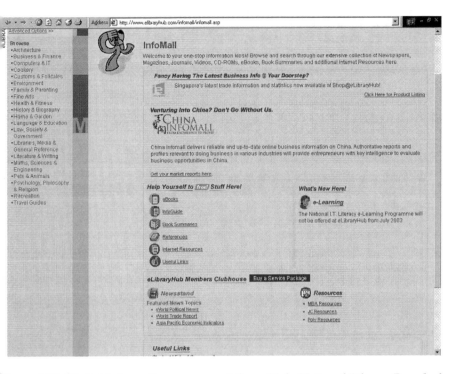

Figure 9.16 Digital information sources, eLibraryHub, National Library Board of Singapore (reproduced courtesy of the National Library Board, Singapore)

d) specialized libraries – in order to meet the information requirements of specific sets of users specialized libraries of digital sources are being developed for niche markets. The first such library, the China Resource Library, provides information for business people in Singapore wishing to enter the Chinese market. Information is available in both Chinese and English.

Since 2001 staff at NLB have been running courses for members of the public as part of Singapore's National IT Literacy Programme, as described in Chapter Two. In addition courses on information literacy have also been developed. These comprise:

- User Education Programme: to introduce the general public and students (from primary to junior college levels) to the library services, policies, facilities and resources.
- Basic Information Literacy Programme: aimed at equipping users with the necessary lifelong learning skills needed to locate information from NLB's sources.
- InfoPaths: Pathways to Information: aimed at enabling users (who might include corporate clients or government workers) to efficiently and effectively manage information in the knowledge-based economy of Singapore.

These programmes are designed, developed and delivered by a team of qualified and experienced professional librarians who specialise in information literacy and knowledge management training.

In describing the challenges facing the development of the Digital Library at NLB Cheng (2003) describes the following:

- Matching online content with users and 'repackaging' as appropriate. Careful studies of users' needs are carried out in order to ensure that the content available is appropriate for the information needs of all users. In some cases this means that information must be re-packaged.
- Ensuring that librarians face the challenge of their changing roles. Issues such as negotiating with content suppliers and dealing with intellectual property rights are skills required by library and information professionals who must be able to adapt to their new roles.
- Costing resources. The time and money involved in choosing and providing appropriate sources of digital information must be analysed to ensure that a return on investment is provided.
- Promoting in a competitive environment. As in many institutions the NLB finds that its users 'surf' the Internet for information and are not aware of the range of sources and services that have been made available via the Digital Library. A strong promotion programme is seen as vital.

Cheng notes that the NLB's Digital Library strives to be a strategic information system that provides convenient, accessible and useful services to its patrons. It plans to change the public's view of the NLB from a physically accessible institution to one that brings the library to the user.

The range of digital developments within public libraries in Singapore is impressive. Singapore is a small country with a population of four million. Those working in Singaporean public libraries have embraced a range of new technologies and methodologies in order to provide improved and innovative services for their users.

9.7 The International Children's Digital Library, University of Maryland, US

9.7.1 Background to the institution

The International Children's Digital Library (ICDL) (http://www.icdlbooks. org) is being designed and constructed by researchers in the Human-Computer Interaction Lab (HCIL) at the University of Maryland (http://www.cs.umd.edu/hcl) in College Park, a northern suburb of Washington DC. The HCIL conducts research through interdisciplinary teams on advanced user interfaces and their development processes. Its current work includes new approaches to information visualization, interfaces for digital libraries, multimedia resources for learning communities, zooming user interfaces, instruments for evaluating user interface technologies, and technology design methods with and for children. In developing the ICDL, HCIL is working alongside The Internet Archive (http://www.archive.org), a public, non-profit organization founded in 1996 to build an 'Internet library' for researchers and scholars that would provide permanent access to historical collections in digital format and support open and free access to them. The project is also supported by the Library of Congress, the NSF, the US Institute of Museum and Library Services (IMLS) (http://www.imls.gov), Adobe Systems (http://www.adobe.com), Octavo (http://www.octavo.com) – a company that offers access to rare works through digital imaging services, the Kahle/Austin Foundation, and the Markle Foundation (http://www.markle.org).

9.7.2 Background to the ICDL

The ICDL researchers were originally supported through a DLI-2 grant from the NSF to explore how children search, select and use digital materials. In 2002, with renewed NSF funding and a new grant from the IMLS the team expanded its focus to develop an online library of children's books from around the world (Druin et al, 2003). The overall vision for the project is "to use technology to help strengthen existing libraries worldwide by providing a large-scale digital archive of literature for children ages three to thirteen" (http://www.icdlbooks.org/adults/exec.html). The benefits of a well-stocked library for children are obvious, but equally obvious is the fact that not all children have access to such a library. The ICDL is one way to combat this problem.

9.7.3 ICDL implementation and use

The HCIL interdisciplinary team, led by Druin, draws researchers from Library and Information Science, Computer Science, Education, Art and Psychology. Over several years the team has explored how children search, select and use digital materials. In summer 2002 the adults and children in the team observed other children in local public libraries and conducted interviews with them to find out how they choose books. They then developed prototype interfaces that were tested and retested in local schools, libraries and homes. In November 2002 ICDL was launched on the Web, and by late 2003 included 272 books (selected in part because they are free of copyright restrictions) donated from 20 different countries (it is intended eventually to grow to 10,000 books in at least 100 languages).

A critical premise behind the ICDL project is that children need appropriate digital tools if they are to access information successfully. The needs of young children in particular can be very different from those of adults. A notable feature of this project is its intergenerational, participatory approach that includes children aged seven to 11 in the design team: in order better to understand the unique needs of children the adults have chosen to work alongside children (Druin, 2002).

Two interfaces have been implemented for the ICDL: an Enhanced version written in Java (it requires Java 1.4) deployed in November 2002, and a Basic HTML and Javascript version deployed in June 2003 that makes lower

technological demands and therefore should be more widely used internationally (in practice it has been the most heavily used version). In future the
team plans to bridge the differences between the two with a new version
of Basic.

The most interesting aspects of the ICDL are the interface designs that
have been developed for children, and the ways in which the books are categorized. Both will be considered here. Figure 9.17 shows the homepage of
the ICDL from where users are asked to opt for either the Basic or the
Enhanced version of the interface. The succeeding screens are from the Basic
version (it excludes the zooming feature and the options for visual Boolean
searching found in the Enhanced version but offers keyword searching and
multiple ways to look at search results, absent from Enhanced, as well as
quicker access for people with slow dialup connections).

Books can be found using several techniques, as Figure 9.18 shows. Users
can enter a keyword into a search box, and the search can be restricted to
individual fields. Alternatively, children can browse by category or scroll
through all the books (feasible given the present size of the collection, at
least); their covers, titles and the language in which they are written are
displayed 12 books at a time.

The categories used in ICDL are not those conventionally employed in
libraries, that is, based on subject content; instead they are categories that

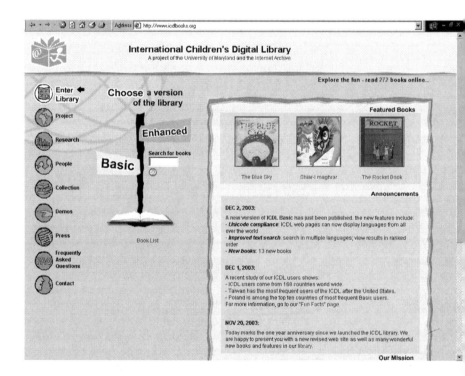

Figure 9.17 Homepage and version selection, International Children's Digital
Library (reproduced courtesy of the International Children's Digital Library)

Figure 9.18 Looking for books, International Children's Digital Library (reproduced courtesy of the International Children's Digital Library)

children themselves proposed to the researchers, as seen in Figure 9.19. These categories are broken down into greater detail on subsequent screens (not shown here). For example, the 'Feeling' top-level category comprises the subcategories: happy, sad, scared and funny.

Alternatively, children can browse the collection by place. If 'Find books in the world' is chosen (see Figure 9.18) the globe will turn and the child can click on one of six areas: Asia, Oceania, South America, North America, Africa and Europe. Figure 9.20 shows a portion of the book covers displayed when Asia is selected. Information on the language of the book is also included in the display and examples are shown in Figure 9.20 of books written in Arabic, Chinese, English, Farsi/Persian and Khmer.

Once found, the books can be previewed. Figure 9.21 shows a preview of one of the Asian books: a story from Iran written in Farsi. Brief metadata plus a summary (both in English only) are displayed alongside the cover. The next step would be to display an overview of the book (Figure 9.22), and finally the individual pages (Figure 9.23), which can be further enlarged for easy reading. Farsi is a language that is read from right to left on a page and the layout of the overview of the book in Figure 9.22 reflects this.

Information can also be displayed more conventionally as hyperlinked lists; Figure 9.24 shows an excerpt from the list of authors and illustrators.

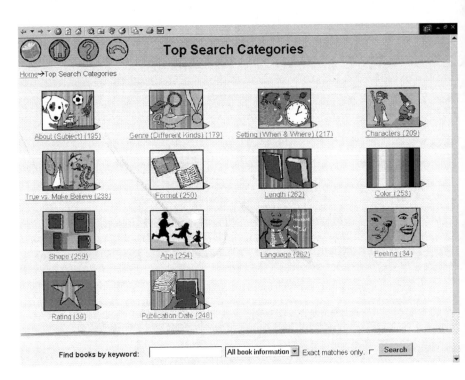

Figure 9.19 Top-level search categories, International Children's Digital Library (reproduced courtesy of the International Children's Digital Library)

Figure 9.20 Display of book covers for books set in Asia, International Children's Digital Library (reproduced courtesy of the International Children's Digital Library)

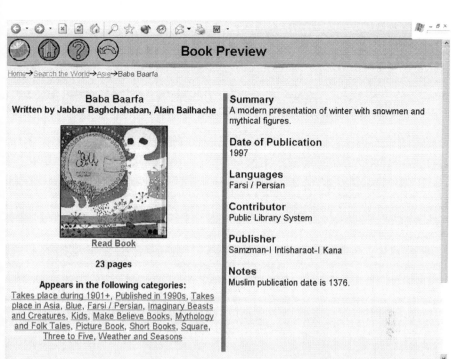

Figure 9.21 Book preview with metadata, International Children's Digital Library (reproduced courtesy of the International Children's Digital Library)

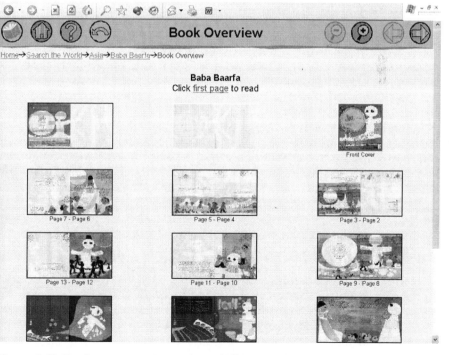

Figure 9.22 Book overview, International Children's Digital Library (reproduced courtesy of the International Children's Digital Library)

Figure 9.23 Pages from a book, International Children's Digital Library (reproduced courtesy of the International Children's Digital Library)

Help pages are offered, written in a way that is intended to be straightforward for children to understand. All the texts in the various languages have been encoded using Unicode, and advice is offered for any users that are encountering problems with it.

A number of methods are being used to evaluate the impact of the ICDL, including web log tracking, an online questionnaire, and working with children in local schools. Web log analysis shows that between its launch in November 2002 and September 2003 over 60,000 unique users visited the ICDL and read books.

As the ICDL Executive Summary expresses it, ICDL is:

> focused on the inherent promise of the Internet to provide direct and global access to quality content for children. With the creativity of designers who devise tools that make content enjoyable and easy to access, and the commitment of a coalition of experts to put together all the essential pieces of this creative puzzle, the largest bookmobile in history can be made available to children around the world (http://www.icdlbooks.org/adults/exec.html).

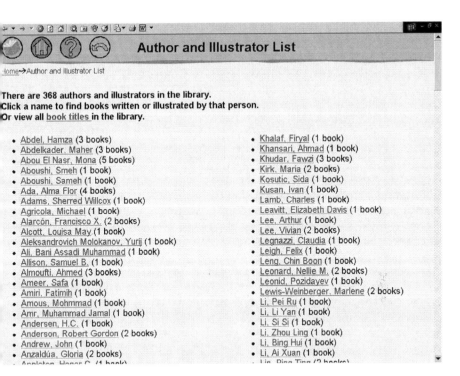

Figure 9.24 Author/illustrator listing, International Children's Digital Library (reproduced courtesy of the International Children's Digital Library)

9.8 Archives, McGill University, Montreal, Canada

9.8.1 Background to the institution

McGill University (http://www.mcgill.ca) is one of four universities located in Montreal, Canada. It was founded by James McGill, a wealthy merchant originally from Scotland, and received its Charter in 1821. In the academic year 2002–2003 it had 22,915 undergraduate students (18,164 full time) and 6895 graduate students (5073 full time). The distribution by mother tongue was English (54%), French (20%) and other (26%). The University's staff comprised 1436 tenured or tenure-tracking professors, 3992 other research, part-time and visiting academic staff, and 2853 administrative and support staff.

9.8.2 Background to the Archives

McGill University Archives (http://www.archives.mcgill.ca) was established in 1962 along with the appointment of McGill's first University Archivist. In 1971 it moved to consolidated storage, access and administrative offices located in the McLennan Library (home of the University's Humanities and Social Science collection). The staff comprises two professional archivists, four full-time clerical staff and one temporary staff member.

The objective of the University Archives is to select, collect, preserve and provide services based upon the institutional records raised by administrative officers, officers of instruction and research and their staff in the performance of their duties as University officials or employees. Examples of archival materials include minutes of meetings, correspondence, legal records, curricular and student records, University and student publications, personnel and fiscal records, drawings, paintings of a documentary character, electronic and other record types, sound recordings, microforms, motion pictures, still photographs and prints, posters, letter-press and near-print publications, teaching aids, special and annual reports, calendars, manuals and scrapbooks. These comprise more than 4,000 metres of records of permanent value generated over the last 180 years. Approximately 2000 boxes of records are acquired annually, and an average of 900 boxes of records per year are destroyed after their retention periods have expired. The University Archives, in the Canadian tradition of total archives, has also acquired the private records or fonds of both individuals and non-McGill institutions to complement institutional holdings. The papers of professors and students figure prominently in recent acquisitions. The University Archives has had no policy for the safeguarding of information located in university-based websites, but a project currently is establishing a new policy for all kinds of electronic records, including websites.

The key functions of the Archives service are the transfer of relevant records, their inventory and appraisal, the establishment of retention policies for these records and their eventual destruction if deemed appropriate, the arrangement and description of records according to archival standards, including the preparation of electronic finding aids, the preservation of records, and the delivery of a service to users via a reading room, website, and via telephone, fax, e-mail and written queries from users. As a part of such services the archival staff have undertaken inhouse digitization projects, some with special funding, as well as mounting virtual and actual exhibitions based on the archival holdings.

9.8.3 Implementation and use of the digitized collections

Digitization activities within McGill University Archives have taken two forms: the provision of digital information about the archives service, including collection finding aids, and the actual digitization of some material. The homepage, offering access to various services, is shown in Figure 9.25 (http://www.archives.mcgill.ca).

The Reference Services page includes a list of questions frequently posed by users that gives an indication of the breadth of requests received by staff (Figure 9.26). From this page can be found information about the Reading Room services and how to submit requests for assistance, as well as hyperlinks to other archival services such as the Library and Archives of Canada, and the Canadian Council of Archives.

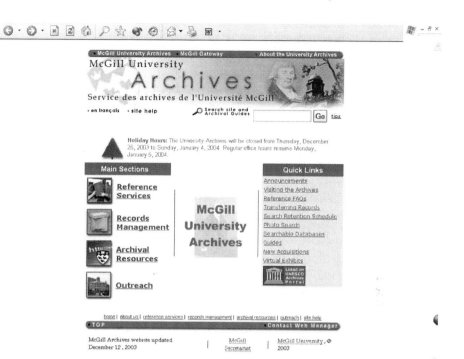

Figure 9.25 Homepage, McGill University Archives, Canada (reproduced courtesy of McGill University)

Information about the various information sources available from the Archives are listed on the website (Figure 9.27), including both metadata and in some cases the objects they describe. A three-volume Guide to Archival resources at McGill University is available online; Figure 9.28 provides an overview of the contents in Volume 1. An excerpt from the Finding Aid for one Faculty, Dentistry, is shown in Figure 9.29. The finding aids prepared by the archivists are at different levels of detail. Many were compiled before national or international descriptive standards existed in the archival world, and their arrangement or organization is based upon provenance or the individual structure of the parent institution (in this case, McGill). In some cases the finding aids for special media such as photographs have been created based upon the archivists' understanding of their users' needs. McGill University Archives does not adhere to the EAD standard, but its more recently generated finding aids do follow the Rules for Archival Description (RAD) that are widely employed in Canada.

The University Archives also provides online database access to metadata relating to its holdings. Figure 9.30 lists some of these databases. The Photo Collection is noteworthy because it has been digitized inhouse, and can therefore be viewed from the website. It comprises over 14,000 separate images that can be searched using keywords linked with Boolean operators (the

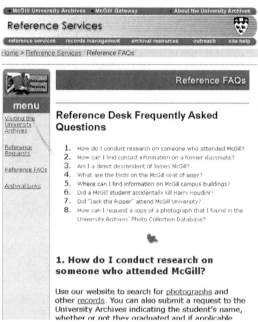

Figure 9.26 Frequently Asked Questions, McGill University Archives, Canada (reproduced courtesy of McGill University)

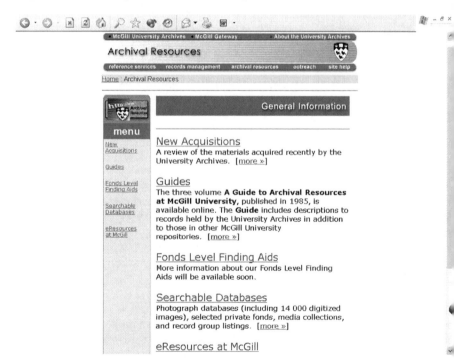

Figure 9.27 Digital information sources available from McGill University Archives, Canada (reproduced courtesy of McGill University)

McGill University Archives · McGill Gateway · About the University Archives

Archival Resources

reference services · records management · archival resources · outreach · site help

Home > Archival Resources > Guides : Volume 1

menu

Guides

Fonds Level Finding Aids

Searchable Databases

eResources at McGill

Volume 1

Volume 1

The Archival Records of McGill University

The Archival Records of McGill University are split into four parts:

1. Executive and Administrative Bodies
2. Faculties
3. Colleges, Schools and Services
4. Associated Institutions.

guide intro

guide help

Each unit has been listed according to its unique record group number and opens in a new window.

I. Executive and Administrative Bodies

RG no.	Record Group Name

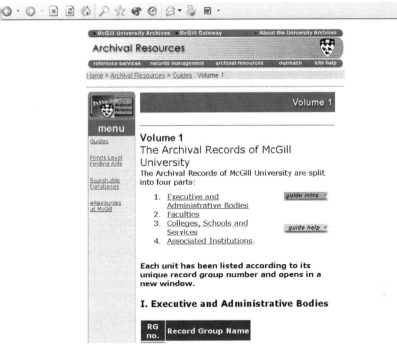

Figure 9.28 Online Guide (Volume 1) to the Archival Records of McGill University, Canada (reproduced courtesy of McGill University)

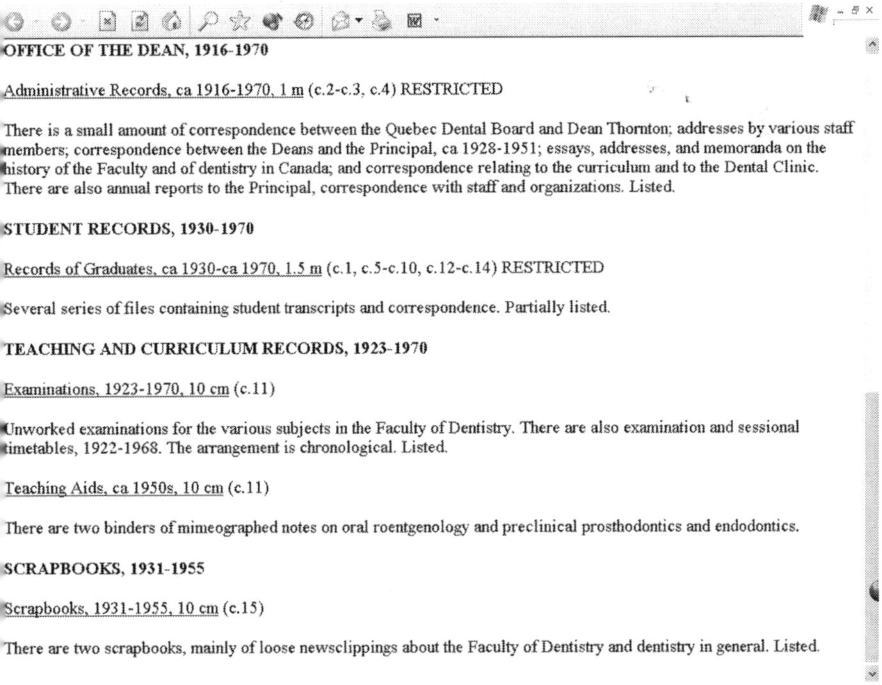

OFFICE OF THE DEAN, 1916-1970

Administrative Records, ca 1916-1970, 1 m (c.2-c.3, c.4) RESTRICTED

There is a small amount of correspondence between the Quebec Dental Board and Dean Thornton; addresses by various staff members; correspondence between the Deans and the Principal, ca 1928-1951; essays, addresses, and memoranda on the history of the Faculty and of dentistry in Canada; and correspondence relating to the curriculum and to the Dental Clinic. There are also annual reports to the Principal, correspondence with staff and organizations. Listed.

STUDENT RECORDS, 1930-1970

Records of Graduates, ca 1930-ca 1970, 1.5 m (c.1, c.5-c.10, c.12-c.14) RESTRICTED

Several series of files containing student transcripts and correspondence. Partially listed.

TEACHING AND CURRICULUM RECORDS, 1923-1970

Examinations, 1923-1970, 10 cm (c.11)

Unworked examinations for the various subjects in the Faculty of Dentistry. There are also examination and sessional timetables, 1922-1968. The arrangement is chronological. Listed.

Teaching Aids, ca 1950s, 10 cm (c.11)

There are two binders of mimeographed notes on oral roentgenology and preclinical prosthodontics and endodontics.

SCRAPBOOKS, 1931-1955

Scrapbooks, 1931-1955, 10 cm (c.15)

There are two scrapbooks, mainly of loose newsclippings about the Faculty of Dentistry and dentistry in general. Listed.

Figure 9.29 Finding aid, Faculty of Dentistry, McGill University Archives, Canada (reproduced courtesy of McGill University)

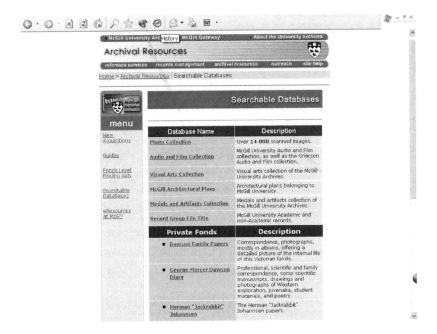

Figure 9.30 Searchable databases, McGill University Archives, Canada (reproduced courtesy of McGill University)

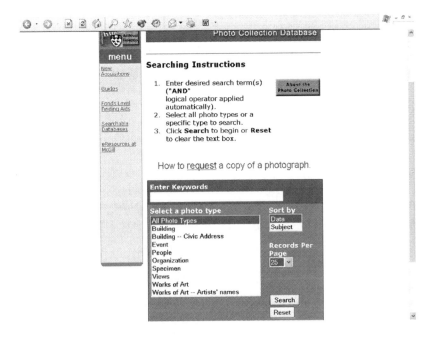

Figure 9.31 Searching the Photo Collection, McGill University Archives, Canada (reproduced courtesy of McGill University)

default operator is AND) either across the entire collection or within specified subject categories such as 'Event' or 'People' (Figure 9.31). An excerpt from the results of a search on *James McGill* is shown in Figure 9.32. The 29 retrieved images then can be displayed one by one.

Digitization is expensive to undertake, and McGill Archives has only been able to proceed relatively slowly in capturing its large holdings in this way. It decided to begin with the Photo Collection to improve access to an important collection that hitherto had been difficult to use effectively. It was also influenced in this decision, however, by the critical role that digitization can play in preservation; with the digitization of its photo collection there is much less need either for staff or users to handle the fragile photographs themselves. The next collection to be digitized by the Archives staff demonstrates another advantage that digitization can offer. It is planned in the near future to digitize the videotapes of lectures given by McGill professors in the 1970s. This is an urgent task as the equipment required to view the original videotapes now is obsolete, but digitization offers a way to preserve them at the same time as being able to use them on a new generation of equipment.

The Archives staff also prepare online exhibitions, and at the time of writing four were available: the McGill Football Photo Gallery, the Installation of Principals at McGill since 1821, University Records and Family

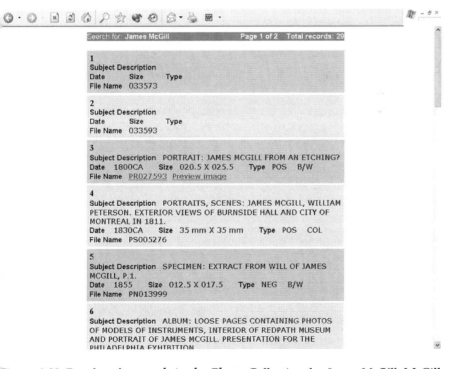

Figure 9.32 Results of a search in the Photo Collection for *James McGill*, McGill University Archives, Canada (reproduced courtesy of McGill University)

History, and Student Life at McGill, 1829–1997. An excerpt from the thumbnail sketches of the latter exhibit is shown in Figure 9.33.

McGill University Archives, then, are exploiting the advantages offered by a digital library approach to storage, access, dissemination and preservation of archival records of various kinds. Although most of the collections themselves are still unavailable in digital form, a start has been made on the digitization of non-text holdings. More generally, descriptive cataloguing tools are available online to help users identify and find relevant archival documents, and the McGill Archives website is an important means of publicizing its services and notifying users of its rich collections.

9.9 National Library of Wales, Aberystwyth, UK

9.9.1 Background to the institution

The National Library of Wales (NLW) was founded in 1911 and is located in Aberystwyth. It is one of the six legal deposit libraries in the UK and Ireland and has the right to collect, free of charge, copies of material published within the UK and Ireland. In late 2003 the Legal Deposit Libraries Act (of 1911) was amended to enshrine the principle that e-publications be deposited as well as printed materials. Over 50,000 books and 120,000

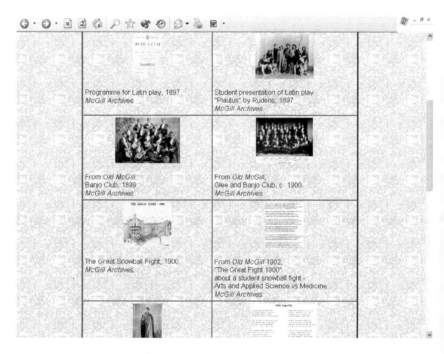

Figure 9.33 Excerpt from the Student Life at McGill Virtual Exhibit, McGill University Archives, Canada (reproduced courtesy of McGill University)

periodical parts arrive in the library each year as a result of the legal deposit. The collections within NLW comprise over four million printed volumes – books, periodicals, newspapers, official publications, maps and music. In particular Welsh and Celtic material is acquired so as to form a comprehensive collection covering all periods from the first Welsh book printed in 1546 to a current range of Welsh local publications. The NLW also houses manuscripts and archives, pictures and photographs, posters, ephemera, radio and TV recordings, films, videotapes and sound recordings to reflect Wales and the Welsh people throughout the world and acts as a national repository for Wales. There are some 262 members of staff at NLW. The language used within the library is Welsh and its website is fully bilingual (Welsh/English); the homepage shown in Figure 9.34 (http://www.llgc.org.uk). Users can choose from the menu using their language of choice and future screens will be presented in that language although an option to switch language is always available via a radio button at the top right hand corner of each screen.

9.9.2. Background to digital library development

In 2002 a 65-page corporate plan for the forthcoming five years (2003–2007) was published (*Digital library, open library*, 2002) comprising two main initiatives: the digital library and the open library. Within the digital library three programmes were identified which aim to:

* prepare a complete online listing of the library's content;
* mount digital online copies of items from the collection;

Figure 9.34 Bilingual homepage of the National Library of Wales, UK (reproduced courtesy of Llyfrgell Genedlaethol Cymru/The National Library of Wales)

- collect, make available and preserve non-print (mainly electronic) publications that will flow from the new legislation extending the scope of legal
deposit (Green, 2002).

Within this case study only the second aim, that of digitization, will be
discussed. Digitization formed a key part of the NLW's previous five year
plan and a strategy document for digitization 2001–2004 was produced
(*Crossing the threshold*, 2000). This strategy identified a number of key policies
and procedures relating to the digitization programme. The General
Statement of Policy stated that:

- The Library will digitize items from its collections (and, where resources
are made available, from external collections) for the purpose of enhancing
access for current and future users. It will also, where appropriate, use
digitization as a preservation tool.
- The Library will aim to produce, preserve and present its digital collections
to the highest recognized standards.

Other policies specified included:

- users requirements will determine the content to be digitized;
- digitization that is likely to lead to IPR difficulties will be avoided;
- metadata will be created and maintained for all digital objects;
- high standards of security will be strived for, both in the creation of digital
files and in their delivery;
- a budget will be allocated for a programme to train appropriate staff.

9.9.3 Implementation and use of the digitized collections

Staff within the NLW started work on digitization of some collections in
1999. The first two projects were:

a) Framed Works of Art. This database, developed using the CAIRS software,
covers NLW's holdings of 4,000 art works mainly of Welsh interest;
an example of the metadata and a thumbnail for one item was shown in
Figure 5.2.

b) *Ymgyrchu/ Campaign/ ¡Campaña!* This trilingual site (Welsh, English and
Spanish) presents social and political campaigning in Wales during the twentieth century through digitized images of original documents, photographs
and sound and video files mainly housed in the Welsh Political Archive
within NLW. Themes covered include: War and Peace; The Ballot Box; and
Labour Struggles. Annotations were included so as to explain the import of
various printed, image and sound archives, as can be seen in Figure 9.35.

In 2001 NLW staff also worked on another special digitization project,
Gathering the Jewels (http://www.gtj.org.uk). Its goal was to digitize the
'cream' of Welsh cultural history from repositories throughout the princi-

Figure 9.35 Sample output in English from the Campaign! digitized collection, National Library of Wales, UK (reproduced courtesy of Llyfrgell Genedlaethol Cymru / The National Library of Wales)

pality. NLW's digital imaging unit was contracted to do a fair amount of the imaging work on the materials from other institutions as well as from NLW. In addition, NLW metadata staff prepared the NLW materials for imaging and the NLW computer section was contracted to support the ICT aspects of the project. By the end of the project (late 2003) some 20,000 images had been digitized (of which over 7,000 were created by the NLW digital imaging unit) and this material is now available online via Culturenet Cymru – a new body working to promote Welsh heritage and culture online (http://www.culturenetcymru.com).

Following a major re-structuring of staff within NLW in 2002 a Digitization and Retroconversion section was set up comprising 25 members of whom, in the digitization branch, five are involved in creating metadata, five in imaging and two in encoding material using the TEI format. Decisions such as which collections should be digitized are taken by the digitization strategy group – Digistrat, which comprises representatives from various sections of the Library (Systems, Sound and Screen Archive, Computer Centre, Exhibition) as well as a selection of staff from the Digitization and Retroconversion Section (Head, Metadata Manager and Imaging Supervisor). Digistrat meets regularly to review progress on all the digitization projects that are underway and to deliberate on future projects.

A number of digitization projects were in progress at the time of the visit. Details of a selection of these, with examples, are given here classified by type of material:

- *Archives*, including the 1886 diary of the British Prime Minister David Lloyd George.
- *Manuscripts*, including The Black Book of Carmarthen – a thirteenth century manuscript written solely in the Welsh language.
- *Maps*, including sea charts of Wales from the eighteenth century.
- *Paintings*, including 122 etchings of Tenby.
- *Photographs*, several Welsh photographers have deposited their collections in NLW. The collection of one, Geoff Charles, comprises 120,000 photographs from the 1930s-1970s and these are in the process of being digitized.
- *Printed materials*, including *Brython* – a nineteenth century periodical in Welsh.

The above can all be accessed via the Treasures option on the NLW website. Figure 9.36 shows an example of a page in the diary of David Lloyd George. Further projects are 'in the pipeline', including:

- the full and searchable text of *Y Bywgraffiadur Cymreig* and its English equivalent, *The Dictionary of Welsh Biography;*
- a million images of pre-1858 wills (actually about five images per will for 200,000 wills) and associated documents of particular interest to historians and genealogists.

Staff have adhered to the basic principles for digitization laid down in *Crossing the Threshold*. Metadata are seen as an essential component of all the digitization projects as they support the discovery, use, storage and migration of digital objects over time. The design of appropriate metadata for each project is a critical part in planning for that project. The digitization metadata generally comprise three elements:

- Descriptive metadata – for describing and identifying sources.
- Structural metadata – for facilitating navigation and presentation of the source.
- Administrative metadata – for facilitating both short-term and long-term management and processing of digital collections.

Although MARC21 was used for descriptive metadata, with associated structural metadata also incorporated, for the early digitization projects, it was decided that METS would be the appropriate standard to use in the later projects and staff at NLW were early adopters of METS in Europe. The trilingual (English, French and Spanish) tutorial on metadata used at Cornell University (*Moving theory into practice*, 2000) has been used for training purposes. Staff at NLW are also considering using open source software, such as Greenstone, for publishing and making their digitized collections accessible.

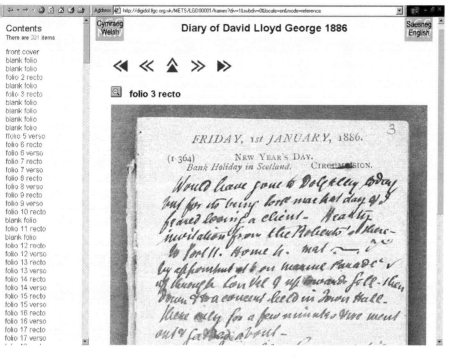

Figure 9.36 Screenshot of a page of David Lloyd George's diary, National Library of Wales, UK (Reproduced courtesy of Llyfrgell Genedlaethol Cymru / The National Library of Wales)

At the start of every digitization project there is a 'benchmarking' session involving metadata staff, imaging staff and the curator of the particular collection being digitized. The basic steps involved are:

- assessment of the original;
- knowledge of output requirements;
- critical digitization requirements and choice of conversion process;
- setting specifications and tolerances.

Further details about the imaging standards and benchmarking are given in *Crossing the Threshold*.

There have been many lessons learnt by staff at NLW during the implementation of an impressive range of digitization projects that form part of the digital library. These include:

- digitization is more complex and expensive than might be imagined;
- proper planning is needed to ensure sustainability and scalability;
- it is easy to scan objects but it is necessary to have the structure, in the form of appropriate metadata, to support the digitized objects;
- a variety of new skills are needed by staff involved in digitization projects.

References

(2000) *Dros y rhiniog: Crossing the threshold. The National Library of Wales' digitization strategy, 2001–4.* Aberystwyth: National Library of Wales. Available at: http://www.llgc.org.uk/drych/digido_s01.htm

(2002) *Digital library, open library: next steps. Corporate Plan 2003–4 to 2005–6.* Aberystwyth: National Library of Wales. Available at: http://www.llgc.org.uk/adrodd/index_s.htm

(2000) *Moving theory into practice: digital imaging tutorial.* Cornell University Library. Available at: http://www.library.cornell.edu/preservation/tutorial/contents.html

Druin, A. (2002) The role of children in the design of new technology. *Behaviour and Information Technology,* 21 (1), 1–25

Druin, A., Bederson, B. B., Weeks, A., Farber, A., Grosjean, J., Guha, M. L., Hourcade, J. P., Lee, J., Liao, S., Reuter, K., Rose, A., Takayama, Y. and Zhang, L. (2003) The International Children's Digital Library: description and analysis of first use. *First Monday,* 8 (5). Available at: http://www.firstmonday.dk/issues/issue8_5/druin/index.html

Gamage, R. (2002) Introducing a library automation package as a customer care system – a case from University of Moratuwa Library. *Journal of the University Librarians' Association of Sri Lanka,* 6, 101–119

Giordano, T. (2002) Library co-operation on ICT in Italy: an overview. *Program,* 36 (3), 144–151

Green, A. (2002) Digital library, open library: developments in the National Library of Wales. *Alexandria,* 14 (3), 161–170

Lunati, G. (2003) Progress report from Italy presented at 27th ELAG seminar, Berne, April 2003. Available at: http://www.elag2003.ch/pr/pdf/pr_it_ifnet.pdf

Payne, G. and David B. (2002) An automated approach to online digital reference: the Open University Library OPAL project. *Program,* 36 (1), 5–12

Ramsden, A. and O'Sullivan, U. (1999) ROUTES: creating a tailored learning resource for distance learning students at the Open University. *Program,* 33 (4), 339–346

Ramsden, A. (2003) The OU goes digital. *Library +Information Update,* 2 (2), 34–5

Seneviratne, G. P. and Amaraweera, J.A. (2002) Automation of library operations in Sri Lanka: a cost-effective solution. *Information Development,* 18 (2), 111–115

Tai, A.C. (2003) NLB's Digital Library services. In *Information resources empowerment: enhancing knowledge heritage CONSAL XII.* Bandar Seri Begawan: Dewan Bahasa da Pustaka Brunei. 59–64

Urs, S. and Raghavan, K.S. (2001) Vidyanidhi: Indian digital library of electronic theses. *Communications of the Association of Computing Machinery,* 44 (5), 88–89

Urs, S. (2003) Copyright and libraries: balancing rights of stakeholders – authors, publishers and libraries in the digital age in *Information resources empowerment: enhancing knowledge heritage. CONSAL XII.* Bandar Seri Begawan: Dewan Bahasa dan Pustaka Brunei. 84–89

List of Acronyms

A&I	Abstracting and Indexing	CAIRS	Computer Assisted
A2A	Access to Archives		Information Retrieval
AACR2	Anglo-American		Software
	Cataloguing Rules, 2nd	CAMiLEON	Creative Archiving at
	edition		Michigan and Leeds
AAP	Association of American		Emulating the Old on the
	Publishers		New
ACM	Association for	CBIVR	Content-Based Image and
	Computing Machinery		Video Retrieval
AMC	(MARC) Archival and	CD	Compact Disc
	Manuscript Control	CDL	California Digital Library
ANSI	American National	CD-ROM	Compact Disc-Read Only
	Standards Institute		Memory
ARL	Association of Research	CEDARS	CURL Exemplar in Digital
	Libraries		Archives
ARPANET	Advanced Research	CELT	Corpus of Electronic Texts
	Projects Agency Network	CERN	European Particle Physics
ASCII	American Standard Code		Laboratory
	for Information	CGIAR	Consultative Group on
	Interchange		International Agricultural
			Research
BOAI	Budapest Open Access	CILEA	Consorzio
	Initiative		Interuniversitario
BSI	British Standards		Lombardo per
	Institution		l'Elaborazione
			Automatica
CAIRNS	Cooperative Academic	CIMI	Consortium for the
	Information Retrieval		Computer Interchange of
	Network for Scotland		Museum Intelligence

CLIR	Council on Library and Information Resources	EAD	Encoded Archival Description
CM	Content Management	ECDL	European Computer Driving Licence
CMS	Content Management Software	eCUIP	Digital Library Project of the Chicago Public Schools / University of Chicago Internet Project
COBISS	Cooperative Online Bibliographic System and Services		
CONSAL	Congress of South East Asian Librarians	eIFL	Electronic Information for Libraries
CORC	Cooperative Online Resource Catalog	ELFNI	Electronic Library for Northern Ireland
COPAC	CURL OPAC	elib	Electronic Libraries Programme
CORE	Chemistry Online Retrieval Experiment	EMu	Electronic Museum
CSA	Cambridge Scientific Abstracts	ETD	Electronic Theses and Dissertations
CURL	Consortium of University Research Libraries	EZB	Elektronische Zeitschriftenbibliothek
		FAIR	Focus on Access to Institutional Resources
DAMS	Digital Asset Management System	FAQ	Frequently Asked Question
DARE	Digital Academic Repositories	FinELib	Finnish Electronic Library
DARPA	Defense Advanced Research Projects Agency	Gabriel	Gateway and Bridge to Europe's National Libraries
DBMS	Database Management System	GAINS	Gateway to Internet Information Sources
DDC	Dewey Decimal Classification	GIF	Graphics Interchange Format
DELIVER	Digital Electronic Library Integration within Virtual EnviRonments	GNU	GNU's Not Unix
DISA	Digital Imaging South Africa	HCI	Human-Computer Interaction
DLESE	Digital Library for Earth System Education	HCIL	HCI Laboratory (University of Maryland)
DLF	Digital Library Federation	HEDS	Higher Education Digitisation Service
DLI	Digital Libraries Initiative		
DOAJ	Directory of Open Access Journals	HTML	HyperText Markup Language
DOI	Digital Object Identifier	HTTP	HyperText Transfer Protocol
DPC	Digital Preservation Coalition		
dpi	dots per inch	ICDL	International Children's Digital Library
DSIR	Department for Scientific and Industrial Research	ICIMSS	International Centre for Information Management and Systems
DSLIS	Department of Studies in Library and Information Science (University of Mysore)	ICT	Information and Communications Technology (or Technologies)
DVD	Digital Video (or Versatile) Disc		

IEEE	Institute of Electrical and Electronics Engineers	MDA	formerly Museum Documentation Association
IFLA	International Federation of Library Associations and Institutions	MESH	Medical Subject Headings
		METS	Metadata Encoding and Transmission Standard
ILO	International Labour Office		
IMLS	Institute of Museum and Library Services (US)	MIMAS	Manchester Information and Associated Services
INASP	International Network for the Availability of Scientific Publications	MIT	Massachusetts Institute of Technology
		MLE	Managed Learning Environment
IPR	Intellectual Property Rights	MOSAIC	Making Sense of Information in the Connected Age
ISAD(G)	International Standard Archival Description (General)		
		MPEG	Moving Picture Experts Group
ISBN	International Standard Book Number	MSDN	Microsoft Developer Network
ISSN	International Standard Serial Number	MT	Machine Translation
ISO	International Organization for Standardization	NACESTID	National Center for Scientific and Technological Information Documentation (Vietnam)
IZUM	Institute of Information Science (Slovenia)		
JISC	Joint Information Systems Committee	NASA	National Aeronautics and Space Administration (US)
JPEG	Joint Photographic Experts Group	NCIP	NISO Circulation Interchange Protocol
JSTOR	Journal Storage	NDIIPP	National Digital Information Infrastructure and Preservation Programme
KERIS	Korea Education and Research Information Service		
		NDLTD	Networked Digital Library of Theses and Dissertations
LC	Library of Congress		
LCSH	Library of Congress Subject Headings	NeLH	National electronic Library for Health
LEARN	Library Electronic Academic Resources Network	NGO	Non-Governmental Organization
		NIH	National Institutes of Health (US)
LITA	Library and Information Technology Association	NISO	National Information Standards Organization (US)
LIUC	Università Carlo Cattaneo		
LMS	Library Management System	NISSAT	National Information System for Science and Technology (India)
LSE	London School of Economics and Political Science	NLB	National Library Board (Singapore)
		NLM	National Library of Medicine (US)
MARC	Machine-Readable Cataloguing	NLW	National Library of Wales

nof   New Opportunities Fund

NSF   National Science
         Foundation (US)

NZDL   New Zealand Digital
         Library

OAI   Open Archives Initiative

OAI-PMH Open Archives Initiative
         Protocol for Metadata
         Harvesting

OAIS   Open Archival
         Information System

OCLC   Online Computer Library
         Center

OCR   Optical Character
         Recognition

ODL   Oxford Digital Library

OPAC   Online Public Access
         Catalogue

OPAL   Online Personal Academic
         Librarian

OSI   Open Society Institute or
         Open Source Initiative

OU   Open University

PADI   Preserving Access to
         Digital Information

PARC   Palo Alto Research Center

PC   Personal Computer

PDA   Personal Digital Assistant

PDF   Portable Document Format

PERI   Programme for the
         Enhancement of Research
         Information

PUC   Permanent UNIMARC
         Committee

PURL   Persistent Uniform
         Resource Locator

RAD   Rules for Archival
         Description

RDF   Resource Description
         Framework

RDN   Resource Discovery
         Network

RKMS   Recordkeeping Metadata
         Schema

RoMEO   Rights Metadata for Open
         Archiving

ROUTES   Resources for Open
         University Teachers and
         Students

SAFARI   Skills in Accessing,
         Finding and Reviewing
         Information

SciELO   Scientific Electronic
         Library Online

SCONUL   Society of College,
         National and University
         Libraries

SCRAN   Scottish Cultural
         Resources Access Network

SFX   Special Effects

SGML   Standardized General
         Markup Language

SHERPA   Securing a Hybrid
         Environment for Research
         Preservation and Access

SIDA   Swedish International
         Development cooperation
         Agency

SL   Source Language

SME   Small and Medium
         Enterprises

SPARC   Scholarly Publishing and
         Academic Resources
         Coalition

SPIE   The International Society
         for Optical Engineering

SQL   Structured Query
         Language

STM   Scientific, Technical and
         Medical

SunSite Sun Software, Information
         and Technology Exchange

TASI   Technical Advisory Service
         for Images

TCP/IP   Transmission Control
         Protocol/Internet Protocol

TEEAL   The Essential Electronic
         Agricultural Library

TEI   Text Encoding Initiative

TiARA   Timely Information for All
         Relevant and Affordable

TIFF   Tagged Image File
         Format

TL   Target Language

TRIS   Trials Support

TULIP   The University Licensing
         Project

UGC   University Grants
         Committee (Sri Lanka)

UKOLN	UK Office for Library and information Networking	W3C	World Wide Web Consortium
UMI	University Microfilms	WAI	Web Accessibility
UniMARC	Universal MARC format		Initiative
URL	Uniform Resource Locator	WIPO	World Intellectual
URN	Uniform Resource Name		Property Organization
		WS-I	Web Services
VL	Virtual Library		Interoperability
VLE	Virtual Learning Environment	XML	Extensible Markup
VLmp	Virtual Library museums pages		Language
VRC	Virtual Reference Canada		

Index